Kings for Three Days

**INTERPRETATIONS OF CULTURE
IN THE NEW MILLENNIUM**

Norman E. Whitten Jr., General Editor

*A list of books in the series appears
at the end of the book.*

Kings for Three Days

The Play of Race and Gender in an Afro-Ecuadorian Festival

JEAN MUTEBA RAHIER

UNIVERSITY OF ILLINOIS PRESS

Urbana, Chicago, and Springfield

Library of Congress Cataloging-in-Publication Data
Rahier, Jean Muteba, 1959–
Kings for three days : the play of race and gender in an Afro-
Ecuadorian festival / Jean Muteba Rahier.
pages   cm. — (Interpretations of culture in the new millennium)
Includes bibliographical references and index.
ISBN 978-0-252-03751-1 (cloth : alk. paper)
ISBN 978-0-252-07901-6 (pbk. : alk. paper)
ISBN 978-0-252-09472-9 (e-book)
1. Blacks—Ecuador—Esmeraldas (Province)—Rites and
ceremonies. 2. Blacks—Race identity—Ecuador—Esmeraldas
(Province) 3. Epiphany—Ecuador—Esmeraldas (Province)
4. Sex role—Ecuador—Esmeraldas (Province) 5. Esmeraldas
(Ecuador : Province)—Race relations. 6. Esmeraldas (Ecuador :
Province)—Social life and customs.
I. Title.
F3741.E6R34   2013
305.8009866'35—dc23   2012040474

To Mariama

Contents

List of Figures

Preface and Acknowledgments

The work included in the following pages has been conducted over many years, from the mid-1980s until 2012. While the final writing has taken place at various stages between 2007 and 2012, fieldwork was carried out between 1986 and 1991, and in late 2002 and early 2003.

• • •

I became fascinated by the Afro-Esmeraldian *Fiesta de los Reyes* (Festival of the Kings) in 1985. I was already living in Ecuador at the time, with the objective to stay there and do some research on Afro-Ecuadorian realities. While at the Université Libre de Bruxelles, before early 1990s doctoral work at the Université de Paris X at Nanterre, France, I had been advised by Luc de Heusch who wanted me to engage in a Herskovits-inspired research on African cultural survivals in Ecuador. Needless to say, that didn't work for me. I ended up conducting my first research on European cultural influences on, or European cultural origin of, an Afro-Esmeraldian cultural institution: the Décima, an oral poetic tradition (Rahier 1987, 1999a). The idea that African diaspora cultures and cultural politics are always the products of cultural encounters and mingling, of lending, borrowing, and re-creations of various kinds, began to make sense to me. When I learned about the Festival of the Kings, it right away excited my interest and appeared to be the kind of focus my next research should logically have. Nothing could be better to discuss this conception of African diaspora cultures than a three-day carnivalesque festival in which black folks disguise as "whites," as "Indians," and as "blacks" whom they parody amid laughter. The importance of particular contexts for the performance of cultures and for cultural politics became crystal clear to me once I understood the quite notable differences in the festival as it was performed in different villages of the province of Esmeraldas. Juan García Salazar brought me to La Tola in 1984. There, I made acquaintances who introduced me to Santo Domingo de Ónzole, a village that was known for its fervent Play of the *Cucuruchos* (another name given to the Festival).

I should thank all the people in La Tola, Santo Domingo de Ónzole, the city of Esmeraldas, and so many other villages of the province of Esmeraldas who generously welcomed me into their lives, even if only briefly, and who allowed me to enjoy experiences that have changed me forever. In Ecuador, special thanks must go to countless people, among them Juan García Salazar; the brothers Oscar and Pepe Chalá; Edgardo Prado and his former colleagues at the Centro de Investigación y Cultura of the Esmeraldas branch of the Banco Central del Ecuador; Antonio Preciado, Rocío Rueda Novoa, María Alexandra Ocles Padilla, Jacqueline Pavón Espinoza, Catherine Walsh, Hernán Ibarra, Iván Saltos, Nelson Estupiñán Bass, Argentina Chiriboga, Manuel Mancheno; and all the colleagues of the Department of Anthropology at the Pontificia Universidad Católica del Ecuador in Quito who in the late 1980s welcomed me and gave me a job and collegial support. Here I must also mention the support and friendship of Philippe Buck and his wife Stéphane, and of Marc Franck, the ambassador of Belgium in Ecuador at the time, his wife, Marie-Paule Bastin, and their children. Many thanks as well to Carmen Bernand at the Université de Paris X, Nanterre, France, and to Philippe Descola, Anne-Marie Losonczy, and France-Marie Renard-Casevitz. In the United States, special thanks go to Norman Whitten for his critical engagement and for having encouraged me in more ways than one, and sometimes unknowingly, to put my years of research in a book format and to publish it; to my colleagues in the Department of Geography & Anthropology at Louisiana State University, from 1992 to 1998; and to my colleagues in the Department of Global & Sociocultural Studies and the African & African Diaspora Studies Program at Florida International University, from 1998 to the present. A special mention should be made of Martina Carla Louis, my graduate assistant, who helped me prepare the page proofs and the index. I am also grateful for all the support I have received from my institution, Florida International University, and particularly from its African & African Diaspora Studies Program, School of International and Public Affairs (SIPA), College of Arts and Sciences, and Latin American and Caribbean Studies Center (LACC).

This work is the product of my interactions with all who are named here. I remain solely responsible for its many imperfections.

Kings for Three Days

Introduction

Although relatively small in size, the republic of Ecuador is known for its remarkable geography and cultural diversity. Ecuador's indigenous peoples have long drawn the attention of ethnographers, historians, and political scientists,[1] but with a few outstanding exceptions (West 1952, 1957; Whitten 1965, 1970, 1974; de la Torre 2002a; Walsh 2010a, 2010b; Walsh and García Salazar 2002; Antón 2007a, 2007b, 2009, 2010),[2] Ecuadorians of African descent have not. The province of Esmeraldas in Ecuador, which has been associated with blackness since the colonial period, borders Colombia and faces the Pacific Ocean. As I explain more extensively in chapter 1, most of today's Afro-Esmeraldians are descendants of black migrants who came from Colombia in two waves of immigration—the first in the early twentieth century, during a period of economic growth usually referred to as the *tagua* boom (a particular palm nut very popular at the time, which was sometimes called "vegetal ivory" on the world markets and was used to produce buttons and other objects before the mass production of plastic), and the second in the 1940s during a period of economic bonanza called the banana boom. This post-abolition migration explains in part why the province constitutes the southernmost extremity of a vast cultural area called the Pacific lowlands of Colombia that stretches north to cover the entire Colombian Pacific coast and that includes, as its northern extremity, the Panamanian province of Darién (West 1957). The Pacific lowlands host one of the most concentrated black populations of South America, after the northeastern region of Brazil.

While 70 percent of the population of the province of Esmeraldas are said to be blacks and mulattos, the Esmeraldian elites are mostly composed of whites, white-*mestizos*, and white-mulattos who either migrated from Colombia, the Ecuadorian Andes, or the province of Manabí. Being able to identify with such migratory movements and their attendant connection with modernity constitutes a source of prestige. Their rule in the province relies on the power of the national elites, who usually reside in Quito and Guayaquil—the two major urban centers of the country. Esmeraldian elites reproduce the national ideology of *mestizaje* (see chapter 1) at the provincial level and apply a racist reading of the map of provincial territory. They consider the city of Esmeraldas to be the major, if not unique, center of "culture and civilization," with secondary status given to the towns of Quinindé, Atacames, and Muisne. The northern sector of the province, usually referred to as *El Norte*, the north, is seen as a place of backwardness because it is the home of the *negros azules*, "the blue blacks," so called for the darkness of their skin color (no race mixing). The "blue blacks" or northerners are considered by most of the urban population of Esmeraldas as people without "culture," untouched by modernity, who maintain traditions from another age, do not mind living within the dense rain forest, with no electricity or running water, with mosquitoes and wild animals, and who—when they come to town—have "no manners" and can sometimes behave as social predators. In the numerous villages on the riverbanks of the northern sector, subsistence economy continues to prevail: cultivated parcels in the forest, hunting, and fishing, along with a few other economic activities directed toward cash markets.

In the city of Esmeraldas (the provincial capital), as elsewhere in Ecuador and in Latin America, the process of *blanqueamiento* (whitening) is a dominant theme of the social fabric of life (see Whitten 1974; Quiroga 1994; Rahier 1999b). The popular expression *mejorar la raza*, "to improve the race," denotes whitening by pointing to the publicly acknowledged ideal followed by many darker-skinned people to try to marry lighter-skinned individuals to secure upward mobility. The city of Esmeraldas has a phenotypic typology that ranges from the most negative category to the most positive one. The bottom category is the blue blacks, the top is the whites, with a series of intermediary types such as, non-exhaustively: the *morados* (dark-skinned individuals with "fair" [non-kinky] black hair), the mulattos (brown-skinned with kinky hair), the *trigueños* (lighter-skinned than the mulattos with softer dark hair), the *zambos* or *colorados* (light-skinned persons with light and fair brown, red, or even blond nappy hair). There exists the tendency, for example, when it is required in a conversation to refer to the body type and skin color of the individual with whom one is talking, to call this person, by politeness, with a more "respectable" term than what the person actually is—that is to say, to refer to a lighter skin and "fairer" hair type. Indeed, body types and skin colors are interpreted within the framework provided by the racial-spatial order. Black people, and particularly darker-skinned ones, have their bodies marked as "the body of the Other" (see Rahier 1999b, 1999c).

The Afro-Esmeraldian Festival of the Kings

The principal objective of this book is to examine playful African diasporic performative representations of racial and gender identities in the Afro-Esmeraldian Festival of the Kings, locally called *La Fiesta de los Reyes, La Fiesta de los Santos Reyes*, and also *El Juego de los Cucuruchos* (the Play of the Cowls), as it has been celebrated from January 6 through January 8 in two different villages of the northern sector of the Ecuadorian province of Esmeraldas, Santo Domingo de Ónzole and La Tola (see figure 1). Hereafter, I will refer to the fiesta as "the Festival" or "the Play."

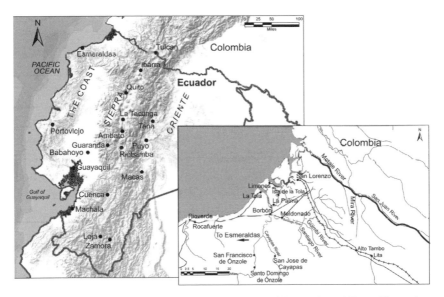

Figure 1. Ecuador and its three regions, the northern sector of the province of Esmeraldas, and the villages of Santo Domingo de Ónzole and La Tola. (Maps by the Florida International University GIS Center; locations and roads are approximate.)

During these three days, Afro-Esmeraldians disguise themselves as "whites," "Indians," and "blacks," and perform in the midst of great laughter, often through sexual cross-dressings, parodic representations of these racialized identities—including themselves—and satiric commentaries about Ecuadorian society.

By paying attention to the Afro-Esmeraldian Festival of the Kings as it is performed in the villages of Santo Domingo de Ónzole and La Tola, one of my main objectives is—above and beyond understanding the Festival and its many representations—to emphasize the importance that should be given to specific contexts in the study of festivities, since festivities repeat or represent these contexts with a "critical distance" (Drewal 1992). As we will see, references to the particularities of the two village contexts considered here explain the originality of the representations of racial and gender identities and of the Ecuadorian racial-spatial order in each village.

The Festival of the Kings is the Afro-Esmeraldian celebration of the Catholic festivity of the Epiphany. The dates January 6, 7, and 8, as well as the term *Reyes*, or "Kings," evoking the expression *los reyes magos* or "the magi-kings" and "the wise-men," leave no doubt about that origin. In order to ease the reading of the following pages, I will hereafter use the expression "the Kings" to refer to the Magi-Kings, unless the discussion centers on Magi (wise men) as opposed to Kings, as is the case at some point in chapter 1.

We should, however, not see the Afro-Esmeraldian Festival of the Kings as a simple copy of European folklore of the Epiphany, which is itself rather diverse. In Santo Domingo de Ónzole, the tradition of the Kings has actually not included any King until very recently. In the tradition of the Festival in La Tola, three teenagers have been dressed up as Kings on the morning of January 6 for two or three hours. They represent Gaspar, Melchior, and Balthazar: the black, "Indian," and white Kings, respectively.

Sexual dichotomy is one of the principal foundations of the Festival—that is, a committee of women organizes and prepares the Festival. In Santo Domingo, they are called *fiesteras*, *reyeras*, or *cucuruchos* and *cucuruchas*. In La Tola, although the expression *fiesteras* is also used, they prefer the expression *cucuruchos*—masculine in gender despite the fact that the term refers to women. In the following pages, I use fiesteras, reyeras, and cucuruchos as synonymous.

During the three days of festivities, and also—to a lesser extent—since December 28, daily conflicts and problems are mocked. Laughter pervades all aspects of life; nothing and no one can escape from it. Men, above all, are dominated good-humoredly—particularly in Santo Domingo.

The Festival Is a Play for Adults,
a Carnivalesque Festivity

The Festival is an adult "play": a number of behaviors more or less informed by "traditions" and everyday reality, even if only with a certain and necessary critical distance, which are performed with the objective of provoking joy and laughter. Plays, and adult plays in particular, point to the openness of sociocultural and political reality. They indicate that we can talk about, think about, and do the same things in different ways or talk about, think about, and do different things in the same way (see Schultz and Lavenda 2001, 127–28). In that sense, plays have a subversive potential because of their power to evoke how things could be, or how things could have been. However, as scholarship has also shown, adult plays have most of the time consisted in rather well-framed, let-off-steam processes that have ended up not so much subverting the sociopolitical order of daily life as reinforcing it by reminding everyone involved in the performance or in the surrounding audience of the existence of specific social rules and regulations.

Carnival is most certainly the adult play par excellence. As revealed in Mikhail Bakhtin's work, carnival has its undeniable origins in Medieval Europe, as a secular pre-Lenten festival grounded in folk humor, that is to say a humor that constitutes a second reality, a reality that exists off to one side of the official realm: "[I]t is a complex system of meaning existing alongside and in opposition to the 'authoritarian world' of dominant orthodoxy. Its most powerful mode of expression is laughter, but it stems from a comprehensive way of seeing human existence that cannot be isolated in any particular aesthetic form or practice" (Bakhtin 1994, 194). Carnival and its spirit, which also overflow in literature (see Rabelais and Frame 1991), informed a great many festivities and cultural traditions that took place in Europe between early January and Ash Wednesday. In the Catholic calendar, the latter marks the beginning of the forty-day period of fasting and penance that lasts until Easter Sunday. Through rituals, masquerades, and plays, which all exaggerated and also inverted daily or "normal" behaviors, medieval carnival and carnivalesque festivities opened up a space filled with irony, disguise, laughter, and revelry, of which end-of-winter symbolism has been interpreted in terms of renewal and rebirth (see Morris 1994).

> Despite the regional differences, by the fifteenth and sixteenth centuries some basic characteristics were prevalent in Carnivals throughout Europe. The season for the festival generally began in January with preparations and events

that grew in intensity and excitement as the time drew closer to Lent. For the elite members of society in the larger cities and royal courts, the celebrations generally consisted of raucous masked balls, comical theatrical performances, and sponsorship of various forms of public competition. . . .

A prominent activity in the rural celebrations, known as charivari, featured groups of merrymakers traveling from house to house singing songs or ballads that criticized or made fun of the occupants. Charivari was sometimes accompanied by loud, rough music, such as the playing of pots and pans. In return for the mock serenade, the homeowner would often douse the troupe with a bucket of water or ashes. A related activity carried out in other communities was known as mumming, in which wandering groups performed a begging ritual in exchange for food and other items. (Mauldin 2004:3–4)

In the sixteenth and seventeenth centuries, Spain, Portugal, and France colonized parts of the Americas. These colonizing enterprises brought about colonists who carried with them a number of religious and festive traditions. At first, local indigenous communities and the African slaves who had been brought to work on plantations and in mining activities might have observed these celebrations, without being, for the most part, authorized to join in (see Mauldin 2004; Real 2004; Nunley 2004; Cosentino 2004). In the first half of the nineteenth century, after the wave of American independences, upper- and middle-class citizens of the newly formed nations kept many European festive traditions alive. By the mid- to late nineteenth century, "freer" lower-class indigenous people and "emancipated" Africans began participating regularly in carnivals either in their own, very often rural, communities or in larger urban celebrations (see Mauldin 2004; LeCount 2004; Real 2004; Nunley 2004; Cosentino 2004; Berry 2004). What precedes justifies my use of the expression "carnivalesque festivity" when I refer to the Afro-Esmeraldian Festival of the Kings.

The Village of Santo Domingo de Ónzole

Santo Domingo is located in a remote area of the Esmeraldian rain forest, in the northern sector of the province, on the left bank of the Ónzole River. The river provides the exclusive avenue for traveling in canoes to other villages and to the towns of Borbón and Limones. When Santo Domingeños want to go to the city of Esmeraldas, they must transit by Borbón, where begins the partially asphalted road to Esmeraldas, in order to take the bus which assures public transportation.

The entire population of the village is black. It totaled 361 between December 1989 and January 1990. The size of the population had not really changed in the early twenty-first century following outmigration. Although a slight socioeconomic differentiation can be observed in the village—some are more entrepreneurial than others—Santo Domingo's way of life, more communitarian than in La Tola, is mostly characterized by subsistence economy. The entire village population would enter in the social category of the "poor peasants of the black lower class" proposed by Norman Whitten some time ago (Whitten 1970, 1974). Forest agriculture, hunting, and river fishing are the most important activities, with only partial involvement in the cash economy when selling agricultural surplus and wood in surrounding towns or to the local sawmill in Borbón.

Just as in other rural black communities of Latin America (see, among others, Smith 1956; Smith 1969; Smith 1962; Gonzalez 1970; Prior 1997; Wilson 1969), Santo Domingo is characterized by a marked sexual dichotomy. Men are in charge of most of the official, social, political, and economic matters, while the responsibilities of women are confined mostly to the household. Men are esteemed for their virility and enjoy a greater sexual and geographic mobility than women. Indeed, very few couples officially marry. They usually prefer, at men's requests, common law unions. This allows men to leave a woman and engage in a relation with another without major difficulty. Norman Whitten understands this lack of enthusiasm for legal marriage as a consequence of, or prerequisite for, "serial polygyny" (1965, 122).

In traditional Afro-Esmeraldian contexts, women are expected to be modest and faithful to their husbands. A man who is incapable of keeping his mate happy will not be considered macho enough. Afro-Esmeraldian men, when living in northern contexts, seem convinced of women's inferiority, or at least of their women's inferiority, to the detriment of whom they construct their *machista* reputations. The traditional Afro-Esmeraldian kinship system is matrifocal: Women are the households' stable figures, and it is around them that other people regroup. When members of the extended family live in a given household, they are most of the time relatives of the mother rather than of the father or the man in the position of "husband-father." Daily contacts with matrilateral kin are more frequent than with patrilateral kin. Most of the time women—who are the primary source of affection and comfort for their children—occupy as well the disciplinary role (see Rahier 1994).[3]

A small community of indigenous people of the Chachi ethnic group live not too far away from the village, mostly upriver. They sometimes come down to Santo Domingo to sell some of their products or to buy things they need in one of the village's small stores. During a trip downriver, Chachi men might spend the night in the village, in the house of one of their Afro-Esmeraldian compadres, or fictive male kin. Such fictive kin are also beneficial to Santo Domingeño men when they go upriver to hunt.

Outmigration from Santo Domingo is quite important. According to a census I conducted in December 1989 and January 1990, there were 125 outmigrants representing 34.6 percent of the population of inhabitants. Most of them went to the cities of Esmeraldas and especially Guayaquil. These numbers show that even if Santo Domingo is relatively isolated geographically deep in the Esmeraldian forest, it remains nevertheless in sustained contact with urban centers, through the visits of outmigrants who sometimes return to the village for a short period, as well as because of the occasional travels of Santo Domingeños to Esmeraldas and Guayaquil to visit a relative or to go to a hospital for healthcare (see Rahier 1994; Whitten 1974). The trend had not changed in the early years of the twenty-first century. At both times when the fieldwork was conducted, no Ecuadorian radio station or Ecuadorian newspaper regularly reached the village. However, once in a while, somebody could tune in to a Colombian radio station if he or she had the necessary batteries.

The Village of La Tola

La Tola is quite different from Santo Domingo. It is located at the mouth of the Santiago River and is the capital of La Tola Parish. It constitutes a social, economic, and political center for the surrounding villages. A partly asphalted road begins there, joining with the road from Borbón at a point called the "Y" and then goes on to Esmeraldas. During the dry season, the trip from La Tola to Esmeraldas by bus lasts four hours. It can last more than six hours during the rainy season. A cooperative of large, outboard canoes assures the transportation of goods and passengers to Limones and San Lorenzo. Thus, La Tola has been an obligated passing point for passengers coming from and going to Esmeraldas. The village is therefore more accessible to influences from the national white-mestizo (urban) society than Santo Domingo is.

La Tola's population is larger than Santo Domingo's. There were 1,016 inhabitants in December 1989–January 1990. In January 1990, there were 278 outmigrants who had left La Tola mostly for the cities of Esmeraldas and Guayaquil.

In contrast with Santo Domingo, La Tola's population is multiracial. For the census I conducted in December 89–January 90, I used only three categories: the Esmeraldian white-mestizos (EWM); the non-Esmeraldian white-mestizos (NEWM); and the Afro-Esmeraldians (AE). Results showed 20.8 percent of the household heads entered in the first category, 7 percent in the second, and 72.2 percent in the third (see Rahier 1994, 163 and following).[4] No Chachi indigenous people leave in La Tola parish.

Another major difference with Santo Domingo is that the intracommunity social differentiation is much more complex in La Tola. The social sectors I have identified follow racial identities quite closely:[5] the small-scale peasant-fishermen (mostly AE, and a few EWM), the poor proletariat (mostly AE, and a few EWM), the fishermen from the cooperative Buena Esperanza (all AE), the fishermen-workers (all NEWM), the small local entrepreneurs (mostly EWM), the local entrepreneurs (mostly NEWM), the absenteist elite (NEWM).

This greater racial and socioeconomic diversity of La Tola's population comes with a series of tensions between the different sectors and racial groups. This situation diminishes the extent of communal life and of Afro-Esmeraldian traditions such as the funerals (*alabados* and *chigualos*), saint days (*arrullos*) (Barrero 1979a, 1979b; Whitten 1970, 1974), and the Festival of the Kings, which are all looked down upon as marks of "non-modernity" and backwardness. The more important exposure of La Tola to the social values of white-mestizo urban society explains why gender relations are quite different than in Santo Domingo. La Tola's women enjoy a greater freedom and mobility than Santo Domingo's. Although most women are still engaged in "women's activities," some Afro-Esmeraldian women (as well as EWM and NEWM women) residing in La Tola have a high-school education or even slightly more, and they work as cashiers for the transportation cooperatives or as teachers in the local schools.

The Importance of "Place" and "Space" for the Study of Festivities and for African Diaspora Studies

My insistence on the importance of the notions of "place" and "space" for the study of festivities in general, and for what I think is a successful place-informed analysis of the Afro-Esmeraldian Festival of the Kings in two different villages of the province of Esmeraldas, allows two kinds of critique.

The first one consists in engaging critically with colleagues in festivity studies who have not paid enough attention to "place" in their respective research and who have written about the festivity they have studied as if the location or place were the performances were observed were irrelevant. This book shows that no one should write about a festivity without remaining aware of the fact that what one is observing in one location, village, or town might not be characteristic of the performance of the same festivity in another location, village, or town of the same cultural area. In other words, one should be extremely cautious before making generalizations about a festivity that one has observed in only a single location.

The second critique supported by the material presented in this book is aimed at what could be called "the Herskovitsian model" in African diaspora studies. Indeed, for Melville Herskovits, the only acceptable approach to African diaspora cultures consisted in exclusively looking for, and analyzing these cultures in terms of, cultural continuity. For him, the cultures of the African diaspora in the Americas were nothing but—fundamentally—emigrated African cultures. This is the reason he thought anthropological research had to focus solely on "Africanisms," "African retentions," and "cultural reinterpretations" that allowed Africa to survive in the Americas. He wrote:

> In the organization of our scientific endeavor, it is important to consider the geographical divisions as well as the political borders as simple titles of chapters that are useful for the classification of data and for the organization of our research. But if the data that we possess do not agree with these categories, we have to follow them where they lead us. This is the reason why we have to acknowledge in our research that the numerous black populations of the New World, African in origin, African in various degrees in their physical types and, much more than we thought so far, African in their traditions, must be considered an integral part of the field of study of Africanists. (1938, 66; author's translation)

His spaceless conception of African diaspora cultures could not be better illustrated. In various ways, his interpretations actually denied any real importance of the socioeconomic histories, political processes, and the geographies of the Americas. This book wants to underscore the erroneous nature of this orientation, which survives today in the work of historians and anthropologists that Richard and Sally Price have called "neo-Herskovitsian" (2003).

The Book's Chapters

Chapter 1 provides additional and required contextual information that should facilitate the reading of the analyses of the Festival. It begins by revisiting briefly the theoretical discussion begun in this introduction about the importance "place" should have in festivity studies. It then goes on with the presentation of a brief history of the celebrations of the Catholic Epiphany, which leads to a historical explanation of how it became a festivity with which African slaves associated. It ends with historical accounts of the black presence in the province of Esmeraldas, which come infused with bits of provincial, national, and transnational economic history.

Chapter 2 is dedicated to the nine-day period of preparation of the Festival in the village of Santo Domingo de Ónzole and to a first ethnographic discussion of the village's marked sexual dichotomy. This ethnographic information will help explain why gender is so important in that village's Festival performances.

Chapters 3 and 4 provide ethnographic interpretations of the performances of the three-day-long Festival in each village—Santo Domingo de Ónzole and La Tola, respectively.

Chapter 5 provides additional contextual information that allows for a better appreciation of why race and race relations are the main source of inspirations for the Play in La Tola, while by contrast gender relations instead are central to the Play in Santo Domingo.

Chapter 6 zeroes in on more recent developments around and during the Festival in both villages.

The conclusions complete the actual analyses of the Festival while also opening up the opportunity once again to engage critically with the subfield of festivity studies.

1

Setting Up the Stage
Contextualizing the Afro-Esmeraldian
Festival of the Kings

My approach consists of viewing festivities as nonstatic texts always embedded in ever changing or evolving sociocultural, economic, and political realities. Thus, my concern here is not the discovery of the origin of the various aspects of the Festival in order to identify more or less "pure" and "authentic" forms, or to interpret the festival as if the only way to read the content of African diasporic festive performances would be to evaluate the intensity of their "africanisms," or as if whatever expression of African diasporic, political resistance in a festive celebration should always and automatically involve Africa or so-called "African culture" (used in the singular). Rather, walking away from the placelessness of Herskovits's model and of the rigidity of his understanding of "culture" (see Rahier 1999c, xiii–xxvi), I propose to relocate the Festival's "texts" within the webs of social relations and social practices that constitute its "contexts." In doing so, I emphasize the importance of "place" and "space" for the study of carnival and carnivalesque festivities, with the declared objective to remind performance studies and cultural studies scholars alike (Browning 1998; Harris 2003) that it might not be quite right to take into consideration exclusively the transnational dimensions of festivities to the detriment of local contexts when trying to make sense of performances and representations. For a while already, academic fashion has turned on the (mostly urban) global and transnational. In this particular scholarly moment I want to argue that specific places—even if rural—remain tremendously important for our analyses, despite the existence of otherwise fascinating and complex transnational processes that constitute what is often called "globalization," and which also impact rural places and rural realities. To make sense of festivities, a multidimensional approach that takes into consideration the local, regional, national, and transnational must be elected.

Joseph Roach (1996), for instance, is one of these cultural studies scholars I want to take distance from here. His work has been inspired by, among other things, the reflections of Paul Gilroy in *The Black Atlantic* (1993), as Roach analyzes a series of performances taken from the history of London, New Orleans, and other locations. In his otherwise interesting and intellectually surprising and enriching work, he downplays the importance that specific "places" have within regional, national, and transnational "spaces" by defining his master concept of "circum-Atlantic world" as "the geohistorical locale [in the singular] for my thesis about memory and substitution . . ." (emphasis added) (Roach 1996, 4). Too often, his analyses enthusiastically jump over places and times, from London to New Orleans and elsewhere, and from the seventeenth century to the twentieth. His deciphering of the symbolism of the various performances under scrutiny (New Orleans Mardi Gras; Mardi Gras or Black "Indians"; French, Australian, and American nineteenth-century paintings; Iroquois' visit of the Royal Court in London; London cemeteries) seem to have no other goal but to justify his "circum-Atlantic approach" instead of making sense of the performances and objects themselves. With this book, I want to face Roach and object that analyses of such complex sociocultural events as carnivalesque festivities may not erase the participants' experiences and agencies. Any macro-level comparisons of festivities taking place in very different parts of the world should be grounded in serious ethnographic research and embrace local particularities. Indeed, festivities are "multilocal" and, thus, they must be approached within their specific space/time contexts.

In paying careful attention to the local contexts of two Afro-Esmeraldian villages—Santo Domingo de Ónzole and La Tola—in my analyses of the Afro-Esmeraldian Festival of the Kings, my intention is not to assert that La Tola and Santo Domingo present realities completely closed to, or definitely separated from, what is going on in the rest of the country and the world. On the contrary, I am well aware of the sometimes intense circulation of peoples and goods that has characterized the history of the northern sector of the province of Esmeraldas, linking it to national and international markets through processes of globalization.

This book is an attempt to analyze the festive perspectives grounded on specific cultural traditions that folks who have been living in the periphery of national and transnational centers, and on the margin of full citizenship, have on the world and on their place within it. Indeed, as I think this book demonstrates, interesting processes—which are not necessarily unrelated to global forces—do take place in "rural areas" and deserve detailed and contextualized analyses.

Most scholars who have worked on festivities have, in fact, focused on the performance of a festivity in one given location. From the data they gathered using a number of research methods and techniques, including participant observation, they then generalize their findings to the festivity as it would exist in the entire cultural area in which their chosen location is seated: a province, a transnational cultural area, a continent, a transcontinental circuit. I contend that they, operating in this fashion, erase the possibility of local variations and originality in the performance of the festivity in focus; they show that they are unaware of the very hard fact that festivities are multilocal. One given festivity is performed differently and might carry completely different meanings in different micro-contexts and at different times, within one single cultural area or region.

The notion of "multilocality" as understood here opens up the door to the possibility of the existence of profound differences among the performances of one specific festivity in a given cultural area's different locations. This is what my research on the Festival in two Esmeraldian villages illustrates.

I follow the work of David Guss (2000) and Olga Nájera-Ramirez (1997) when they state that festive behaviors and their symbolisms are always multivocal, in the sense that they always involve a series of negotiations among the different perspectives held by the various agents involved. As I show in the following chapters, the Afro-Esmeraldian Festival of the Kings provides sites for multiple voices to be heard, to negotiate, and eventually to clash in a general humoristic ambiance (in Santo Domingo) or in relatively tense situations (in La Tola). The specificity of each one of the two village contexts explains why the principal focus of the Play tends to be on race relations in La Tola, while gender relations have prevailed as a master theme in Santo Domingo de Ónzole.

Brief History of the Catholic Epiphany

There is no doubt that there are some connections between the Afro-Esmeraldian Festival of the Kings and the history of the celebration of the Epiphany in the Catholic calendar. The very name of the Festival, *Fiesta de los Reyes*, or *Fiesta de los Santos Reyes*, as well as the days of celebration or play—January 6, 7, and 8—are unambiguous about its origin. While undertaking my fieldwork in the late 1980s and early 1990s, I found no one disguised as any of the three Kings in the village of Santo Domingo de Ónzole; the Play in La Tola, by contrast, always begins on January 6 with a performance that represents the scene of the adoration of Melchior, Gaspar, and Balthazar. Moreover, as I explain below, during my fieldwork of December 2002–January 2003 I was surprised at the insistence of an older woman of Santo Domingo to have young boys from the village disguise themselves as the three Kings because, as she repeated, she wanted the celebration to be "more truthful to the Catholic tradition." In any case, the very fact that the three "racial groups" of the province, the whites (and white-mestizos), the indigenous people (Chachi), and the blacks (Afro-Esmeraldians) are represented during the three days of festivity clearly indicate—even in the absence of any presence of the Kings—a connection to the Catholic Epiphany.

As a result of both the tolerance (or even encouragement) from the power in place and of the activism of Catholic missionaries, the celebrations of the Epiphany in the Americas during the colonial period very often reinterpreted the racial identity of the three Kings according to the "racial composition" of the local populations: whites, Indigenes, and blacks (see Moreno 1997, 52). These celebrations also integrated and continue to integrate—and this is the very argument developed in this book—a number of local peculiarities due to local socioeconomic, cultural, and political processes. These local peculiarities explain the great diversity of the forms taken by the celebrations of the Catholic Epiphany or Festival of the Kings around the globe and call for an informed appreciation of local contexts in any analysis of the festivity. Obviously, the folklore of the Catholic Epiphany is very diverse. One may not assume that these varied folklores will all reproduce identically nothing more than an official story of the three Kings imagined in, let's say, Ancient Rome. The differences between the play in Santo Domingo de Ónzole and La Tola, two villages situated in the same province, illustrate the point.

The Afro-Esmeraldian Play of the Cowls is a direct product of a folklore most certainly developed by missionaries. As such, it could fall within one of the two types of what Roger Bastide called *le folklore nègre*: a folklore invented by Europeans for their slaves (Bastide 1972, 49), and which clearly evokes processes of creolization.

The word "epiphany" is derived from the Greek *epiphaneia*, which stands for the action to show oneself, the appearance, the coming out, the physical revelation of a God, the manifestation of the divine power, the emergence of a thing. As a Christian festivity, Epiphany has been linked to the commemoration of three different events (Vacandard 1912, 49; Botte 1932, 82–83;

Van Assche 1974, 11–20): the adoration of the Magi (see Trexler 1997), the Baptism of Jesus in the Jordan River (see McDonnel 1996), and the miracle of the transformation of water into wine at Cana. The first, adoration of the Magi, is mostly associated with the Occident and is found in areas under the influence of the Roman Church, while the other two are characteristic of Oriental churches.

The Oriental Epiphany was originally the celebration of the Incarnation, of the Nativity. For some historians, it began in Alexandria; for others it originated in Syria or Palestine. It was opposed, just like Christmas in the Occident, to a pagan celebration that commemorated the birth of a God—either Aion, Dionysos, Onisis—which was identified with the sun and which appeared to have been connected with an ancient date of the winter solstice (see Botte 1932, 9–12). For Robert Van Assche, the Epiphany has the same origin as Christmas. The difference in dates (December 25 and January 6), he says, would be due to astronomers' errors (1974, 4–6). That celebration spread throughout the Orient and even penetrated part of the Occident. It is quite probable that Rome was inspired by it when it created Christmas (Botte 1932, 82).

In the Orient, the pagan festivity of January 6 also comprised another aspect: there were traditions centered on certain fountains and rivers, and people used to take water from those because it was supposed to have, on that specific day, supernatural and marvelous properties. This custom continued even after the conversion to Christianity, although it received a new interpretation: some attributed it to the anniversary of the wedding feast at Cana, while others attributed it to the baptism of Jesus.

The baptism of Jesus was first considered as his manifestation to the world, his Epiphany, by the testimony of his Father. Later, the sanctification of water took on much greater importance. After the advent of the Christmas celebration, the Epiphany became exclusively a festivity around the memory of Christ's baptism. Oriental Christian churches still perform a solemn benediction of the waters on January 6.

When the Epiphany emerged in Rome at the end of the fourth century, it was entirely dedicated to the memory of the adoration of the Magi, quite different from the Oriental Epiphany (Botte 1932, 34–39). Saint Augustine had been a pivotal figure in the propagation of the Epiphany as the celebration of the adoration of the Magi. He wrote six sermons on the Epiphany that do not deal with anything else but the Magi (see Trexler 1997). The Epiphany has a different history in the various regions of Europe where it was implanted. In Spain, for example, the two festivities, Christmas and the Epiphany, were established by 380 A.D. There, the Epiphany first began as the celebration of the adoration of the Magi, although the two other aspects of the festivity, the celebration of the baptism of Jesus and the miracle of Cana, were also adopted later in a peripheral way (Botte 1932, 53).

Matthew's is the only gospel that mentions the adoration of the Magi, without ever referring to their respective age or to the fact that they were kings. From Matthew's gospel, we could deduce that the three Magi were in fact living in the regions around Palestine. The transformation of the Magi into three kings of various ages and racial identities constitutes a Eurocentric reinterpretation of Matthew's gospel. The three Kings came to represent all the races and all the generations of the people of the world who came to pay their respect and to acknowledge the universal preeminence of the white baby God, "the only one there is."[1]

The Roman liturgy recalls these three mysteries in the office of the Epiphany. "That is on that day that the Star guided the Magi to the crib; on that day that water was changed into wine at Cana; on that day that Christ wanted to be baptized in the Jordan River" (Vacandard 1912, 52). Although the Roman Church inscribed these three different manifestations of Christ in the rubric of the Epiphany, only one of them has dominated the celebration of January 6: the adoration of the Magi.

The Epiphany Becomes "Day of the Blacks"

The Spanish historian-anthropologist Isidoro Moreno has shown how both the indigenous and black brotherhoods and confraternities that existed in the regions of the Americas that were colonized by the Spaniards had their origin and direct precedent in Adalusian "ethnic confraternities" predating the conquest (Moreno 1981; 1985; 1999, 4–5). At the end of the fourteenth century, the Guadalquivir Valley area of Andalusía, which had been incorporated into the kingdom of Castile more than a century before, was a multiracial and multiethnic society with Jews, Moriscos, blacks, mulattos, and an emerging gypsy community. "The slave population was composed primarily of Moriscos and blacks, the former as a result of the capture of prisoners in periodic wars between Castile and the Nazari kingdom of Granada—which was independent until 1492—and the latter as a result of Castilian incursions onto the coast of Africa and, especially, of an active slave trade that had its center in Lisbon" (Moreno 1999, 4). At that time, during the reign of Henry III of Castile, the activities of blacks were regulated in such a way that they were granted some rights, including the right to gather on certain Sundays and feast days and to dance at the sounds of percussion instruments of "autochthonous tradition."

> This concession set the precedent for those that were granted centuries later to blacks of diverse American cities and that would be preserved even during the nineteenth century in the Caribbean colonies. As the Cuban anthropologist Fernando Ortiz correctly observed, the African American cabildos[2] of the island were assemblies or meetings centered on dance, similar to those which were organized centuries before in Seville and whose directors were, in the early years, blacks from Seville who had come with their masters to Cuba. (Moreno 1999, 4)

Moreno notes that confraternities of blacks and mulattos also appeared in various other Andalusian cities: Cádiz, Jeréz de la Frontera, El Puerto de Santa María, Huelva, Jaén, and the Sevillian suburb of Triana. Their most common patron was *Nuestra Señora de los Reyes* or "Our Lady of the Kings" (Moreno 1997, 49–56; 1999, 7–10). The title of *Virgen de los Reyes* ("Virgin of the Kings")—which can also be found in the ex-colonies of Spain in the Americas—referred to the mother of Jesus when adored by the Magi. She was represented iconographically with the Infant Jesus in her arms as the three "Kings" paid homage (see also Trexler 1997). This particular association of Andalusian blacks with the legend of the three Kings should not surprise, since it was only through the representation of a black king—sometimes identified as Melchior, other times as Gaspar or as Balthazar—that blacks could actively participate in the Catholic faith by identifying with one of his legendary figures (see Devisse and Mollat 1979, 7–58; Trexler 1997, 102–7).

> Indeed, this selection was fostered by the church which had already established the iconography of the three Magi in the twelfth century and had supported and popularized it during the time of the increase in numbers of Oriental and African slaves in Europe as a means of symbolizing the unity of all the races in the common adoration of the Christian God. The Three Kings reflected perfectly the "universal" Christian Order. The attribution to them of the characteristics considered proper to the three races of the then-known continents, the European, the Asian, and the African, and of each of the three ages, youth, maturity, and old age, symbolized the fact that all humanity, without exception . . . had as its destiny to follow the religion of the true God, the Christian God.
>
> The identification of the blacks with a holy king was thus promoted by the late medieval church as one of the means of facilitating the integration of peoples of color into the Christian faith. And since the liturgical feast of the

kings is January 6, the blacks of Seville and later, for centuries in Spanish America, held on that day their principal Festival of the year. (Moreno 1999, 8; see also Moreno 1997, 49–56)

By incorporating black slaves within the Christian faith, albeit through a structure that reproduced the inequalities existing in the society at large, the power in place was neutralizing in the collective imagination of most of the members of the dominated "ethnic group" the very realization that these inequalities were unjust. It was doing that at the same time that it reinforced the consent of the dominated group. Their suffering was sublimated in the identification with religious symbols, which were presented as valid for all "ethnic groups,"[3] social sectors, and classes, above and beyond whatever position one might occupy within the societal structure. This brought about a process of naturalization of the social structure as part of a unique and divine order, which is both eternal and earthly (Moreno 1997, 40–56).

The iconographic importance and the symbolic meaning of the Kings was complemented with the ludic character that the festivity of January 6 had all over Europe during the late Middle Ages and the Renaissance to become the most important festive day for blacks, both slaves and free. The ludic aspect of the festivity was maintained through centuries: January 6 being the last day of the period of twelve days—a period that symbolically represents the twelve months of the year—which began with the winter solstice, which was itself Christianized through the adoption of Nativity. That is why, Moreno writes, during the celebration of the Epiphany

> there is most of the time a postponement [*una puesta en paréntesis*], and sometimes even an inversion, of the established social order through the momentary suspension of social controls and the practice of greater permissiveness, identically to what was happening during the Classic Antiquity and the Festival of the *Saturnales*. During the latter, slaves enjoyed a greater freedom—although within pre-established limits—without being directly subjected to the authority of their owners, being instead under the authority of a burlesque king whom they elected on that day. (1997, 53)

There is evidence of the existence of a Festival of the Kings in nineteenth-century Cuba (Ortiz 1920), in colonial Brazil (Pereira de Magalhães Gomes and Pereira 2000; Ramos Tinhorão 2000), in Colombia (Atencio Babilonia and Córdoba 1982), and in colonial Peru (Pradier-Fodéré 1897), and there is no doubt that the celebration of the *Tres Juanes* of Mexico and Cuba have their origin in the Catholic Epiphany (Moreno 1997, 52).[4]

The most notorious descriptions of an African diasporic Festival of the Kings are probably those reported by Fernando Ortíz, which were first published in 1920[5] under the title: *"La fiesta afrocubana del 'Día de Reyes'"* (Ortiz 1920). Ortiz's article is nothing but a commented recompilation of descriptions of the Afro-Cuban *Día de Reyes* in Havana by journalists, artists, travelers, and writers of the nineteenth century. The Day of the Kings was celebrated in the biggest cities of Cuba by Afro-Cubans, both slaves and freed. It was their special holy day, which was spent in dancing and parading in the streets. The last recorded Day of the Kings in Cuba would have taken place in 1884 (Stubbs 1993, 6). The accounts of the Afro-Cuban Día de Reyes reproduced in Ortiz's article give a good idea of what the festivity consisted of. They illustrate well the processes of creolization that have characterized African diaspora cultures in the Americas. Ortiz writes, "The 'Day of the Kings' was a free day for the Africans in Cuba, and the Creole *negros* were equally enthusiastic in joining the clamor of celebrations. . . . That Day [January 6], black Africa, its people, its costumes, its music, its tongues, its songs and dances, its ceremonies, its religions and political institutions, were brought across the Atlantic to Cuba, especially Havana" (Ortiz 1993, 8). Ortiz then reproduces the fragment of a description written by Cuban scholar Ramón Meza, which was initially published on January 11, 1891, in the Cuban paper *El Hogar*. The passage shows that the Afro-Cuban Día de Reyes was indeed an event marked by Afro-Cuban multivocality or diversity of perspectives:

> From daybreak, all over can be heard the monotonous beat of those big drums made out of hollowed tree trunk and covered on one end by a patch of ox-hide tempered by fire. The house servants would leave very early in the morning. The plantation slaves would come in from the nearby estates: some jammed into rear railroad wagons, others crammed onto carts that carried the enormous barrels of sugar, and not a few came on foot. All were hurrying to join their respective cabildos whose chief was generally the elder of the tribe or nation to which they belonged.
>
> But not all the negroes joined the cabildos, which the creoles and certain of those belonging to the nation thought the less of. Rather than attire themselves in the outlandish dress that made up the costumes of their countrymen, they would dress as Paris dandies. Elegance consisted in the exaggeration of fashion, which is why the weaker sex showed a preference for ribbons, baubles, tassels, large earrings, fancy shawls, a profusion of rings, bracelets, and contrasting bright colors. In the strongest sex this preference found marked form in wide

collars, frilled shirtfronts, large cravats and a choice of the most brightly colored jacket and pantaloons. Others would be dressed as sailors, carrying a small, constantly moving boat on a piece of crumpled canvas, painted green and white, representing the seaspray and waves, asking for their *aguinaldo*[6] at more or less acceptable intervals. (1993, 8–9)

Another account reproduced by Ortiz, which was written by Pérez Zamora and which was published in *El Abolicionista Español*—a paper published in Madrid, Spain—on January 15, 1866, presents a more somber and negative picture of the Día de Reyes:

Countless groups of *comparsas*[7] of African negroes go through the streets of the capital; the crowd is huge; its aspect horrific . . . the noise of the drums, horns and whistles is everywhere deafening to the ear of the passerby; here is to be seen a mock *Lucumí* king amidst his negro phalanx, there a *Gangá* or *Carabalí*; all kings for a day, they chant in disagreeable monotone, in African language, the memories of their peoples; and hundreds of voices, some shrill, some hoarse, all wild, respond in chorus to the African king, forming a diabolical concert that is difficult to describe . . .

The negroes of Cuba have no greater joy at any other time of the year than on the Day of the Holy Kings. They spill out in all directions like a black cloud over the city: from the morning hours, it is as if the slave servants were spirited away from the house of their masters; those who have achieved their freedom also partake of the enthusiasm and general frenzy; all, in short, snatch these moments of madness from the heavy yoke that is their fate. Because man in all countries, under all conditions of life, in all states, of all ages, needs a certain palliative to strengthen the spirit so as to bear the bitterness of existence. . . .

On the "Day of the Kings" in Havana, dear readers, your pockets must be continually open. Do you know why? To give . . . should you go to a café, should you sit down to rest on the bench of some public promenade, should you enter the home of a friend or one who is not of your acquaintance, you will be accosted by negroes, adults and children of both sexes, coming up to you, insistent and importune in asking for the popular gift: "El aguinaldo! El aguinaldo!" (1993: 14–15)

Some of my descriptive analyses of the sketches of the Afro-Esmeraldian Festival of the Kings in subsequent chapters sometimes evoke aspects of the Afro-Cuban Día de Reyes. I must, however, emphasize major differences between Ortiz's Cuban context and my Ecuadorian contexts. The nineteenth-century Día de los Reyes that Ortiz was dealing with is an urban festivity performed by Afro-Cubans who were organized in nations (*naciones*) and *cofradías* (see Moreno 1997; 1999; see also note 2 herewith). On the other hand, the Afro-Esmeraldian Festival of the Kings or Play of the Cowls is a twentieth- and twenty-first-century rural festivity performed by Afro-Esmeraldians whose ancestors in Ecuador and in Colombia were never organized in nations, cofradías, or brotherhoods.

After having spent some time with the history of the Catholic Epiphany and its emergence as the Day of the Blacks in Spain, it makes sense to get closer to the contemporary moment in order to explore other facets of the Festival's contexts: contemporary identity politics in the Ecuadorian nation.

National Identity and the Ecuadorian Racial-Spatial Order: From Monocultural Mestizaje to Multiculturalism

In Ecuador, as elsewhere in Latin America, the official imagination of national identity has been constructed by the white and white-mestizo elites around the reified notion of *mestizaje* (race mixing) (Stutzman 1981; Rahier 2008; Hale 1996, 1999; Miller 2004). These elites have reproduced an "Ecuadorian ideology" of national identity that proclaims the mestizo as the prototype of modern Ecuadorian citizenship (Polo 2002). This ideology is based on a belief in the indigenous population's inferiority and on an unconditional but contradictory admiration and identification with Occidental civilization (see Whitten 1981, introduction; Stutzman 1981; Silva 1995; Rahier 1998; Whitten 2003b; Carrillo N. and Salgado 2002; Lane 2003). Despite this obvious attempt at racial and ethnic homogenization, this Ecuadorian ideology of national identity results in the drawing of a racist map of national territory: rural areas are places of racial inferiority, violence, backwardness, savagery, and cultural deprivation. These areas, mostly inhabited by nonwhites or non-white-mestizos, are seen as representing major challenges to the full national development toward the ideals of modernity. As the editors of *Knowing Your Place: Rural Identity and Cultural Hierarchy* write in their introduction: "The utility of the countryside as a locus of national essence is more complicated in plural societies where rural populations are ethnically or racially marked, hence hardly a national unifier. In these cases, rural/urban differences often qualify ethnic and/or racial ones, demanding that all three be examined in tandem" (Ching 1997, 25).

In this official imagination of Ecuadorian-ness, there is logically no place for blacks: they must remain "peripheral." Afro-Ecuadorians—who today represent around 10 percent of the national population—constitute the ultimate

Other, some sort of a historical accident, a noise in the ideological system of nationality, a pollution in the Ecuadorian genetic pool. The best example of "non-citizenship," "they are not part of Mestizaje" (Stutzman 1981, 63). Indeed, unlike indigenous groups—who also have been victimized and in many ways excluded from understandings of citizenship (de la Torre 1996; 2002b; Guerrero 2003)—Afro-Ecuadorians are not part of what I call the "ideological biology of national identity" (Rahier 2010), which incorporates elements of indigenous-ness within a notion of Ecuadorian-ness/mestizo-ness (see also Rahier 1999c, 2010; Hooker 2005).

The national development plans of the Ecuadorian elites see the cities (mainly Quito, Guayaquil, and Cuenca) as the epicenters from which civilization radiates to the rural and frontier areas. Thus, Ecuadorian society, spatially constituted, is organized in a racial-spatial order within which the various ethnic and racial groups (indigenous peoples, blacks, mestizos, white-mestizos, and whites) occupy their "natural" places. Blacks and indigenous peoples are found at the bottom of the socioeconomic hierarchy and in the periphery of national space; and the two "traditional"[8] regions of blackness, the province of Esmeraldas and the Chota-Mira Valley, are looked down upon by the white and white-mestizo urban citizenry. The two largest cities of the country, Guayaquil and Quito, are associated with white-mestizo-ness, and of course with modernity, and the black people who live there are often conceived as being "out of place" (de la Torre 2002b; Rahier 1999c, 2003b). Elsewhere, I document how, in the Ecuadorian press, Afro-Ecuadorians have been represented as social predators in urban areas while their presence appears as less threatening and as remnants—if not accidents—of a historical past in rural areas (Rahier 1998, 1999c, 2008).

In the last two decades, following the adoption of "multicultural" policies targeting indigenous and African diasporic populations by institutions of international development and global governance such as the United Nations and the World Health Organization (Hale 2002, 2004, 2005, 2006), and as a result of the political activism of indigenous and African diasporic communities, many Latin American nation-states revised their constitutions and passed special laws that express a concern for greater inclusion of African diasporic and indigenous populations. It is in this context that emerged what Charles Hale (2004) called *el indio permitido* (literally, the "allowed Indian," or the "permitted Indian identity") and that Latin American African diasporic populations gained relatively greater agency compared with the marked exclusion or construction as (ultimate) Others (see Rahier 1998, 1999c) that characterized their situation during "monocultural mestizaje" (Silva 1995;

Polo 2002; Espinosa Apolo 2003; Rahier 2003b). That period extended for Ecuador, from the early twentieth century until the major indigenous uprisings of the early 1990s (Whitten, Whitten and Chango 2003; Clark and Becker 2007), culminating in the adoption of a multicultural constitution in 1998 by a National Constituent Assembly (Rahier 2011). Elsewhere (Rahier 2008, 2010), I argue that in fact with multiculturalism, mestizaje—as an ideological technology of the state and as a project of the Ecuadorian elites—has not disappeared from the political landscape but instead continues to do its work both within and around multiculturalism. Thus, for Afro-Ecuadorians, the passage of the official or national stance from "monocultural mestizaje" to "multiculturalism" has not been accompanied by the transformations that the change of vocabulary might suggest. Instead, it has reinscribed the prevalent racial order in a "new" narration of the nation.

The Three Regions of Mainland Ecuador

Ecuador, like Colombia and Peru, can be sharply divided into three distinct regions extending from north to south: the coast, *la Costa*; the highlands or the two cordilleras of the Andes, *la Sierra;* and the Amazonian region, *el Oriente* (see figure 1). Because of the two cordilleras that separate the coast from the Oriente and the proximity of the equator, these regions present three very distinct climates.

The coast, between the Pacific Ocean and the Western cordillera of the Andes, is a fertile alluvial plain from 0 to 1,200 meters above sea level, which enjoys a tropical climate year round. Few indigenous communities live on the coast: mostly the Tsachila—in the area of the city of Santo Domingo de los Tsachilas (in the province of Pichincha), and in the province of Esmeraldas (the Chachi and the Awa-Kwaiker). The province of Esmeraldas constitutes the northern extremity of the coast and borders the Colombian department of Nariño. It is covered by two major river basins: the Esmeraldas River (with its most important tributaries, the Guayllabamba, the Blanco, and the Quinindé at the center of the province) and the Santiago River, in the north (with its tributaries the Bogotá, the Cayapas, and the Ónzole). The northern sector of the province of Esmeraldas is covered by a dense rainforest that goes northward and covers the Pacific lowlands of Colombia (West 1957).

Guayaquil—located at the mouth of the Guayas River, and capital of the province of Guayas—is the most populous city of the coast (and of the country), and that is where the regional economic and political powers are concentrated. It is often called *el Puerto Principal*, "the country's principal port," which it is and always was (see Phelan 1967). Many Afro-Esmeraldians have migrated to Guayaquil in the past few decades.

The Sierra is a region of about 390 miles long and 45 miles wide. Its altitude varies between 1,200 and 6,300 meters above sea level. From the perspective of physical geography, the two cordilleras of the Andes are the regional backbones. Numerous snowcapped volcanoes are located on both the eastern and the western chains. Many indigenous communities live in the inter-Andean valleys. Most of them had fallen under the rule of the Incas less than a century before the beginning of the Spanish conquest. From the early colonial period on, the Spaniards established their principal settlements in the Sierra. The "abundance" of indigenous labor and a climate depicted in tourists' brochures as an eternal spring probably provided decisive encouragement. The Chota-Mira Valley, the site where the other "traditional black community" lives, is a warm inter-Andean valley (from 1,300 to 1,800 meters) situated in the northern Sierra (figure 1). It enjoys a quasi-tropical microclimate very different from the tempered climate of the surrounding areas. The production of sugar cane with slave labor was the successful economic project for the valley during the colonial period. The sugar cane plantations, principally owned by the religious order of the Jesuits, were installed on the banks of the Chota and Mira Rivers (see Costales Peñaherrera and S. 1959, 1964; Colmenares 1969; Klumpp 1970; Stutzman 1974; CESA 1977, 1982; Coronel 1987a, 1987b, 1988; Savoia 1988, 1992). Many Afro-Choteños have migrated to Ibarra, the capital city of the Andean province of Imbabura, and to Quito.

The Oriente is covered with dense, tropical rainforests and constitutes a part of the drainage basin of the Amazon River and its tributaries (principally the Napo River). Until the mid-twentieth century, after the 1940s conflict with Peru and the beginning of oil exploitation—accompanied by governmental programs of colonization—it did not play a significant role in the colonial and early republican economic history of the country. Explored during the heroic age of the conquest, it became the site of a few missionary settlements in the 1600s, but a difficult climate and the hostile indigenous population "have kept mastery of the upper Amazon country an unfulfilled dream exciting the imagination and the cupidity of merchants, conquerors, and missionaries from the sixteenth century to the present" (Phelan 1967; Whitten 1981, 1–44). Diverse indigenous communities live in the Oriente. From the 1970s on, oil has been extracted from the Oriente by a series of foreign (U.S. and European) oil corporations, sometimes in partnership with Ecuadorian companies (Kimerling 1991). The internal migration into the Oriente has grown, and indigenous organizations have become more successful in having their voices heard in their struggles to stop the extension of oil exploration and production (Whitten 2003a, 1–45; Whitten, Whitten and Chango 2003; Vickers 2003). Afro-Esmeraldians and Afro-Ecuadorians living in Guayaquil have migrated to various towns of the Oriente in the past few decades.

The colonial and modern history of Ecuador is clearly marked by a strong antagonism between the Sierra, with Quito as its center, and the Costa, dominated by Guayaquil. It would be impossible to comprehend Ecuador and its history without keeping in mind this particular opposition but also the complementary relationship between the elite of the Sierra and the *guayaquileño* merchants and their allies (Lane 2003). During the colonial and the early national periods, highland landowners dominated the political scene. And despite the fact that the merchants of Guayaquil could sometimes have their voices heard by the Viceroy of Peru, for instance (Phelan 1967), most of the local powers were concentrated in Quito (*Real Audiencia de Quito* and Kingdom of Quito). It is only at the end of the nineteenth century that the Costa was successful in challenging the power of the Sierra, when its production of tropical products (bananas, cacao, rice, sugar, coffee, and *toquilla* palm) became the principal exports of the country. In the liberal revolution of 1895 led by Eloy Alfaro, the *guayaquileño* merchant class and its allies—the bankers and the *costeño* landowners (the liberals)—challenged the control of the state by the *serrano* landowners, who were supported by the Church (the conservatives) (Fernández 1994; Donoso Pareja 2000).

The opposition between the Costa and the Sierra is not limited to the economic and political history of Ecuador. Culturally, these two regions differ as well by the way costeños and serranos speak Spanish, the music they like, the food they prefer and with which they identify, and their politics (see Donoso Pareja 2000).

Brief Notes on the History of the Black Presence in the Province of Esmeraldas

The black immigration in Esmeraldas began in the sixteenth century, along with the commerce between the Spanish colonies of Central America and the Caribbean on one hand and the Vice Kingdom of Peru on the other. This commerce transited via Panama. Cartagena de Indias was the main port of the slave trade, which provided all the colonies of the region, the Pacific side of South America included (Bowser 1974; Curtin 1969; Palacios Preciado 1978). In the sixteenth century, the number of slaves transported was considerably reduced. The merchants who traveled between Panama and Callao (Peru) were transporting mostly merchandise. Sometimes they completed their loading with one or two slaves, rarely more (Bowser 1974). The first black immigration originated in the province in 1553, in the context of these commercial activities, and as a result of a shipwreck.

The facts were immortalized in the chronicle of Miguel Cabello Balboa (Cabello Balboa 1965 [1577]), who obtained the information in 1577 from shipwrecked ex-slave Sebastian Alonso de Illescas, who had become the leader of what the historians called the "Republic of Zambos"[9] (Phelan 1967; Rueda Novoa 1990, 2001; Lane 2002). The ship in question belonged to the Spaniard Sebastian Alonso de Illescas, from whom the slave had borrowed the name after his confirmation in Seville, Spain. The ship was en route to Callao (Peru) and had merchandise on board, as well as twenty-three slaves, a substantial number for the time (seventeen men and six women). After thirty days of navigation, the ship anchored off the Esmeraldian coast. The Spanish crew debarked with the slaves to hunt some game and refill the reserve with drinking water. Before they had the chance to return to the ship, a powerful thunderstorm wrecked the ship against the reefs. The slaves did not let the opportunity go and escaped into the forested central area of the province after having (probably) killed the Spanish crew.

In 1553, various small indigenous groups inhabited the region of Esmeraldas: the Niguas, the Yumbos, the Campaces, the Lachas, and the Malabas. The first indigenous communities with whom the maroons established contact were the Niguas and the Yumbos. The Chachi, the Malaba, and the Lacha were situated north of the Esmeraldas basin, while the Campaces resided in the south. The zone of influence of what became the zambo society was limited to the central part of the actual province, which corresponds more or less to the coast and the inland of Esmeraldas canton (see Rueda Novoa 1990). Other shipwrecks provided more runaway slaves, who joined Illescas's group (Rueda Novoa 2001; Lane 2002).

The control of the province of Esmeraldas was realized in two stages. The first was the trip by two zambo leaders to Quito: "Captain" Don Francisco Arobe (son of Juan Manguache, another shipwrecked runaway slave who occupied a position of leadership [Cabello Balboa 1965 (1577)] and "Captain" Don Sebastian Illescas (son of Sebastian Alonso). Arobe arrived in Quito before Sebastian Illescas, in 1599. His two sons, Pedro and Domingo, accompanied him.[10] The second stage of pacification saw the creation of villages according to a standard colonial model (church, parallel and perpendicular streets, central plaza). The foundation of villages was important for the control of what was to become the indigenous and zambo "labor force." At the turn of the seventeenth century, the total population of the Province did not exceed a few thousand. Consequently, any colonial project had to secure the control of the scarce labor force. This pressure for the control of the population provoked permanent conflict between the zambos and the colonial authorities. The celebration of the pact allowed the latter to progressively take control of the Province to the detriment of the zambo autonomy. At various occasions, the zambos escaped inland from the projects of relocation that were forcing them into labor. By the second half of the seventeenth century, the Republic of Zambos disappeared as a political power in the region (Rueda Novoa 2001).

The limited placer mining activity (of alluvial gravels) in the province was, and still is, principally located in the north, in the basin of the Santiago River and its tributaries. The mining incursions of the colonial period can be re-grouped into two: the first decades of the eighteenth century, primarily during incursions for prospecting, and also between 1815 and the beginning of the twentieth century, when successive penetrations of *señores de minas* (owners of concessions and slave gangs or *cuadrillas*) disposed of relatively important capitals and stimulated the creation of villages on the banks of the rivers. For the most part, capitalists of the mining region of southern New Grenada (Barbacoas and Popayán, in today's Colombia) financed these enterprises; the participation of capitalists from Quito was very limited and practically marginal (Rueda Novoa 2001). At the turn of the twentieth century, a few Americans and Europeans invested in Esmeraldian mining concessions.

After the confrontation in the early nineteenth century between royalists and Republicans, most of the few Esmeraldian mines, which never produced in the expected quantity and with a slave population of only a few hundred, were in a state of complete abandonment. In 1826, with the help of an ecclesiastic, the captains of the slave gangs of the mines of Playa de Oro, San José, and Güimbí (Santiago River basin) complained to the colonial authorities regarding the deplorable living conditions of the slaves: they had not received clothes for months, and they did not have salt (*Cuaderno Afro-Ecuatoriano* n7: *Documentos de la esclavitud*, 9).

The Esmeraldian goldfield production of the colony cannot be compared to the important production of the New Granadian Pacific lowlands[11] (Sharp 1976; West 1952, 1957; Wade 1993; Taussig 2004). One of the most important factors responsible for the limitations of the Esmeraldian gold production was without a doubt the absence of a practicable road, which isolated the slave gangs. Moreover, the lands of the northern sector of the province had not been truly colonized, which made the production of the necessary alimentation very difficult. The colonial mining project of Esmeraldas resulted in a failure (Rueda Novoa 2001), and during the eighteenth century most of the limited numbers of blacks living in the province were typically, at one point or another, left to themselves. Thus, Esmeraldian blackness remained characterized for the most part by a frontier situation in which blacks enjoyed more autonomy than in other American contexts of slavery, and in which black nucleation was possible (see Whitten 1974).

In the first quarter of the nineteenth century, the project of opening a road passing through the province of Esmeraldas to the ocean still preoccupied the elites of Quito and Ibarra. There was, however, a novelty: for the first time, they added to the road project the idea of colonizing the Esmeraldian lands to develop an agriculture inclined toward exportation (Rueda Novoa 2001). After the war for independence in which zambos and blacks (some free, some slave) were involved on both sides, the economic situation of the province—from the point of view of the white-mestizo society—was a disgrace because of its isolation and its limited population. Thus around 1850, and especially under the administration of President José María Urbina, the serrano elite made a series of decisions that resulted in the first binding of the province to the international market.

In Ecuador, the abolition of slavery followed a long process over several decades, which began in 1821 and ended with the Urbina Decree signed on July 25, 1851. The Convention of Guayaquil ratified the decree on September 18, 1852. Slavery was then in direct contradiction with the new republican institutions. For the liberals of the mid-nineteenth century who were controlling the institutions of the state, modernization and the development of international commerce was seen as the principal means to energize the Ecuadorian economy. To this effect, the national government took specific measures in each province. In 1846, a decree tried to encourage the colonization of Esmeraldas (Estupiñan Tello 1977, 95–96). The hope of a provincial economic development that would finally integrate Esmeraldas into the national economy was also the fundamental reason for the signing of the Convention Espinel-Moncatta by the government in 1854, aimed at reimbursing Ecuador's debt to the British Crown for the support received during the independence war of the *Gran Colombia*. Three years later, in 1857, the government signed the Icaza-Pritchett contract with its English creditors, who constituted the "Ecuador Land Company." This contract engaged the Ecuadorian government to place at the disposal of the British company one hundred thousand *cuadras* (a Spanish colonial unit of measure that varied by region) in the region of Atacames (near the city of Esmeraldas), and one hundred thousand supplementary cuadras in the Santiago basin, in the vicinity of the town of San Lorenzo, in exchange for part of the interest of the debt and at a location price of three pesos per cuadra. In the minds of the Ecuadorian government, this surrender of extended lands to the British creditors over which they legally lost control did not at all constitute treason to the national honor. In doing so, they wanted to maintain a good image on the international financial market by reimbursing a debt as well as give an impetus to the progress of the region, "because the British, where they go, they make roads, they install printing shops . . . and everywhere they bring their advanced technology and their strong capital" (Terán 1896, 646–47). In reality, things happened quite differently, and the hopes of the Ecuadorian government were never realized. The Ecuador Land Co. did not actually invest in the province; it subleased sections of its lands to other foreign or national commercial companies. These companies dedicated themselves to the export of forest products (tagua,[12] rubber, tobacco, gold) they bought from farmers and black gatherers who resided in the forest areas. Thus, despite the lack of investment, the Esmeraldian concessions to the Ecuador Land Co. gave an important boost to the provincial commercial activities. This was the first boom in the economic history of Esmeraldas, which is characterized by a cycle of booms and busts (CONADE 1980; Jácome B. 1978, 1979; Montaño 1982; Whitten 1965, 1974). That first boom was called "the tagua boom." The tagua boom put in place a system of gathering-export that functioned chiefly with black gatherers. The products (tagua, rubber, gold, tropical wood, tobacco) exported were gathered in the forest. They were not produced on plantations.

In addition to the blacks and zambos who already inhabited the province—which was then sparsely populated—the labor force necessary for gathering immigrated according to two mechanisms: immigration of ex-slaves from the Colombian region of Barbacoas and from the Ecuadorian province of Imbabura from 1850 to 1920 (West 1957), and immigration organized by a British company of Jamaican blacks to work in alluvial mines on the Santiago River (West 1957).

After a depression in the 1940s, the province of Esmeraldas experienced another economic period of development, the banana boom, which began around 1948. The American companies that had invested important capital in the banana plantations of Central America suffered great losses following a series of cyclones and the proliferation of nematode tread worms (*sigatoka negra*) (Jácome and Martínez 1979; Striffler 2002). These companies decided that Ecuador presented the most favorable conditions to replace their Central American plantations. And if there was indeed an Ecuadorian banana production in previous years, it is nonetheless only since 1948 that, because of the determination of the international market, Ecuador engaged in credit and incentive programs. Rapidly, the banana production augmented at a faster rhythm than the other traditionally exported coastal agricultural products, such as cacao, coffee, and sugar. "Because of this new situation, the agricultural frontier was extended to most of the regions suitable for the production of bananas. More regions of the country, principally along the Coast, were opened to new cultivation and forest regions were colonized" (Jácome and Martínez 1979, 115). This new "favorable" economic conjuncture integrated the province into the rest of the country. Many banana-producing haciendas emerged, particularly in the central area of the province.

The development of banana production in Esmeraldas presents some peculiarities compared with the production in other coastal provinces. A foreign trust (the Fruit Trading Company) controlled, through the intermediary of a local company (Aztral), an ample territory and dominated the export business. The controlled lands constituted a kind of enclave in the province. This transition of the provincial economy from a model of subsistence agriculture to a commercial one turned toward exportation did not happen in the entire province but principally in the Quinindé and Esmeraldas cantons. The most distant region of the north did not really participate in the banana boom.

At the beginning of the 1950s, the provincial population was composed of the following groups:

1. A reduced number of landowners (white-mestizos) who had settled during the gathering-exports period and whose most important activity was the breeding of animals for the local market;
2. A small sector of capitalists dedicated to commerce (principally white-mestizos);
3. The banana enclave turned toward exportation;
4. A sector of "small peasants"—principally blacks, contrary to the previous groups—who engaged especially in subsistence agriculture, who constituted the reserve of gatherers, and who participated in the boom as small producers in a marginal fashion (they planted in small quantities without really transforming or modernizing their production techniques).

With the boom, the last sector diversified progressively into

1. wage-earning workers for the enclave under the control of Aztral;
2. small producers who were selling their production to Aztral but who rapidly experienced serious difficulties because of a lack of capital necessary to acquire quality seeds, land, and modern technology;
3. domestics and nonagricultural workers residing primarily in urban areas (principally the city of Esmeraldas);
4. a relatively important group who stayed confined in a subsistence economy and who also stayed involved, on a small scale, in the gathering for exportation (the northern sector) (Jácome and Martínez 1979).

The commercialization of the bananas and the strength of the exports depended for the most part on the position the Fruit Trading Co. could obtain on the world market. That is why between 1948 and the end of the 1950s Esmeraldas experienced the peak of its banana boom following the deterioration of the Central American plantations, which belonged mostly to the competition (United Fruit and Standard Fruit). By the end of the 1950s, the sale possibilities of the Fruit Trading Co. on the world market diminished progressively following the recuperation of the Central American plantations and the strong comeback of the rival companies. The Fruit Trading Co. reacted to this new situation by reducing its investments in Esmeraldas and by paying lower prices for the production from its local companies. The difficulties of the Esmeraldian banana production augmented even more after the development of plantations in other coastal provinces. Between 1965 and 1970, the Esmeraldian participation in the Ecuadorian banana exports was insignificant, and the crisis reached its culmination.

The banana boom encouraged the immigration of various ethnic groups: blacks from the Colombian region of Barbacoas (West 1957) and white-mestizos principally from the provinces of Manabí and Pichincha, who settled mainly in the Esmeraldas and Quininde cantons. The banana bust provoked internal migrations from the region of Muisne to Esmeraldas and Quininde; some migrations also took place from the northern sector to Esmeraldas and Quininde but in lesser proportions (Jácome and Martínez 1979). The latter were not measured with precision.

With the banana crisis, northern black gatherers migrated to the city of Esmeraldas to constitute what is usually called by Ecuadorian social scientists "the urban popular strata," *el estrato popular urbano* (Jácome and Martínez 1979). They resided particularly in three entirely black neighborhoods: *el*

Pampón, la Isla Piedad, and *Barrio Caliente*. This migration continues to-day, and new black barrios were created principally through invasions of unoccupied lands. The in-migrants try to secure their survival with subal-tern jobs in the provincial administrations (if they are lucky enough to get them), as domestics in private houses, or as workers in the informal sector. The Esmeraldian elite, which resides in the city of Esmeraldas and is mostly white-mestizo (from the highlands or other coastal provinces), "Esmeraldian white-mestizo," and Lebanese, control all the instances of power (political, economic, and social).

This first chapter has provided necessary contextual information that should allow the reader to better appreciate the interpretive descriptions included in the following ethnographic chapters.

2

The Village of Santo Domingo de Ónzole and the Period of Preparation of the Festival of the Kings

The Centrality of Sexual Dichotomy and Role Reversal

Santo Domingo de Ónzole is located deep in the Esmeraldian rainforest on the left bank of the Ónzole River, an affluent of the Cayapas River, which itself reaches the Santiago River near Borbón (see figure 1). It does not differ much from the other small Afro-Esmeraldian villages established deep inside the rainforest (Concepción, Güimbí, Telembí, Selva Alegre). Although these villages might have benefited in the past from the gold, tagua, and banana booms, their inhabitants continue to live principally from subsistence products (agriculture, hunting, and fishing). Their cash economy is more limited than in San Lorenzo, Limones, and Borbón, which are the three most important towns in the northern sector of the province of Esmeraldas. These economic booms—the tagua boom is at the origin of the foundation of Santo Domingo de Ónzole—reinforced the subsistence economy.

Rivers constitute the only means of traveling. The entire population of most of these villages is black (nonracially mixed), and until the late 1980s they had not been threatened by a white or white-mestizo in-migration. The members of the provincial elite, who reside in the city of Esmeraldas, the provincial capital, often refer to the people who live in the small villages along the banks of the Santiago and Ónzole Rivers with the expression *los negros azules* (the blue blacks), to underscore the darkness of their skin color. It is true that members of the local elite (and many others with them) are preoccupied with the "improvement of the race" (*mejoramiento de la raza*)—a popular expression that evokes the whitening of the skin color of their children or the maintaining of family "whiteness" through "appropriate marriages" (Rahier 1999b).

Figure 2. View of Santo Domingo de Ónzole from the upper part of the barrio "Quito." (Photograph by Jean Muteba Rahier)

Between December 1989 and January 1990, I conducted a census covering the entire population of the village with the help of two research assistants, anthropology students from the Pontificia Universidad Católica del Ecuador (PUCE)–Quito. At that time, the total population of Santo Domingo was 361: 184 males (51 percent) and 177 females (49 percent). The average age was 24.08 years, and the proportions of the classes of age were the following: from 0 through 20 years, 53 percent (191 people) of the population; from 21 to 40 years, 24.4 percent (88 people); from 41 to 60 years, 17.7 percent (64 people); and those older than age 60 were 4.9 percent, or 18 people. As was the case in other Afro-Esmeraldian villages of the north of the province where I had the opportunity to visit, children were numerous in Santo Domingo: one-third of the total population was between birth and ten years of age.

The Subsistence Economy in the Northern Sector of Esmeraldas

The population of Santo Domingo presents a slight intracommunity differentiation: some men (whom I call the "leaders") have been more entrepreneurial than others and consequently more successful in accumulating economic resources. The village population has a way of life much more communitarian than in La Tola. It is still greatly characterized by subsistence economy.

Subsistence agriculture takes place in the form of agroforestry. It is based on a system of slash-mulch, which is probably of indigenous origin. The slash-mulch system functions as follows: at the beginning of the process, the land to be cultivated is not burned. The seeds, corms, and stem cuttings are planted, after which the vegetation is cut down and used as mulch. It is only after the planting that the leaves of the old plantain and other growth are cut. This vegetal debris is then left on top of the growing plants to decompose quickly. The mulch forms a thick cover through which the small sprouts emerge after about two weeks. Plants grow rapidly, as the decomposing vegetal cover provides a natural fertilizer. The machete is the only indispensable tool. It is used to cut the branches out of trees, to harvest the plantains and the sugar cane, to dig in the ground. To cut the coconuts and the clusters of *chontaduros* (peach palm, *Guilielma Gasipaes*), they use, when they have one, a "half-moon" (*una media luna*), which is a kind of sickle with a very long wooden handle up to six feet long.

The products cultivated in all gardens are relatively varied: several kinds of plantains provide the basic foodstuff. Plantains are eaten in different forms, for breakfast, lunch, and dinner. Other crops include sugar cane, avocados, pineapples, peach palm fruits, mangos, oranges, lemons, *guanábanas*, *caimitos*, cacao, and a great variety of other fruits, a diversity of roots, such as manioc and corm and old- and new-world taro. Many Santo Domingeños also plant "tropical trees" for wood in their gardens. When these trees are cut down, the trunks are transported downriver in big rafts and then sold to the sawmills in Borbón.

Afro-Esmeraldian gardens have an appearance quite distinct from the monocultures and their orderly crops. Gardens are sometimes located far away from the village, deep in the forest. When I visited gardens with Santo Domingeños, I remember always being surprised when the man I was accompanying was telling me that we had arrived at our destination. Nothing distinguishes the garden from the rest of the forest, to the eyes of the ignorant foreigner that I was. This impression is due to the thick vegetal cover on the ground, but also to the great variety of plants and trees, arranged in what appears to uneducated eyes as a somewhat "disorganized way." In a corner, there are pineapples growing on the ground. Farther away, there are a few sugar cane plants alongside scattered banana trees. Fruit trees have been planted in various spots and, just as in the noncultivated area of the forest, one has to walk around the garden to avoid branches and trees, being careful not to step into a hidden swamp before finally reaching a spot where a series of manioc plants are growing next to taro (another corm of a purple hue).

Hunting provides most of the protein in the people's diet. The four animals most hunted, and therefore the most abundant, are the *guanta* (a paca or *Cuniculus paca virgatus*, which looks like a large guinea pig, with a delicious white meat); two species of savage peccary—the *tatabra* (collared peccary or *Peccari tajacu bangsii*) and the *saíno* (white-lipped peccary or *Tayassu pecari spiradens*); and the *venado* (deer). Hunting is strictly a male activity. Men often prefer to hunt in groups of two, usually with another male family member.

Fishing is much less important for the daily diet than it has been in the past. The use and abuse of dynamite to fish is responsible for a drastic decrease of the fish population in the river. A provincial decree was passed in the late 1980s to forbid the use of explosives as a fishing technique. The ban has for the most part not been respected. As various men told me, the fish that the Santo Domingeños are able to catch with the *atarraya* (a casting fishnet), in the *corrales* (large bamboo fish traps installed underwater on the bank of the river), or with dynamite are generally smaller than the fish they caught before the advent of explosives. With the *catanga*, a cylindrical trap made out of tree bamboo, they trap river shrimp. More so than in past years, they have to buy fresh or salted fish during a trip to Borbón, from one of the small stores of the village (salted), or from traveling salesmen (fresh and salted). These are usually fishermen from villages of the coastal area, including La Tola.

The Foundation of the Village at the End of the Nineteenth Century

The in-migration that led to the founding of the village began at the end of the nineteenth century. The first migrants were all either Afro-Esmeraldian *santiageños* (persons born in a village located on one of the banks of the Santiago River) or Afro-Colombians coming primarily from the Colombian Nariño Department (see West 1957).

At that time, the region of the upper Ónzole was practically unpopulated. The Chachi indigenous people farthest up the Ónzole River lived in the community of Loma Linda, which is situated in the parish of San Francisco de Ónzole, about forty-five minutes by canoe downriver from Santo Domingo.

Some villagers indicated, somewhat contradicting the previous statement, that there were already a few Chachi living on the lands that were going to become the village of Colón (upriver the Onzole from Santo Domingo). The arrival of black people in the region of the upper Ónzole at the same time as—and even perhaps before—the Chachi is an argument that was often used by Santo Domingeños in their struggle to have their land officially recognized as communal land by the Ecuadorian state. In 1989, the Chachi of the northern sector of the province of Esmeraldas (which includes the upper Ónzole) had already obtained from the national government, through its appropriate agencies, a communal title of ownership of their gardens and of specified forest areas (*bosques*), which these documents termed *territorio tradicional* (traditional land):

> Black people came to the Ónzole before the Chachi. All of us we have forefathers and foremothers who came from the Santiago River, the Cayapas River, or Colombia. The Chachi, when they entered in the Ónzole, they were very few. They were in Loma Linda. Later, they went upriver closer to the source of the river, in Pambíl, Ónzole, Gualpí or Capulí.
>
> When we came here (*los negros*), there were only Cayapas downriver. Very few of them had already reached Colón. (Fragment of a conversation with an elder from Santo Domingo de Ónzole)

The oral testimonies I have gathered from San Francisco de Ónzole, Santo Domingo de Ónzole, and Colón show that the arrival of black people in the upper Ónzole was a direct consequence of the tagua boom. The unoccupied land of that area of the Esmeraldian rainforest was attractive at a time when the price of tagua was at its highest. This favorable economic situation encouraged the exploration and the colonization of new lands for the gathering of forest products, including the tagua nuts.

The origin of the first immigrants was rather surprising to me. I was expecting to see the thesis of Robert West (1957) confirmed: the Afro-Esmeraldian villages of the Eloy Alfaro Canton were principally founded by Afro-Colombians from the mining areas around Barbacoas, following the abolition of slavery. As it appeared, West's thesis is mostly valid for the foundation of villages along the banks of the Santiago River. The establishment of villages along the banks of the Ónzole River took place later, and although some came directly from Colombia, most people migrated from villages on the Santiago. There had therefore been, at the end of the nineteenth century and at the beginning of the twentieth, a movement of internal migration within the northern sector of the province, which redistributed or extended the black presence—until then concentrated on the Santiago—to other areas of the canton:

> MARCIANA MEDINA (M. M.), from Santo Domingo de Ónzole: My parents were from the Santiago, from Playa de Oro more exactly. They came here before the Concha war. I was a little girl during the Concha war.
>
> JEAN MUTEBA RAHIER (J. R.): And why did your parents leave Playa de Oro?
>
> M. M.: I don't know why they came. They liked it here. At that time, many people were coming here. They came to see, they liked it, and they stayed. My grandparents also came here. My mother came here as a little girl. She got together with my father here.

The flux of migration into what was becoming Santo Domingo intensified during the Concha Revolt (1912–16). It was in fact easy to escape from the "Conchista commissions" that conscripted Afro-Esmeraldian peasants by force in their ranks.

La Guerra de Concha, or the Concha revolt, from the name of Colonel Carlos Concha who led it, was one of the most famous liberal rebellions against the conservative national government in Quito. As shown by this interview, it had great effect on the lives of Afro-Esmeraldian northerners (see Chávez 1971; Estupiñán Tello 1977; Montaño 1982).

Kinship Networks in Santo Domingo

In Santo Domingo, ritual, fictive, or real kinship is of great importance for the exploitation of the natural resources (agriculture, hunting, fishing). Kinship-organized networks of solidarity constituted the social capital of any individual. When coming back from a hunting journey, for example, a man first sold the parts of the animals he has caught and that he did not want to keep or smoke for his own family, to his brothers, sisters, cousins, sons, and uncles before eventually considering selling them to a nonrelative. The construction and repairing of houses are always made with the help of relatives. And when a man wants to sell the surplus of his harvests in Borbón to obtain the cash necessary to purchase a variety of products (rice, kitchen oil, *aguardiente* [distilled sugar cane alcohol], gun powder) while avoiding the cost of a trip because the amount of his surplus did not justify such an expense, he arranges in advance, with one or more relatives, to regroup their surplus and make only one trip for the benefit of all of them.

The repetition of certain family or last names reflects the existence of these networks of kinship. In the village, at the time of my census, 328 individuals, that is to say 90.9 percent of the total population of inhabitants, shared nine last names (I took into consideration only the first last name, which is given by the father): 109 persons were called Medina (30.2 percent); 82 Quiñonez (22.7 percent); 50 Corozo (13.9 percent); 26 Borja (7.2 percent); 19 Caicedo (5.3 percent); 15 Ayoví (4.2 percent); 12 Valencia (3.3 percent); eight Montaño (2.2 percent); and seven Preciado (1.9 percent). The rest of the population, 33 people (9.1 percent), was divided between 18 other last names.

It is then possible to conceive the population of the village as being "localized" (see Whitten 1970), in the sense that they have established intracommunity networks to exploit economic resources, to the point of rendering the geographic mobility difficult.

Outmigration from Santo Domingo de Ónzole

During the census, we asked questions only about the children of current inhabitants who had outmigrated. We did not ask questions of the heads of families about their brothers and sisters, or about any other person who had migrated and who did not have, at the time of the census, at least one of his or her parents living in the village. In that way, we identified 125 migrants who were all children, wives, or husbands of living Santo Domingeños. This number would be higher if we had included in our calculations the parentless outmigrants.

The 125 outmigrants represented 34.6 percent of the total population of inhabitants: 21 went to live in two other villages of the Santo Domingo Parish (10 in Colón and 11 in Zancudo); 21 left the parish to make a living in other villages of the Eloy Alfaro Canton (Limones, Borbón, San Francisco de Ónzole, and Selva Alegre); 24 went to the rest of the province (21 in the city of Esmeraldas and 3 in the village of Lagarto); 45 went to Guayaquil; 13 went to other parts of the country; and only one person emigrated internationally, to Caracas, Venezuela.

Women outmigrated more than men (76 and 49, respectively). The 14 women who outmigrated to another village of the parish kept the same daily activities as the women of Santo Domingo: housekeeping and help with agroforestry. However, as soon as they left the parish, although some continued to be housekeepers, most of them became domestic employees (as cooks and other domestic employees, and doing temporary work) in Borbón or Limones, in the city of Esmeraldas; and in Guayaquil, in the rest of the country, or in Caracas. Two women who had completed their secondary education were employees, and three of them had professional jobs (in nursing and teaching) after having been exposed to some higher education.

During the six years I resided in Ecuador, from 1985 through 1991, I had more than once the opportunity to meet Santo Domingeños in the cities of Esmeraldas, Quito, or Guayaquil. I was then able to evaluate the enormous economic difficulties that they had to face daily. Some, who had been referred to during the census as "workers" or "domestic employees," were in fact in prison or were sexual workers, and when they realized that I was going to visit the village after our conversations, they insisted that I not reveal their real occupations, which I of course promised not to do.

The people who migrated outside of the canton only came back very rarely to the village, usually when a close parent died. In 1989–90, the trip from Guayaquil by bus and by *lancha* (large, wooden canoes with outboard motors), which was relatively costly, could take up to two days.

During the tagua and banana booms, migration out of the small Afro-Esmeraldian villages located in the forest seems to have been much less important than the outmigration that began in the 1970s and continues until today. The eventual migrants were then going primarily to the city of Esmeraldas, which was in full expansion, attracted by the growing demand for unskilled laborers. I could not measure that migration. The parish and canton archives are simply nonexistent or they are kept in such a way that it is impossible to extract from them any valid information. But the numerous oral testimonies I have gathered during my visits to various villages of Eloy Alfaro and San Lorenzo cantons allow me to interpret the consequences of the economic booms in reinforcing the traditional subsistence economy. The "poor peasants" had no reason really to migrate. They obtained relatively good prices for the products they cultivated in their gardens. In the 1950s, the development of commercial banana production attracted numerous Afro-Colombians to the province (West 1957, 103 and elsewhere; Striffler 2002). On that issue, Grace Schubert wrote: "As opportunities stimulated by the world market presented themselves to the non-indigenous coastal people (Blacks), they participated in a cash economy in return for securing the raw material called for by foreign entrepreneurs. When this demand no longer existed, they adjusted by returning to their time-honored subsistence economy" (1981, 564).

Since the end of the 1970s, without real interruption, the economy of the province has been in decline, encouraging migration. In Santo Domingo, the situation of the youth has become more and more difficult. Progressively, the lands closer to the village are occupied by the older men (land usually belongs to men), which obligates the younger men to establish gardens on lands that are quite removed. And after having to face the difficulties involved with transporting the harvests from the gardens to the rivers, and then from the rivers to the village in dugout canoe, and then with transporting the surplus from the village to Borbón or Limones, their income is not sufficient to provide for the needs of their families. The effort appears too great for the meager income.

Young people have a worldview that is quite different from that of their parents. The influence of schools, battery-powered radios, relatives who had migrated and who later visited the village, or even the experience they have had when visiting Esmeraldas or Guayaquil are having a great influence on their conceptions of the world. It is not rare to hear them talk of their parents, although with affection, as people—most of them illiterate—who have, in a way, lost contact with reality.

The brother of Santo Domingo's political lieutenant in the 1990s, known by the nickname of *el abogado* ("the lawyer") because he had come back from a stay in Guayaquil with a way of talking that was somewhat refined, explained to me one day that he would not take a woman in the village to establish a family. He planned to go back to Guayaquil: "Why would I get 10 kids if I cannot educate them? If I cannot give them anything? Moreover, when you live here in the village, you don't have a lot of options. At least in the city, you have more options, even if you have to struggle a lot there too."

The Village Leaders and the Socioeconomic Reality

To describe the socioeconomic differentiation in Santo Domingo, I find it more useful to use, in addition to the category of "poor peasants"—which corresponds to most of the village population—a category that I call the "individual leaders," because they enjoy some respect from the rest of the population. The middle class of local entrepreneurs identified by Whitten is more appropriate for the socioeconomic description of the small towns of the region (Borbón, Limones, and San Lorenzo), where the individuals included in that category manipulate more cash and are more involved, on a daily basis, in the political and economic life of the region than the people from Santo Domingo whom I have chosen to call "leaders." The "leaders" are, in their community, also more entrepreneurial than the others. They are themselves peasants who also play the role of intermediaries for the village commerce. They usually have larger gardens than the other men of the village, although the extension of their gardens is not great enough to qualify them as cash farmers. They might have a few cows and obtain a major part of their income by buying the harvest surplus of their fellow villagers who do not want to make the trip themselves to Borbón or Limones because their individual surplus is not sufficient to justify the cost of a trip. They usually have a small store (*una tiendita*) in the village, in which they sell various articles of daily need (rice, aguardiente, cigarettes, matches, bandaids, sweets, sugar, tomatoes, kitchen oil, beer, a few pieces of clothing, machetes, which they bought in Borbón, Limones, or even sometimes in Esmeraldas), to members of the "local middle class of entrepreneurs" who own larger and more varied stores. The leaders of the Afro-Esmeraldian villages of the rainforest are always black, whereas there are more and more "light-skinned Costeños" and Andean white-mestizos among the "local entrepreneurs" in Borbón, Limones, La Tola, or Esmeraldas.

In Santo Domingo, the leaders are those who could benefit from the periods of economic boom to put together, with their tienditas, a system of intermediary commerce. They have access to the social capital necessary for the possession of bigger gardens, mostly through the labor of others (usually kin). They enjoy relatively greater economic security that allows them to somewhat buffer away the effects of the periods of bust. During my visits to Santo Domingo in the period between 1988 and 1991, I could identify four men who were clearly much more entrepreneurial than the others and whom I include in this category.

Four Santo Domingeños were salaried: the schoolteacher, Neyra; the political lieutenant, Childo Corozo (until January 1991); the employee and the janitor of the *dispensario médico* (small clinic; see the village map), respectively Trífilo Corozo (one of Childo's older brothers), and Doña Flora, who was Childo's and Trífilo's sister. All these positions were relatively recent. Before Neyra came back as schoolteacher, all the teachers came from other regions of the province. Before May 14, 1982, there was no teniente político[1] (political lieutenant) since the parish of Santo Domingo did not exist. Its territory was included in the neighboring parish of San Francisco de Ónzole, and the two employees of the clinic were hired through the "Project of Medical and Spiritual Health," funded by U.S. and Dutch Protestant churches.

The Geography of the Village

For Santo Domingeños, the village is clearly divided into three neighborhoods (barrios). These neighborhoods were each given a name with regard to the respective elevation they had in the village topography, in a humorous attempt (as we shall see) to recall the three most important cities of the country: Quito, Guayaquil, and Cuenca.

The first neighborhood, called "Quito," is the most elevated of the three, just like the city of Quito in relation to the other two largest Ecuadorian cities. It constitutes the southern part of the village and is separated from the other neighborhoods by a small stream, which is almost dry most of the year. Its altitude varies from around sixty-five feet to around fifty feet, relative to the river water level in dry season. Its terrain is therefore inclined: the highest part is its western extremity, near the public toilets, and the lowest its eastern extremity. Quito is the oldest part of the village, where the village's founders installed the first houses.

The second neighborhood is called "Guayaquil" because, just like the country's "principal port," it is the lowest and flattest part of the village: a dozen

Figure 3. Map of Santo Domingo de Ónzole. (Map by Florida International University Web Services Enterprise)

meters from the river water during the dry season. "Guayaquil" was founded mostly by offspring of inhabitants of "Quito" and by new immigrants who came in the 1930s, when the space in "Quito" did not allow for any more expansion westward without bringing the disadvantage of being very far from the point of the neighborhood where there is an access to the river (the stairs in concrete). The founders of the village decided to construct their houses in "Quito" because at the time, the rainy season used to have more precipitation, which caused flooding on the land of "Guayaquil." This had been much less often the case since at least the 1960s.

The third neighborhood is called "Cuenca" because it is higher than "Guayaquil" but lower than "Quito," just like the city of Cuenca actually is. This is the most recent neighborhood: the first houses were built there at the end of the 1940s. It is also on a slope, and its height varies from around fifty feet, to less than sixty-five feet. This is the least densely populated neighborhood: it had, at the time of my visit, only twelve houses.

This naming of the three neighborhoods of the village is ironic in that the Santo Domingeños know very well, from their trips to Guayaquil or Quito (most never traveled to Cuenca) that their village neighborhoods represent the opposite of the three largest urban areas of the country, which are associated in the national racial-spatial order with modernity and white-mestizoness. By giving the names of the three major urban settings of the country to the three constitutive parts of Santo Domingo, the villagers are, as it were, symbolically claiming an Ecuadorian-ness that is denied to them in myriad ways once they leave the village and face everyday life situations in the cities of Esmeraldas, Guayaquil, and Quito.

The Ónzole River, just like the other waterways of the northern sector of the province, on the banks of which Afro-Esmeraldians established villages, is indispensable for the life of the community. It provides drinking water, fish, and river shrimp. It was also a location of choice for hunting paca and other animals at night. It sometimes served as a big garbage recycling system, since many threw their rubbish in it. Women washed the clothes on its banks in the morning. It provided the major way of traveling, in canoe or in lanchas. Many went to relieve themselves in it, while sometimes, not at the same moment hopefully, everyone bathed in it daily, usually in the afternoon, when the temperature is higher than in the morning.

Santo Domingeños distinguished upriver from downriver with the vernacular expression *adentro* (inside) and *afuera* (outside); they sometimes also used the expression, respectively, of *arriba* (up) and *abajo* (down). Strangers—that is to say missionaries, politicians, traveling salesmen, a rare anthropologist, and medical doctors—always have come to the village from afuera or abajo (downriver), while the people who arrive from adentro or arriba are either Afro-Esmeraldians from the village of Colón, or Chachi from the various villages they have established upriver near Colón, and further up at Pambíl and Capulí. The latter are not real strangers, unlike the people who come from afuera. It is meaningful that, for example, the canoe of the "President of the Republic" and his party, who are all "whites," arrive from afuera, from outside, on the morning of January 6, the first day of the Play, while the black and indigenous people, and the forest spirits who visit the village on January 7 and 8, always come into the village from the west (near the public toilets in "Quito"), from adentro, from inside, if we take into consideration the direction of the river flow.

Afro-Esmeraldian houses are constructed on four piles of *guayacán* wood, which is very dense and water resistant. Often, there are four couples of piling, which are installed at what will become the four corners of the house: there is one shorter pole that sustains the beam on which the floor will be installed, and a second one, much longer, on which the walls will be nailed and the structure of the roof fixed. Usually the interior space of the houses is divided into two or three rooms. One or two rooms serve as sleeping rooms as well as living rooms and are also used to receive visitors. A kitchen is installed at the back of the house. Most of the time, the room that serves as kitchen does not have external walls: it is a room by virtue of its floor. That is where the *fogón* (brazing fire) is lit on a wooden structure, and where all the kitchen utensils are kept. The interior walls of the house are made in split bamboo or of wooden boards, which is cheaper and less resistant than the guayacán. The wooden walls give more privacy than bamboo, which has cracks. The bamboo or the wood is nailed on the foundation beams, although in the past they were fixed to these beams with vegetal fibers (see West 1957). The external walls are usually in split bamboo as well. The flooring is made of irregular peach palm wood, which is very dark and very hard, and which is also used for the fabrication of the marimba keys (a locally made xylophone). The roof's structure is covered with leaves from a variety of palm trees: tagua, peach palm, or even sometimes, in case of a leak in the roof, with leaves from banana trees, which resist water very well when green. During the life span of a house, the walls and the roof are replaced many times.

The houses that have been constructed more recently, by younger people, sometimes have a second floor, which allows for a better separation of the living area from the bedrooms (on the second floor). Their floors and their walls are made of boards of lighter wood, and the roofs are zinc, which makes for a lot of noise when it rains.

The first school of the village was created at the end of the 1920s. It was a school that was financed by the village's heads of families (*padres de familia*), which was a very common situation in the Afro-Esmeraldian villages of the northern sector of the province. Parents agreed on an amount to pay per academic year and per child. The money mostly served to pay the salary of a teacher. At the beginning of the year, the parents paid a down payment and, when they had been able to verify at the end of the year that their children had learned what they were supposed to learn, that their children could read, write, and calculate, they paid the balance to the teacher. During times of economic boom, the family heads did not have too many difficulties paying for the education of their children. Some years later, that first school functioned with two teachers who had come from the Santiago. They had been educated by Catholic priests. It is only in the 1950s that the national government funded the construction of the school in "Quito" and sent three salaried teachers.

The church was also built in the 1950s. It has been in bad shape for a long time. The roof has many leaks. The deplorable state of the church points to the rarity of the visits of Catholic priests and missionaries in the villages of the upper Ónzole. Santo Domingeños, as do most other Afro-Esmeraldians, consider themselves Catholics, even though they often perform "Catholic rituals" on their own, without the presence of a priest. In fact, during their visits, Catholic priests often try to transform their traditional rituals: Saint Days (arrullos), and, most important, the funerals for deceased children (chigualos).

The small clinic and the toilets constructed especially for the clinic's personnel were built in 1988. That edifice was the first step of a five-year development project funded by U.S. and Dutch Protestant churches. The actual management of the project was under the responsibility of the NGO *Centro Nacional de Desarrollo* (CENAD). The CENAD provided the funds to build the clinic and pay the salaries of the clinic's personnel, and the Santo Domingeños contributed their labor.

Despite their charitable intentions, the white-mestizos who were the leading personnel of the clinic had difficulties establishing good communication with the Santo Domingeños. I must say that they behaved a bit arrogantly with Afro-Esmeraldians, as if the latter were completely ignorant, as if they were schoolchildren in need of learning how to behave properly in life. They never manifested any interest in Afro-Esmeraldian ways, customs, and the traditional knowledge they had accumulated during the many decades of their presence in the forest. They viewed Afro-Esmeraldians as completely deprived of any medical knowledge and as pagans when considering their spiritual life. Their approach was in all ways completely opposed to mine. I sometimes had the feeling that the fact that I was black provoked a certain malaise in the interactions I had with them. On the one hand, I shared some physical characteristics with those whom they called, with an air of superiority, *los morenos*; on the other hand, because I had at the time Belgian nationality, I came from the much-admired Europe and therefore deserved respect. I resided in one of the houses of the village; they resided in the clinic, which was rather removed physically from the places where the community life was unfolding. They had their own generator, which they turned on every night at around 6:30 P.M. until they went to sleep. When they were in the village, the noise of their generator resounded loudly, almost violently signifying their presence. It was only on special festive days that the community's generator was turned on. During my episodic conversations with the clinic's personnel, I always surprised them with information I had gathered about the village and its history. I remember how astonished they were to learn that the village was in fact divided into three neighborhoods, which were given the names of the three biggest cities of the country, and that they celebrated every year the Festival of the Kings, on which my research was focused. I also had to explain to them that Santo Domingeños, just like many Afro-Esmeraldians, performed different funeral rituals for adults and for children.

Santo Domingeños refer to the staff of the clinic with the expression *los doctores* (the doctors). Individually, they addressed the medical doctor and the dentist with the term *doctor*, while they used *licenciada* for the two female nurses. On their part, the doctores did not refer to the Santo Domingeños with the expression "the inhabitants," "the people," or "the blacks," but instead with *los morenos*, which is very meaningful in the mouth of a white-mestizo in such a situation. The euphemistic term *Moreno* is generally preferred to *negro* by white-mestizos who find the latter depreciative and insulting, as if to call someone *negro* (black) was obligatorily and directly negative. In the same register, white-mestizos preferred to use the term *indígena* instead of *indio*, for a similar reason: *indio* evoked, to them, insult and disrespect.

The village generator, which has been installed in the neighborhood "Quito" north of the school to limit the annoyance of its noise, the communal house, and the stairs in concrete were gifts to the village community from local politicians during electoral campaigns. The prison was built after the parish of Santo Domingo de Ónzole was created.

The wooden stairs were constructed by various men of "Guayaquil" in December 1989 with wood that had been donated by Childo, who was then, in addition to being a resident of "Guayaquil," the village's teniente político. That donation was also aimed at getting the respect of the doctors, who had suggested such a construction at several occasions to help the families of that part of the village ascend the riverbank, which was often muddy and slippery. Childo and his brother Trífilo were among the few men to attend the Bible meetings organized by the doctores, and who publicly self-identified as Protestants.

The temple, located east of the soccer field, has never been completely constructed. An outmigrant to the city of Guayaquil, who comes back to the village regularly to buy dug-out canoes by the dozen to sell in the province of Guayas where wood is less available, had begun its construction years before the arrival of the missionaries. He was convinced that the Protestant faith would help Santo Domingeños to improve their lives. Until my last stay in the village in 2003, he had never received the help he needed from the rest of the village's population.

Women and the Permit to Play Kings

The Afro-Esmeraldian Festival of the Kings is traditionally organized by a committee of women, called reyeras or fiesteras.

The committee of fiesteras usually gets together for the first time and relatively discretely in one of their houses, a few weeks to a month prior to the beginning of the Festival. During the first meeting, they begin distributing roles or ranks that each one of them will play or hold from December 28 until January 8. They also discuss the various financial aspects of the Festival: What are the things that they will need to buy? Who will bring what? How are they going to buy aguardiente and the gunpowder for the rifles (escopetas) and the *tambuco* (a small canon exclusively used to produce a loud noise)? Who is going to make the *guarapo* (sugarcane beer) for the reyeras to drink during the three days of the Play? Who will invite the *marimberos*, (marimba players) from Timbiré (a small Afro-Esmeraldian village on the Cayapas River) with whom various Santo Domingeños have maintained contact? How are they going to pay for the cost of their trip? Who will prepare and pay for their meals? Some reyeras attending the meeting contribute to the budget with 1,000, 1,500, or even 2,000 *sucres* (the Ecuadorian currency then; at the time, one U.S. dollar exchanged for about 800.00 sucres). Some also make the promise to bring in a gallon of aguardiente *Juan del Monte* (a sugar cane alcohol distilled domestically, and illegally, which is not as strong as the commercial aguardiente) to the house of the "president" or of the "treasurer" before the beginning of the Festival. These ranks, which they call *cargos*, parody the political organization of the national Ecuadorian state, or at least of its most visible aspects, in an Afro-Esmeraldian perspective. In the reality of daily life, nonblack men always occupy these ranks (except for those of political lieutenant and police officers). The cucuruchos do not feminize their ranks when they officially assume their positions. They masculinize their appearances with the use of pants—never worn by women in village context, except by younger women who have migrated to an urban area and who do sometimes visit the village wearing tight jeans or other pants. In a loose hierarchy, the committee has a president (who remains undeclared or secret until January 6); a minister of the interior (*ministro de gobierno*); a governor (*gobernador*); a treasurer; a captain of sea and land (*capitán de mar y tierra*); a *fe de crimen* (this is in fact the name of a legal document); an *escuadrón de la muerte* (squadron of death); a provincial chief of police (*intendente general de policía*); a political lieutenant (*teniente político*); a secretary of the political lieutenant's office (*secretario de la tenencia*); a first police commissioner (*comisario primero*); a second police commissioner; a guard of the communal patrimony (*guardia del estanco*); and police officers. This hierarchy is a loose one. Many ranks seem to concentrate the same amount of power (capitán de mar y tierra; fe de crimen; escuadrón de la muerte); however, everyone agrees that the president is at the top of the hierarchy, while the police officers are at the bottom. Younger women always occupy the lower ranks. Doña Ermelina, an older woman of the village who had not disguised herself for many years, told me about the authority of the members of the committee.

> DOÑA ERMELINA (D. E.): I was the provincial chief of police. I was sitting at a table over there. The other women brought me the "prisoners" and I gave them an arrest warrant (*boleta de captura*). This was for them to pay the fee to be freed. I was always showing a very serious face.
>
> JEAN MUTEBA RAHIER (J. R.): It was not the political lieutenant who gave the arrest warrant?
>
> D. E.: No, not at all! You don't understand, I was the provincial chief of police, I had more power (*tenía más orden*) than the lieutenant. The president came first, then the governor, then me. The lieutenant had a lower rank than the Intendente. The ones with the least power were the police officers.
>
> J. R.: So, you were receiving orders from the president?
>
> D. E.: That's right! The president was giving me orders, the governor as well. That's how the Play of the Reyes was, it was fun!

The beginning of the preparation period is marked by a singular event, which evokes Victor Turner's "framing" (Turner 1977): receiving the permit (*el permiso*) to play Reyes, from the political lieutenant. In the afternoon of December 27, the cucuruchos get together to solve the last small organizational problems: distribute the final ranks, decide whom they will ask, from among the men of the village, for help to construct two punitive stocks or *cepos*[2] (one for the adults and a smaller one for the children), which will serve to imprison men and boys. At the end of this meeting, two or three of them go to the lieutenant to officially request the permit.

The stocks (see figure 20 on page 163) appear in the village only for the duration of the Festival, from December 28 through January 8. It is a wooden structure made of two long beams about fourteen inches long. The first one, very light, is made of balsa wood and lies on the ground. With a machete, men make some slots within the balsa wood, which will serve to place the inferior part of the leg (the calf) of the imprisoned men, who will in that way be forced to remain seated. The second beam is made in the very heavy guayacán wood and is placed above the balsa beam. The prisoners, or *encepados*, in their seating position, cannot lift the weight of the guayacán beam. Only a person standing up could do that. The cucuruchos are the ones who let the prisoners go free after they pay their fines. No men would dare touch the stock to free a friend, brother, or cousin. If they do, they know that they will be arrested. The reyeras always want two stocks to be built. The second and smaller one is for the boys. If boys were imprisoned in the stock for adults, they could easily escape because the slots are too big for their smaller legs. Women are never arrested or placed in the stocks.

The teniente never refuses the permit. The permit is part of the tradition. Every year—and this is independent of who is teniente—it is redacted in the same terms. Before Santo Domingo became a parish, the reyeras went to get the permit from the parish of San Francisco de Ónzole's political lieutenant, downriver from the village, in which Santo Domingo's land was then included. Some years, when San Francisco's lieutenant was not available, they even went to his hierarchical superior to get it: the *Jefe Político* (the canton official) in Limones.

I reproduce below the permit as it was received by the reyeras in Santo Domingo, on December 27, 1989, in the evening. At that time, most of the women did not know how to read or write, which is why the teniente was usually the redactor of the permit. The cucuruchos just had to sign it; some simply drew an "X." The three reyeras made sure that all women named on the permit signed it.

Permiso de Santo Domingo de Onzole
(The original document contains misspellings. I reproduce it as is)

(Stamp of the *Tenencia Política de Santo Domingo de Ónzole*)

Señor:
Teniente Político Principal de la Parroquia de Santo Domingo de Ónzole,
Sirvase concedernos el correspondiente permiso para el festejo de los Santos Reyes.
A la vez que solicitamos nos seda el despacho para sancionar y castigar a cual-
quier ciudadano que cometa alguna anomalía.
Mr. Principal Political Lieutenant of the Parish of Santo Domingo de Ónzole, we
come to you to request the permit for the festivity of the Saint Kings. This is the
reason why we request that you give us your office so that we can sanction and
punish any citizen who will comit an infraction.

(Signature of the *reyeras*)
Florentina Montaño
Leíla Quiñonez
Luciola Corozo
Humbertina Montaño
Rosaura Quiñonez

Tenencia Política de Santo Domingo de Onzole, diciembre 27 de 1989 a las 15H00.

En atención a lo solicitado y en vista que todos los años se lleva a cabo este festejo,
me permito conceder este permiso.
In appreciation of the requested and because this festivity takes place every year,
I concede this permit.

Atentamente,
Sincerely,

(Signature)
Edin Corozo
Teniente Político Principal.
28 de diciembre de 1989.   (Other stamp of the *Tenencia*)

With this permit, which becomes applicable on the following day, December 28, until the evening of January 8, the cucuruchos literally replace
the political lieutenant and become the first authority of the parish. They are
the ones who now have to solve the small conflicts that can emerge (theft,
physical fights) and who have to decide the amount of the fine to be paid.
They also decide the duration of the time to be spent in the stocks by anyone arrested. In the case of a bigger problem, such as a physical fight during
which wounds are inflicted with a machete, for example, they can ask the

actual lieutenant for the key to the village prison, where they lock up both fighters, whom they liberate only after they pay the amount of the penalty the reyeras' political lieutenant or provincial chief of police has established. Instead of giving the amount of the fee to the real lieutenant, they give the money to their treasurer.

In the case of a really bad crime, a murder or a rape—which only happened once during my fieldwork in the early 1990s (a rape)—the actual political lieutenant takes charge of the case.

In fact, the permit gives the reyeras the legal authorization to try to obtain by all means acceptable the financial resources they need for the organization of the Play. Between December 28 and January 5—and to a lesser extent during the three days of the Play as well, when they are busy with the performance of the acts—they charge different kinds of "taxes" or "fees" from men. They stop the canoes and lanchas that go up and down the river when they pass in front of the village to demand from their owners a financial contribution of twenty to fifty sucres, depending on what is in the canoe or lancha. If the owner does not have cash with him, gifts of fruits, plantains, rice, dried fish, aguardiente, or cigarettes are accepted.

The day before the beginning of the play, after everyone has made provision of aguardiente for the three days of the Play, reyeras go from house to house to confiscate (*decomisar*) part of the aguardiente under the timid complaints of their owners who have put most of the aguardiente they own in a secure place, knowing that this confiscation would take place. In the case someone refuses to collaborate or objects when they want to confiscate, the permit gives them the right to arrest the problematic man. When they do so, they often hit him (*dar plán*) on the back or on the buttocks with a wooden machete (*peinilla*), which each one of them carries when walking around as an indication that they belong to the committee of reyeras. The man is then locked up in the stock until he has paid the fine requested.

From December 28 through January 8, the daily social order, within which men assume most of the social and political power, is inverted. During these twelve days, men are subjected to the "dictatorial" or arbitrary feminine authority with, sometimes, a hint of irritation at the beginning of the interaction, although they are joyous once liberated. I once witnessed a situation in which a man prohibited his wife from participation in the committee. The fiesteras arrested him and placed him in the stock until he calmed down and publicly promised to let her play without any restriction. They let him go after he paid the corresponding fine.

At other moments, men subject themselves to the authority of the fiesteras provocatively and mischievously. They verbally or physically provoke them (to add force to the "fire" of the play; *para darle fuego al juego*), knowing very well that they are going to be arrested and placed in the stocks, after having simulated a noisy escape throughout the village. Any arrest always provokes the spontaneous gathering of people who were previously attending to their usual activities, in the midst of laughter and screams. Seeing women exert physical power over men and hearing the dry sound of the wooden machetes hitting their back sides again and again always provokes hilarity in people of both sexes who are witnessing the whole interaction. Once, while I was laughing during such an arrest, a cucurucha came near me and said, "*Don Jean, no rie demasiado, eso le va a pasar a Usted también!* (Don't laugh too much, Don Jean, this will happen to you sooner than later).

Thus, men accept, whether they like it or not, sometimes joyfully, sometimes against their will, the feminine authority particular to this liminal period. Once, when I asked an elder of the village, Don Elio, "Would you like it if women were in charge during the whole year?" he answered, "Absolutely not! I would not like that women have the authority during the whole year. We would be in a big mess if women were in charge all the time. Don't you understand that men were made to be in charge? Women can have authority for certain things, but . . . when they are employees of the government, then they have some amount of authority. But around here, there is no woman in such a position!" (January 1990)

The practical objective of the conformation of a committee of reyeras is the preparation of the material conditions of the Play. Without that period of preparation, the Play could not—materially—take place. By contrast, when they receive the permit and their new responsibilities, they also get the opportunity to metamorphose into men every time they choose to do so, in order to exert with humor an authority that is usually not available to them the rest of the year. Before January 6, they disguise themselves only on specific occasions: December 28—the first day of their "rule"—and January 1, during the celebration of the New Year. The disguises of these two days announce—in a less elaborated way—those of January 6 and of the "act of the president." Their heads, unlike on January 6, are not masked, and the feminine identity of each is clearly revealed to all. They assume a masculine identity through the wearing of pants and male shirts, as well as with the use of rubber boots. They also carry a *peinilla* with them. All these objects (pants, rubber boots and [wooden] machetes) are usually associated with male activities. The holding of wooden machetes is in itself somewhat of a satire: the manipulation of machetes is part of the construction of masculinity in the northern sector of the province. When men physically fight, they often resort to hitting with machetes.

During the other days of the preparation period, the reyeras wear their usual clothes: dresses and skirts. The only visible signs of their membership in the committee of reyeras are their wooden machetes and their hats, on which a piece of paper has been glued (to the superior part) that indicates their respective rank. When they are not engaged in reyeras activities, they usually do not bring these objects with them. They resort to their use only when they publicly "become" reyeras. Then, they do not call one another by their respective first names anymore and only use their official ranks. This allows for the spontaneous marking of the events in which they become involved as taking place on another level of reality. Consequently, reyeras do not assume their masculine quality and their ranks twenty-four hours a day during the preparation period. They do so only in the situations they want to inscribe in the festive time: when they collect taxes at the river or in the village or when they visit a neighboring village on December 28 or on January 1. They are the ones who spontaneously decide to enter or leave liminal time. They spend the rest of the time in their usual daily activities.

I witnessed various sudden openings of liminal time during the preparation period. One afternoon, while I was meeting with many of the reyeras in one of their houses to talk about the Festival, they were patiently answering my questions when the lancha of a fish seller arrived onshore near the barrio "Guayaquil." As soon as we heard the noise of the engine, one of the reyeras, the first to react, jumped to put on her hat and peinilla and shouted to the others, interrupting the conversation: ¡*Vamonos al río, a cobrar el impuesto!* ("Let's go to the river to collect the taxes!") They all got up, grabbed their hats or caps and their peinillas, and rushed to the river. They were no longer *Doña* Humbertina, *Doña* Jacinta or *Doña* Ursula, but provincial chief of police, lieutenant, or police commissioner. As soon as the fish tradesman had paid the tax, they took off their hats and caps and came back, calmly, to their previous personalities and to the conversation, leaving liminal time behind. When they are in such a situation, within the "liminal time of the hierarchy," and they talk to one another using their official ranks, the men involved in the interactions have to acknowledge their authority and their ranks as well, if they want to avoid being locked up in the stocks and paying a higher fine for lack of respect to the authorities. Most men are amused and defer to their ranks with a smile.

These different levels of time, and the switching from one of them to the other, are much more apparent during the three days of the Play because the reyeras, principal actresses of the acts, have the prerogative to move from one level to the next as they so choose, to represent another character, play in an act, or, on the contrary, come back to the quotidian time for a few seconds, when one of them whispers a few words in the ear of another in order to prepare the following act.

On December 28, 1989, five cucuruchos (dressed as men) visited the village of Colón. While they were there, dancing in front of a house, one of the reyeras invited a local woman to dance. A minute later, the cucurucha suddenly stepped back from the other woman while growling and simulating sexual excitement. A piece of wood then emerged from the cucurucha's trouser fly, representing a penis in erection. The reyera, her erected organ in her right hand, then pursued her dance companion, who was running away bursting in laughter. Since she could not get to her, the reyera finally decided to appease her desire by frantically masturbating in front of the audience. After drinking some aguardiente offered by the owner of the house, the group then continued its quest and went to the following house, where they danced and/or performed a similar small act. During these visits, the reyeras also play fragments of the "act of the brothers," which is also taking place at several occasions during the three days of the Play, and most importantly on January 8. These fragments always satirize men, their machismo, and their heterosexual dominance, if not aggression.

Figure 4. "Arrest" of a man in Santo Domingo de Ónzole. (Photograph by Jean Muteba Rahier)

By representing the state's power hierarchy, Santo Domingeñas re-present or repeat official ranks that are never, or extremely rarely, occupied by a black man. This seizing upon the state's political and administrative hierarchy is a negation of, and playful resistance to, the exclusionary practices of the Ecuadorian state vis à vis Afro-Ecuadorians and their reproduction of a racial-spatial order that has constructed the areas where they live as peripheral and frontier regions (the white and white-mestizo men represented—the governor, the provincial chief of police, the interior minister, etc.—never visit their "far away forest lands").

Additionally, the reyeras' performance of the state's power hierarchy also responds to the ordinary gender relations in the area by providing the reyeras not with the authority that men of the village usually hold but, on the contrary, with the authority of white and white-mestizo men who have more social, economic, and political capital than the former.

The reyeras' performances have therefore two targets, one intramural and the other extramural. On the one hand, they try to repeat relatively zealously the relations of power between these different official functions of the state's agencies (the arrest warrants, the orders received by the "policemen"), while on the other hand, they signal an ironic distance by exaggerating the real power held by these ranked characters in everyday life. In that way they underline the arbitrary and unjustified authority these officials have at the same time that they humiliate those in their community who often pay court to them: Afro-Esmeraldian men.

The president is the highest rank of the committee's hierarchy. It is reserved for one of the older women who know well the "tradition of the Reyes." She is the first to be designated by the others when they meet before December 27. Her designation remains secret because on January 6, first day of the Play and "day of the whites," she disguises herself in a way that no one can recognize her. The success of her part—which could be measured by the level of amusement of the surrounding audience—depends in some extent on keeping her identity secret. That is why when they go to request the permit from the teniente político on December 27, the reyeras who sign the permit do not indicate their respective rank. The president usually takes on another rank for the preparation period to better hide the fact that she is going to be the president. And that is for the same reason, they explained, that the president does not appear publicly before the "Day of the first Kings," as January 6 is also referred to. Before January 6, she is the one, in consultation with the others, to call the meetings of the committee. During the meetings, when the reyeras could not agree on a particular issue—the musicians' pay or the purchase of certain products, for example—she influences the final decision. Her authority is based on the consent of the others. She helps the treasurer with the managing of the money collected. The same reyera often occupies the two ranks simultaneously. From one year to the next, a different reyera becomes president. This is justified as a good way to maintain the surprise about the President's identity.

Conclusions

The ethnographic information presented in this chapter underscores the importance of the sexual dichotomy in Santo Domingo de Ónzole and should facilitate a better understanding of the performances that take place during the three days of the Play of the Cowls described and interpreted in the next chapter. Indeed, as a carnivalesque festivity, the Afro-Esmeraldian Play of the Cowls as it is performed in Santo Domingo inverts the order of everyday life where gender is certainly the most important marker for social differentiation. Consequently, it is gender and gender relations that provide one of the most important fields of meaning that one must refer to in order to make sense of the various acts of the Play in Santo Domingo and of the festive events of the period of preparation that begins on December 28. As will continue to be shown in the next chapter, the liminal time of the Play in Santo Domingo provides nothing more than a eleven-day-long (eight days of preparation plus three days for the actual Festival) let-off-steam process during which women rule over men, dominating them and asserting over them an absolute authority that would simply be unacceptable in nonfestive time, as some Santo Domingeño men told me.

Another important field of meaning absolutely necessary to make sense of the Play in Santo Domingo is certainly provided by Santo Domingeños' sense of geography. The distance that separates the village from the urban centers of the country, where those who have political power reside, and from where they assert their authority over the marginalized rural places, is ever present in the lives of everyone in the village. That distance is in fact constitutive of what the village is for them. And the decision Santo Domingeños made to name the three barrios of the village using the names of the three larger cities of the country already denotes a remarkable subversive, humoristic, and even ironic, gaze on their geographic marginalization. This symbolic seizing upon the three most prominent cities of the country to incorporate them and contain them within the space of the village is a way to claiming for themselves an Ecuadorian citizenship that is denied them once they leave the village and go to these cities.

The organization of the committee of cucuruchos in a hierarchy that parodies the state and provincial political structures brings about a satire of these structures at the same time that it provides the very material used to perform the inversion of the gender roles I was referring to earlier. This will be made even more evident in the next chapter.

This brief discussion gives me an additional opportunity to underscore the importance of place in the study of festivities. Indeed, we will see, in chapter four, which is dedicated to the Play in the village of La Tola, that by contrast "race" and race relations in that village provide the main field of meaning that gives its significance to the performances of the Play there. The same festivity must be interpreted referring to different sociopolitical and economic realities as it is performed in different locations of one single cultural area.

3

The Festival of the Kings
in Santo Domingo de Ónzole

Elders told me that in the past, January 6 was called the "day of the whites" and also the "day of the first King"; January 7 was called the "day of the Cayapas" or "day of the coloreds" (*día de los colorados*); and January 8 was called "day of the blacks" or more precisely "day of the little blacks" (*día de los negritos*). This strict division of the festival's three days that allocates one day to each racial group (whites, indigenous people, and blacks) evokes the *folklore nègre* of Roger Bastide (1972), which he saw as a folklore created by Europeans for their slave populations in the Americas. It clearly points to the Eurocentric objective to regroup diverse nonwhite populations and incorporate them within the "universal community" behind the adoration of a white God I briefly discussed in chapter 1.

When referring to themselves, Afro-Esmeraldian northerners use the expression *la gente negra, los negros,* or less often *los morenos,* in opposition to whites and white-mestizos, called also *blancos* or *gente de color* (people of color), and to Chachi, called *cayapas* or also *colorados* (which evoke a lighter, reddish skin color). Thus, black northerners invert the usual terminology found in the urban areas of the country and in most "western" countries in general, where the expression "people of color" or "colored people" refer to black and brown individuals (Yuen 1996). In the northern sector, the term "colorado" is also synonymous with "mulatto." That inversion of the usual typology is meaningful in the sense that it affirms a normality of blackness—which is not considered to be a "color"—vis à vis nonblacks. Santo Domingeños or any other Esmeraldian black who is not formally educated and who is not a political activist never uses the expression *afro-esmeraldeño* or *afro-ecuatoriano* to refer to himself or herself. "Afro-Esmeraldian" and "Afro-Ecuadorian" are expressions that are part of intellectuals', activists', and anthropologists' vocabularies. Afro-Esmeraldians do not consciously claim either an African past or "heritage" and are usually surprised when one discusses their African origin in their presence.

During my fieldwork in Santo Domingo, the expression "people of color," *gente de color*, was most of the time used to refer specifically to the *Manabitas* or *Manaba*, who are white-mestizos with light colored hair and sometimes with light colored eyes, who come from the province of Manabí, located on the Ecuadorian coast, south of the province of Esmeraldas.

Several years before my participation in the Play in Santo Domingo—nobody could tell me exactly when this took place—the "scenario" of the Play changed: January 6 and 7 became the days of the whites, while January 8 is reserved for the Chachi and the blacks, although whites can also be seen on that day. January 7 is also very much the day of forest spirits.

January 6 and the Act of the Arrival of the President

The act of the president, which is rather long, is the principal activity of January 6. It involves, beyond participating with the nondisguised adult population of the village, two groups of disguised actors. The first is the group of cucuruchos. They number about twenty and include the women of the committee who prepared the Play and who assumed the "first authority of the parish" (as the lieutenant is sometimes called) since December 28, as well as a collection of other women from the community who, for one reason or other, did not participate in the activities of the committee. Women from surrounding villages (Arenales, Zancudo, Colón), where the Festival is not played, also join them. They disguise themselves as white men and make every effort possible not to be recognized easily. This is particularly the case with the president. To that end, their faces are entirely covered with masks and when they talk, they modify their voices by emitting higher-pitched sounds than usual. They keep the ranks they had during the preparation period and add other ranks for the women newly enrolled. No man is included in this group, although the characters they play are all masculine.

The second protagonist of the act is the group composed of a dozen adolescents and young men who are disguised as soldiers and called "the troop" (*la tropa*). According to the interviews I conducted, no woman has ever been included in the tropa. In 1990, the tropa was under the leadership of a young man who was often behaving, outside of the festive time, in an exaggerated, manly way with young women. He had gone through the military service, which is a source of great pride for him, and had in that way acquired an experience of the discipline of the military bases. In Ecuador, at that time, military service was mandatory, but a relatively high number of young men found a way to avoid conscription. The young men who have done their military service enjoy, however, a certain prestige in the eyes of the others. They usually return to the village from this obligation, despite the fact that this was completely forbidden, with pieces of military uniforms: shoes, pants, shorts, shirts, t-shirts, caps. They surround the other young men of the tropa and lend them some of the military clothing they have been able to keep in order to give them, as much as possible, a military appearance. Their disguises are therefore exclusively constituted of pieces of military uniforms. Their faces are not covered.

The chief of the tropa has the rank of general and becomes a sort of general-president during the act. The tropa first appears in the village on January 5 at night. They march with discipline, holding a rifle or a real machete to the sound of rhythmic orders: one, two, one, two. Like the reyeras during the preparation period, they arrest a few young men who are not participating in the tropa and lock them up in the stocks so that they can gather some money they will use to purchase aguardiente to drink and gunpowder for their shotguns and the small canon they fire during the act of the president on the 6th. Unlike the cucuruchos, they do not arrest older men, who were their fathers, uncles, and godfathers and whom they have to continue respecting despite the festive time. They do not have the same license as the reyeras to invert everyday rules. The amount of money they are able to gather is quite limited, and they disappear from the festivity as actors as soon as the act is over.

The cucuruchos disguise themselves in the following way: their heads are covered with a piece of cloth positioned to cover the back and both sides entirely. They then fix on their heads a mask made of cardboard with three holes: one for the nose, two for the eyes. There is sometimes a fourth hole for the mouth. Some take the time to draw a Salvador Dali–like moustache and a small triangular beard on the cardboard. They dress in pants and long-sleeved, masculine shirts. Their hands are hidden in socks (to hide their black skin) because they do not own gloves, and they wear rubber boots. Except for their masks, they very much look like Afro-Esmeraldian men ready to go to their gardens or on a hunting trip early in the morning. One distinctive aspect of their disguises is the decorations they place on their masks and clothes. Indeed, they are *poniendo lujo a los disfraces*, which literally means "add some signs of luxury to their disguises," by gluing onto their shirts and masks pieces of packs of cigarettes of a brand that is somewhat more prestigious than the brand of cigarettes that Santo Domingeños usually smoke. That is why, as they explain, they prefer not to attach pieces of packs of *Piel Roja* or "Full Speed," dark tobacco cigarettes without filters, which are cheaper, and prefer instead the brands Marlboro, Lark, and Lider, which are made with lighter tobacco and are more expensive. They also glue on some pieces of aluminum foil, which are usually found in the packs of the most expensive brands of cigarettes. Some add pieces of wool, while others go for chicken feathers and those from other birds. Many attach packages of big leaves around their waist or neck. The disguised women with leaves are said to be *embasuradas* (covered with garbage). The mask of the president is similar to the other masks of whites, with the exception that it has a crown-like cutting on its superior part, as if to symbolize a crown.

Elders told me that in the past, instead of having masks of cardboard, cucuruchos wore masks made out of white cloth which had been sewn in a conic shape (a cowl or *cucurucho*), and which had three holes for the mouth and the eyes and, sometimes, a pointed nose, "just like the nose of white people." Instead of wearing socks of color, as many did when I was there, they wore white gloves, if they had been able to find some. Back then, they said, people were more preoccupied to find white cloth to represent the white color of the president and his entourage.

When disguising, reyeras exchange among themselves the masculine long-sleeved shirts and pants they got from their husbands and sons to better hide their respective identities. Many glue a piece of paper with their ranks on the upper part of their masks. Others wear that piece of paper on their hats, while others still have no rank indication or hat. All move around the village with their wooden machetes and their shotguns.

From talking with elders about the activities of January 6 in the past, it appears that the objective of that day, and of the act of the visit of the president, was to make a mimicry of white people as seen from the perspective of Santo Domingo. Some cucuruchos would disguise as medical doctors, accompanied by one or two nurses (all "whites"), and would parody the provision of medical services to the village's population by white doctors. There was also a dentist walking around with his own nurse performing mock tooth extractions. And the act of the visit of the president was but a parody of a visit by the president of Ecuador and his entourage. Although they admitted that some details of the act could change from one year to the next, according to the preferences of the actors involved, there never was a confrontation between the cucuruchos and the tropa. In the past, the tropa played the role of the Ecuadorian military from a supposedly local military base that was helping to maintain order in the village. The tropa also played the role of bodyguards protecting the president during his visit. The president acted in a "very presidential way" and distributed candies to the children. If the committee had been successful in gathering the necessary money, he also threw small coins of real money that kids and adults alike rushed to pick up from the ground. As one elder said:

> *Y entonces toda la gente estaba felíz. Y después el presidente metía la mano al bolsillo, porque para todo "había partida," y "Crililín," regaba plata, aiiii los muchachos . . ., eran "ayoras," cojíamos plata . . .* (Then, everybody was happy. And later, the president put his hand in his pocket, because there was a budget for everything, and 'Crililín,' he threw away money, and the kids were all excited. They were coins, and we picked them up . . .).

The president represents the political power of the nation-state. Back then, a presidential chair was installed in a central location of the village, usually on the soccer field in the barrio "Guayaquil," and he sat there for a while before making a public discourse that didn't really have a special focus and that often ended up with the sounds "et cetera, et cetera, et cetera," as if to make a satire of white and white-mestizo politicians who are here represented as often talking but saying nothing consistent, and who very often promised things that they never accomplished or provided.

One old man told me that he remembered a Play, a long time ago, when some men had prepared a coup d'état attempt in advance, without informing the cucuruchos. They had fired rifles in the air at a moment when no one expected, *y había sido bien bonito*—"and it had been successful and fun," because it added force to the Play. Everyone had been surprised and scared by the detonation of the rifles and the screams of those conducting the coup d'état: "Death to the president, death to the president!" they shouted. The tropa had reacted by protecting the president and by attacking the plotters, who ended up, after a loud pursuit throughout the village and various rifle detonations later, in the stocks, under the sun, in the middle of the amused and excited population. A man then spontaneously volunteered to represent the guilty conspirators by playing the role of defense attorney who negotiated with the reyeras the amount of the fee for their liberation. Spontaneity and improvisations seem to always have been important characteristics of the Play. They expressed individuals' desire (often men) to surprise the community and add some "force to the fire of the Play" and in that way provoke amusement and laughter.

The act of the arrival of the president as described by the elders was grounded in a series of inversions of daily life situations. Indeed, the first fundamental inversion that was taking place here was the negation of the village as a peripheral or frontier location within the national space. The very fact that the president of the republic was visiting the village—which is a complete impossibility in real life—proclaims a subversive rearrangement of the everyday racial-spatial ordering of things by putting Santo Domingo in the center of the country's political life for the duration of the act, at the same time that it underlined the very nature of the parody, which is, as Linda Hutcheon put it, "to represent with a critical distance" (1985). It is that distance—which is made possible and in a way traveled through by the liminality of the time of the Play—that marked everything that happens during the act as ironic and humoristic. The irony and humor of the performances and the laughter they provoked should not get in the way of our reading of the act as an inversion of the racial othering of Afro-Esmeraldians who, through the playful acting of this presidential visit, refused their marginal condition as "non-citizens" and as "ultimate Others" by becoming, at least for one day, full Ecuadorian citizens who got the attention of their president, whose visit made their village if not the center of the country, at least a full and important component of national territory.

In 1990, on January 6, the various activities of the act of the visit of the president took a peculiar turn. Indeed, it is important to keep in mind that every year, the actual performances of the various acts of the Play follow spontaneous negotiations among the various actors involved, and between them and the very much active and participating audience. This is when changes in the performances from one year to the next do occur. This also points to the importance of contexts in shaping the contents of festivities, which we must approach as always-localized phenomena, even if the targets of their parodies and satires might be found in the provincial, national, and transnational dimensions of Santo Domingeños' lives.

On the morning of January 6, 1990, the group of cucuruchos performed the visit of the president of the republic and his entourage. The president of the committee impersonated the president of the republic and, as has been the case in the past, he took a name typical of the names most commonly heard in the Andean region and which are rare in the province of Esmeraldas. The preoccupation here is to mark the president and his party as white-mestizos, strangers to the village and to the province. The president was named Eduardo Baca. The group of reyeras representing the president and his party (minister of the interior, minister of war, finance minister, chief of police and others) dressed up as white men five minutes from the village, downriver at the hamlet of Baquería. As previously indicated, usually the president was received by the tropa, who represented soldiers of the visiting president's army.

The peculiarity of the act of the arrival of the president of January 6, 1990, is that an improvisation by the character playing the general-president gave an unusual direction to the act. The president of the republic of Ecuador suddenly became the president of the republic of Peru following the improvisation of the general of the tropa, who decided to be a general-president of the "country of here," *el país de acá* (Ecuador), in opposition to Eduardo Baca, whom he called *el presidente del país de allá*, the president of the "country of over there" (Peru). One has to keep in mind here that there was, from the 1940s until 1998, a border conflict between Ecuador and Peru that provoked several military confrontations between the two countries. During these wars—which were mostly border confrontations—many Afro-Esmeraldians enlisted as soldiers.

In fact, the exact identity of the mock president had no real importance. In both cases, he was a stranger to the community. When he arrived with his ministers and other officials, the tropa's general-president organized resistance and threatened to not let the president disembark in the village, which the president finally did, despite the aggressive brouhaha surrounding his dugout canoe when it arrived at the wooden stairs of the barrio "Guayaquil." In the agitation that accompanied his arrival in Santo Domingo, the president was finally able to sit on his presidential chair, which had been installed on the soccer field. It was a sumptuous chair decorated with green, red, black, and blue pieces of paper. A roof made of palm tree leaves and of a big yellow piece of plastic covered the chair. His speech was often interrupted, and following it, there were numerous scuffles between the tropa's soldiers and the cucuruchos. Eduardo Baca, the president, was wounded (even dead, according to some), then resuscitated by the medical doctor (one of the disguised cucuruchos). The two presidents signed a peace treaty, and everybody went to the communal house, where the marimba dancing party was about to begin. The whole act lasted around an hour and a half.

I had accompanied the fiesteras who came back to the village in a dugout canoe with Eduardo Baca (they had gone to disguise themselves in the house of one of the reyeras in Baquería). Before disembarking, soldiers of the tropa asked us to take more time before landing, which we did, because the reyeras who had stayed in the village were not dressed yet. During the trip from Baquería, the reyeras sang songs and repeated mottoes celebrating and praising the presidential visit of Eduardo Baca, interrupted by cheers to the *Santos Reyes*, the cucuruchos, the president, and the 6 of January: *¡Viva el 6 de enero!*

At the arrival of the president, most of the village population was waiting on the river bank, greeting him and his party with mottoes such as: *¡Viva la llegada del presidente!* ("Hurrah for the visit of the President!") or *¡Viva Eduardo Baca!* After his arrival in the village, the president was received by the cucuruchos' welcoming committee, while the tropa was parading with a big Ecuadorian flag. Some of them threatened to attack the president (the soldiers of the tropa had informed us of the plan to attack the president). Shotguns were fired in the air, the tambuco was fired as well, and an atmosphere of coup d'état surrounded the arrival of the president, who was nevertheless able to reach his presidential chair, despite the agitation and under the shouts by the public of *¡Viva la llegada del presidente!*

The president wanted then to begin a speech but was interrupted by the soldiers who were booing and who tried to kidnap him. The cucuruchos defended him, and he was finally able to begin talking. It is important to recall that "president" Eduardo Baca as well as all the members of his party spoke with exaggeratedly high-pitched voices, so as to feminize them. In fact, the

Figure 5. Arrival of the "President" in Santo Domingo de Ónzole. (Photograph by Jean Muteba Rahier)

common idea that men from Esmeraldas have about men from the *Sierra*, the Andes, is that they are not as macho as men from the Costa, and especially not as macho as Afro-Esmeraldian men are. This is in fact a common belief that most men from the Costa have vis à vis Andean men.

Before beginning his speech, the president saluted the public with his two hands covered by white socks. Many took a long time before being able to recognize the actual identity of the reyera who played the role of "Eduardo Baca."

Here are some passages of the dialogue that took place between Eduardo Baca, the public in attendance, and the general-president of the tropa. They show that "in improvisation, each move is contingent on a previous move and in some measure influences the one that follows. Improvisation requires a mastery of the logic of action and in-body codes together with the skill to intervene in them and transform them. Each performance, each time, is generated anew" (Drewal 1992, 7). In order to be appreciated by everyone, these improvisations require from the actors involved, as well as from the audience, what Linda Hutcheon calls "semiotic competence" (1985).

> EDUARDO BACA (E. B.): The President Eduardo Baca salutes you. My intention is to visit you and to give you some economic improvement, since I know you are suffering from the present situation.

People in the audience laughed and applauded. Some nonetheless called the president a liar. Baca sat and continued:

> E. B.: The prices for the alimentation of your children skyrocketed. The price of a pound of rice, of sugar, and of coffee rose ridiculously because the minister, last year, kept us all in the dark situation we are in.

The public applauded, and the president began reciting a poem. Someone in the audience shouted, "Where is the President from?" Someone else responded, "He is Peruvian!"

As soon as these words were pronounced, the tropa's soldiers got agitated. The captain of land and sea began another poem. Someone in the audience wondered what was going to happen now that we knew that the president was Peruvian. Someone else responded, "War!"

The two Presidents began dialoguing:

> E. B.: People are dying of hunger, and things are not developing for the better (*las cosas están muy atrás*). There are families that cannot provide for their children. They cry to get some coffee. The sugar is very

expensive. No one can buy rice because this year the minister left us without any alimentation. My only desire is that the price of goods go down so that poor people do not die from hunger.

After the participation of the public, which wanted to underline the exaggerated price of food items, and after more developments around that central idea, the general-president (G. P.) intervened and changed the course of the dialogue.

> G. P.: In your country, the crisis is very hard. So you have come to our country because you want to sign a treaty with us. What is your objective?

Eduardo Baca spontaneously followed the new development, although he had been a bit surprised by it.

> E. B.: Yes, we have to make peace and do everything in peace to avoid any problematic situation between our two brother countries.
> G. P.: What for? In our country the situation is better than in your country. Therefore we can be friends but we don't want peace!

Figure 6. Dialogue between the "President" Eduardo Baca and the "General President." (Photograph by Jean Muteba Rahier)

E. B.: No, I indeed want peace because I didn't come prepared for those things. I only came to visit these lands to find out about the price of the products, but I am not coming with the idea to attack any nation!

The people in the audience who surrounded the presidential chair where the dialogue was taking place laughed at the high-pitched voice of the president. Some even said that he was afraid of the general-president.

G. P.: We don't want peace, not now. In any case, we are going to give to your country twenty tons of rice, fifty of sugar, one thousand head of cattle to allow a few people in your country to feed themselves; because we are saddened by the fact that people are dying from hunger while here we are throwing food away. Here are the boats that you can take back with you. But we don't want peace!

E. B.: But, I'm not prepared!

G. P.: We thank you for your visit. Don't be afraid, but keep in mind that we do not want peace. . . . We will protect you during your stay. . . . Do your festivity and whatever you want, but we don't want peace!

That is when one member of Eduardo Baca's entourage, the political lieutenant (L. P.), shouted, expressing in that way the preference of many costeños for politicians who are *machos de verdad* (real men) (see de la Torre 1992; Andrade 2001):

L. P.: *¡El Presidente ha venido sin talento, le reputamos!* [sic] (The president is a coward; we reject him!)

G. P.: We want war!

L. P.: We must reach peace today. The president is nervous and I am the political lieutenant, and I am talking to you personally so that we can reach peace.

G. P.: Your president is a bad administrator. He made a lot of propaganda, but he did not accomplish anything.

L. P.: Since we have come here, we can reach peace!

The general then decided to ask the audience what they wanted:

G. P.: Let's see what the country wants, if people accept peace or not.

Various people in attendance shouted:

We do not accept peace, we want Play! (*¡No aceptamos la paz, queremos juego!*)

And a war began between the two nations. A dialogue continued in spite of the agitated combats (cucuruchos and soldiers rolled in the dust, fighting):

L. P.: Peace, give him peace, Mr. President.

G. P.: I have asked my people if they want peace, but they do not want peace because of the bad administration of your president. Now that he is scared, he wants to make peace at any cost, but the citizens don't want it!

The conflict evolved toward another attempt to kidnap the Peruvian president, who suddenly collapsed in the middle of a quarrel, "mortally wounded."

The members of his entourage, the cucuruchos, refused to let him be taken to the "hospital" and demanded a doctor. A doctor and a nurse arrived and began taking care of him. The health of Eduardo Baca then very quickly improved, and everyone in the surrounding public exclaimed with joy to see him alive. He stood up with difficulty, thanks to the help of some ministers; he left with them, limping. The cucuruchos wanted then to take revenge and pursued the general-president throughout the village. He had escaped behind the houses surrounding the soccer field. They finally arrested him. The provincial chief of police came to me and whispered in my ear: "I hope

Figure 7. Eduardo Baca is "mortally wounded." (Photograph by Jean Muteba Rahier)

that we will be able to get back to our country. These people are very bad . . . while we are asking them for peace. If we had known that, we would have stayed in our country. This is our fault, we came here to look for problems." A final dialogue began between the two presidents, who ended up signing a peace treaty. They hugged and invited everyone to go to the communal house for the marimba dancing party. It was then around 9:30 A.M.

The cucuruchos (all women) represented white men who were obviously complete strangers to the village community. At some moments, these white men seemed to be the president of the Ecuadorian republic and his ministers and other officials, while at other moments, the president was the Peruvian head of state, who was visiting with his entourage. Indeed, only the Ecuadorian president could have something to say about the elevated price of the alimentation and could blame one of his ministers for the situation. As soon as the public and the general-president suggested that the president was Peruvian, Eduardo Baca followed the development and "became Peruvian."

This apparent confusion is possible because the origin of the president was never indicated with precision. He had Ecuadorian nationality but, in the perspective of Santo Domingeños, he came from far away. In reality, his precise origin was important. The dichotomy often used to refer to the two groups of masked actors, *los de acá* versus *los de allá*, was more geographical than racial. At no moment during the act was the racial identity of the two groups an issue in the dialogues. It was understood as a matter of fact that the president and his entourage, by being serranos or Peruvians, were white-mestizos. When asking the reyeras after the Play, they were all adamant that the president, his ministers, and other officials were blancos (whites), although they never felt the necessity to underline this fact while playing (unlike what usually happens in La Tola, see next chapter). So, Eduardo Baca became the president *de allá* who came to visit the country of *acá*, because he knew that the president *de acá* does not do a good job with his people.

The internal logic of the Play and of its different acts is not aimed at repeating an eventual traditional scenario. Tradition appears much more as a resource than as an obligation. The unfolding of the acts is consequently far from being the result of a rehearsed mise-en-scène. Before the beginning of an act, nobody can with certainty predict what is really going to happen. Improvisations influence the development of the performances with no preoccupation for the preservation of a logic of ensemble of the act. Improvisations make contradictions appear in the message or meaning of the acts, without in any way provoking a structural anxiety among the various participants who were before anything else determined to have a good time. Improvisations are the stuff of the multivocality I discuss in chapter 1.

By becoming powerful white men, the (female) reyeras occupied a societal domain that is closed to them in daily life. In a way, they humiliated their men through their victory over the young men of their community at the same time that they ridiculed the white men whom they represented: Eduardo Baca was a coward, and the voices of the cucuruchos as white men were higher-pitched than the voices of "normal women."

During the rest of the day, men were arrested and put in the stocks for whatever "crime" the cucuruchos arbitrarily accused them of committing. The musicians interrupted the music around 1:00 P.M. to eat their lunch and relax a bit before playing again in the early evening until around 2:30 A.M. on January 7. Chamita, the older son of Don Chama, who is one of the leaders of the village, organized *a baile de cuerda*[1] in the house of his brother-in-law, the teniente político, Childo Corrozo, where I was housed. At the end of the marimba dancing party, all the people who wanted to continue dancing went to Childo's house. Chamita's baile de cuerda ended at around 4:30 A.M.

In the morning of January 6, a group of Chachi from the community of Colón came to stay in the house of one of the Santo Domingeños who was the compadre of one of them. As they did every year, they had specifically come to participate in the Festival of the Kings. During the afternoon, a Chachi baby was baptized by two Afro-Esmeraldians. The baptism established links of *compadrazgo* among all the adults involved (the Chachi parents and the Afro-Esmeraldian co-parents). Some Chachi men drank a lot with Santo Domingeño men, while their wives remained timidly removed by themselves. In the evening, some Chachi men brought their wives with them to Chamita's baile de cuerda (they knew Childo well and respected him because he never tried to seduce their women). When the marimba dancing ended and the proportion of Afro-Esmeraldian men increased in Childo's house, the Chachi left. The ambiance had become tense when Afro-Esmeraldian men began inviting Chachi women to dance. When invited, the Chachi women of course always indicated that permission had to be given by their husbands, fathers, or brothers, who always refused. When Chamita criticized them for not allowing their women to dance with Afro-Esmeraldian men, the Chachi men got upset and decided to leave with their women.

January 7: A Begging Performance
and the Visit of Forest Spirits

The principal activity of January 7 is the begging performance by cucuruchos going from house to house, which evokes the descriptions of European medieval carnival (chapter 1). They move around in a group. On that day, there are more disguised reyeras than on the previous day. Once the begging is over, another marimba dancing party begins in late morning in the communal house. Just as the day before, the dance is interrupted in early afternoon until early evening, when it goes on again.

During my participant-observation, the reyeras were the only characters to disguise themselves. They initially decided to change their clothes in the village school, situated in the highest part of barrio "Quito," around 8:00 A.M. Most of the cucuruchos dressed in the same way they dressed the day before, since January 7 was also said to be the day of the whites. Other reyeras preferred to take on a new identity and dressed like forest spirits, also called *visiones*. Their masks were quite surprising.

One reyera represented *la tunda*, a female forest spirit who, according to oral tradition, likes to kidnap young boys. She appears generally in the form of the mother or of a female relative of the young boy she wants to take away. She cannot hide the fact that one of her legs is deformed. The other leg is normal. Her behind is more voluminous than the behind of human beings. As soon as the young boys follow her, she breaks stinking winds which *entundan* (hypnotize) the boys who lose all individual will. She brings them where she lives, in the caves of small waterways (*las cuevas*), and gives them river shrimps to eat. She abuses them sexually and keeps them as long as possible. To get her victims back, the parents must go after them with the godparents of the boys, dogs, rifles, and the bombo (everything that can produce a lot of noise to scare the tunda). The tradition says that the victims of the tunda, *los entundados*, never really recuperate their senses and remain somewhat intellectually slow for the rest of their lives.

The cucurucha who was playing the tunda was wearing a skirt made from jute with a piece of red plastic in the back and a piece of green plastic in the front, a black pullover, a collar of empty packs of Lark and Lider cigarettes, fake teeth, a moustache like Abdala Bucaram's (a national politician and later president) or Hitler's, protruding plastic eyes, and a plastic hat. She took great pleasure in scaring the children who ran away from her screaming.

Another reyera represented *el duende*, a forest spirit whom various elders

Figure 8. A *reyera* representing the tunda. (Photograph by Jean Muteba Rahier)

say they had met. The duende is usually described as a small white-mestizo man whose head is always covered with a big hat. He is said to have a big head and, as many Santo Domingeños indicated, two faces: one in the front and one in the back. He is a good musician, an excellent guitar player. He can fight as no other man can, despite his small size. He defends all species of peccary and is sometimes described as the chief of the animals. He is a great thief: if you forget something in your canoe and it disappears, he probably stole it. He likes young girls whom he tries to take away with him into the forest where he lives, to caress their small breasts. He likes only young girls because their breasts are small and hard. When he gets tired of his victim, he sends her back home. It could happen that he sends a young girl back home with some money. He is a very good equestrian: he mounts horses in reverse so that his (frontal) face looks toward the tail of the horse. One can discover that he has been somewhere because he makes braids with the hair of the horses' manes and tails. Just like the tunda, he fears prayers.

The cucurucha who said she was the duende was dressed with nylon shorts, a shirt covered with *damajagua* (bark cloth), and with pieces of jute attached around the calves and knees above her boots. Her hair was covered with bark cloth as well, and she had made out of the mask she was wearing the day before a kind of hat from which hung another piece of damajagua that hid her face.

The disguises of the two cucuruchos who represented the tunda and the duende did not have a lot of resemblance with traditional descriptions of these spirits. Their activities during the quest were limited to scaring children, dancing with the other cucuruchos, and helping them arrest men. They did not really speak but only emitted grave and incomprehensible sounds. Other disguises were quite surprising as well. Two women were wearing a plastic basket on their heads. Their blouses and skirts were made out of bark cloth on which they had placed pieces of paper. They also emitted incomprehensible sounds, said to be representing other forest spirits, without identifying which ones. They chose to call themselves the *muda* (the mute) and the *bobo* (the retarded).

On the morning of that day, the cucuruchos went to dress up at the edge of the forest near the barrio "Quito" and then got down into the village from there. Preceding the group of reyeras were three young men who played the cununo, the bombo, and the maracas. Behind them the walking reyeras were dancing and singing. The songs consisted of sentences or verses first sung by a soloist, and then repeated by the rest of reyeras and young women who were accompanying them and who made up the office of the choir. The melody remained the same, although the verses changed. The excitement that surrounded the fiesteras was intense. Here are some of the verses they were singing (they told me that they were taken from songs and poems that they all knew); most of them celebrated women's agency or reported about passages of Ecuadorian history in which the protagonists were famous white-mestizo politicians:

> *Cuando el hombre es celoso, se acuesta pero no duerme* . . . ("When a man is jealous, he can lie down but he can't sleep").
> *De los hijos de mi padre, yo soy el mejor* . . . *porque bebí guarapo en el perol* . . . ("Of my father's sons. I am the best . . . because I drank sugarcane beer in a cup").

Yo soy la media naranja, yo soy la naranja entera, . . . ("I am the half orange, I am the entire orange"; this makes reference to a couple—where each party is a half orange—and to a woman who is filling both parental roles—the entire orange).

Eloy Alfaro fue un buen presidente, gritaron la independencia, que viva Velasco Ibarra. Velasco se subió a la silla a reclamar sus derechos y le dijo Ponce Enriquez baja con tu culo estrecho. ("Eloy Alfaro was a good president, they proclaimed the independence, hurray for Velasco Ibarra. Velasco sat on the presidential chair and asked to have his rights respected, but Ponce Enriquez told him 'get out of my presidential chair with your small ass.' Eloy Alfaro, Velasco Ibarra, and Ponce Enriquez are three white-mestizos who were Ecuadorian presidents).

Por esta calle me meto . . . El hombre que a mi me quiera le dejo la puerta abierta. ("I enter in this street . . . And for the man who desires me, I'll leave my door open").

From barrio "Quito" they went to barrio "Cuenca," where they mostly stopped at the house of don Chama (one of the leaders of the village's community who was often referred to as the "richest man" of Santo Domingo; he died a few years ago).

During the begging performance throughout the village, which was supposed to go from house to house, they preferred to stop exclusively at the village's small shops where there are more resources to be received. Many men were arrested and locked up in the stocks. One of them attempted to dance with a reyera, another one approached one of the reyeras and made a move as if he wanted to caress her buttocks. Don Aquiles, who had been completely drunk since the day before—he had prepared this with another man—suddenly emerged in the middle of the cucuruchos simulating to be completely infuriated and ready to fistfight with another man. He was gesticulating and shouting and insulted his accomplice, who responded with other insults. Don Aquiles then rushed to his house to pick up his rifle. The cucuruchos—thinking that a real bloody confrontation was about to happen—stepped aside, frightened (Don Aquiles is tall and strong).

His accomplice insulted Aquiles again and brandished his machete. A clamor emanated from the crowd: the songs and dances stopped. Aquiles, back in the space where the altercation had begun, fired a shot in the air with his rifle, then grabbed the other man, and they both rolled in the dust. Some cucuruchos risked trying to separate them, but the two men pushed them away shouting that they should not intervene if they didn't want anything bad to happen to them. Then both men, suddenly, laughed heartily. The tension shared by everyone in the attendance dissipated and was quickly replaced by a general joy. The two fighters were arrested and locked up in the stocks in the middle of the amused crowd. In the evening, while I shared a glass of aguardiente with him, Don Aquiles told me that he enjoyed greatly his giving more strength to the fire-Play.

A reyera was also disguised as a medical doctor and was accompanied by a nurse, just as the day before. The medical doctor was a white man and the nurse a white woman; they were dressed in white, as doctors and nurses in hospitals dress. During the begging performance, they walked with the other reyeras and offered their services for a few sucres to the villagers they met. That is how the muda became the object of their attention. While she was crying, alone, someone got "worried" and called *el cuerpo médico* (medical staff):

A MAN: Good afternoon, doctor. This mute woman is sick, she doesn't stop crying.

THE "DOCTOR": This mute woman doesn't drink aguardiente?

THE MAN: Mute woman, do you drink aguardiente?

THE MUTE WOMAN: . . . (She doesn't respond but emits a sound).

THE MAN: She says that she does.

THE DOCTOR: This mute woman is not sick. She is just drunk. What you need to do to this mute woman is make her a lemonade with a lot of lemon, you put an Alka Seltzer in it, and you give it to her. What you have mute woman is drunkenness. Ha, ha, ha.

As soon as the marimba dancing began, the communal house became the center of activities. The musicians played without interruption, men replaced one another to secure the permanence of the music. People were drinking and dancing. The "medical doctor" and his "nurse" were sounding "patients," the tunda and the duende were dancing together.

Outside the communal house, near the stocks for adult men that had been installed just in front of the communal house's main entrance, Don Alberto played the defense attorney. He wasn't disguised. He just stayed near the stock and offered his services to the encepados. The amount of money that he negotiated with the reyeras were all multiplied by one thousand to increase the dramatic aspect of the situation, at the same time that it underlined the absurd or burlesque quality of the interaction. He expressed himself with grandiloquence as he tried to get from the reyeras' political lieutenant a reduction of the fine they had first requested. If the lieutenant refused to hear him, he then looked for one of his hierarchical superiors until he was able to reach an agreement. His spontaneous interventions were understood for what they were (playful interventions) without hesitation by both the ence-pados and the reyeras. He sometimes entered in long conversations with the cucuruchos about sums of 20,000, 50,000, and 80,000 sucres. When the fee had been paid, he insisted on getting from the reyeras a percentage of what had been paid, for the "legal" services he had provided. The reyeras always refused to pay him anything. He then insisted and provoked them until he was himself arrested, and locked up in the stock.

Just after the begging performance throughout the village had been com-pleted, Don Chama was arrested. He was accused by the fiesteras to be the leader of a gang trafficking marijuana. Arresting Don Chama, the most re-spected man in the community, got the interest of many, to the point that when the reyeras went to arrest him at his house, they were accompanied by a group of women and kids, curious to see what was going to happen. He let them take him away without resisting. On the contrary, he participated in a mischievous way by taking a piece of paper out of one of his pockets, roll-ing it in the form of a conic marijuana joint, and simulated smoking it with great pleasure. It was quite surprising to see Don Chama, who was usually so serious, participate in his arrest with such humor.

After an afternoon recess, the marimba dance began again in the evening and lasted until around 2:00 A.M. on January 8. Chamita organized another baile de cuerda in Childo's house. This time, the Chachi men came alone, without their women.

January 8, the Day of the *Negritos* and of the Cayapas

The last day is dedicated to the negritos and the cayapas, although some reyeras disguised as whites are still participating in the activities. January 8 is also called *el día de todos*, "the day of everybody." During my participant-observation in 1990, the morning was mostly occupied by two activities: another begging performance-visit through the village, and the act of *la parridora* ("the woman who gives birth"). The latter was a prolongation of the act of the hermanitos (the act of the brothers and sisters). There was also the briefer intervention of the *mujer hinchada* (the swollen woman), the *mono* (the monkey)—who is a thief—and the wandering of *damas* (crossed-dressed men).

There were therefore a variety of characters wandering around. The whites were dressed the same way as they were the previous days. The cucuruchos who remained whites during the three days of the Play were usually the younger ones. It was actually easier to keep the same disguise throughout the three days. The reyeras who changed characters from one day to the next were usually the older ones who had greater experience of the Play and who enjoyed playing with more energy, *fuerza*. On that day, three men were disguised as women. They were called damas. They were relatively silent and made sure not to be recognized. In January 1989, 1990, and 1991, their participation was limited to following the reyeras during their quest through the village. The damas never helped the cucuruchos to arrest men. They simply did not have that kind of complicity with the reyeras: no one could forget that in reality they were men. However, as elders told me, a dama was never put in the stocks. Other elders indicated that in the past, there was a greater connivance between damas (who could number as many as ten) and reyeras.

From conversations with various villagers, I was told that usually the Cayapas were represented by a mock "Chachi woman" surrounded by a group of boys and girls of around ten years old, disguised as Chachi. They always moved around as one group. On January 8, 1990, a Chachi woman who accepted the cucuruchos' invitation to play the part dressed up as the "queen" or "mother" of the Cayapas. Around fifteen disguised children accompanied her.

The third group was the group of the blacks, or negritos. They were the most active. They not only performed a begging-spectacle in the various "streets" of the village but were also very much involved in the act of the woman who gives birth and of the "brothers and sisters." There were nine in 1990, and they were the most enthusiastic group of reyeras. Although they were all women, they represented both men and women.

The damas were generally dressed like the cucuruchos except that they replaced pants and masculine shirts with dresses, skirts, and feminine blouses with long sleeves. Their masks in cardboard were similar to those of the cucuruchos.

The Chachi woman was dressed with the traditional piece of colorful cotton (*manta*) that Chachi women used to wrap around their waists. Her head, shoulders, back, and breasts were covered with a cotton shawl. (In traditional contexts, Chachi women used to move about topless; the Chachi had understood that they cannot do this anymore, particularly in an Afro-Esmeraldian village where men tend to interpret this dress code as marks of savagery and sexual availability.) She moved around with a *batea* (a large wooden bowl used for preparing meals and also for panning for gold), a small pot, and wooden spoons. She was barefoot. Her forehead and her cheeks had been reddened with *achiote* (annatto-Bixa orellana). The little girls who accompanied her were dressed with a similar manta wrapped around their bodies, from the breasts to the ankles. They wore a small crown made out of flowers, and their foreheads, cheeks, and sometimes the upper part of their torsos were colored red with annatto. The little boys moved around wearing shorts, their skin colored with white to lighten up their natural color and make *colorados* or lighter-brown kids out of them.

Blacks were dressed with old stained clothes, with holes here and there. They wore a short or long pair of pants if they were men, or a skirt or dress made out of bark cloth or out of an old sack if they were women. As cucuruchos say, blacks were dressed like that because *en la realidad, nosotros los negritos nos vestimos así, con lo que encontramos* ("in reality we, black people, we dress this way, with whatever we find"). They had rubber boots "because they live in the forest," *somos gente de montaña*. The uncovered parts of their skin had been tainted with a black colorant (usually charcoal) to symbolize the black skin of the negritos. They did not wear masks, and their blackened faces were exposed for everybody to see. They often had a hat or a cap. Some had a piece of sack on their heads instead.

La mujer hinchada, or "swollen woman" was completely covered. One could not see any part of her skin at all. A towel had been rolled around her head to cover it completely and later covered by a second layer with a white piece of cloth, which gave the appearance of a balloon. She was wearing a long-sleeved sweatshirt that had been filled up with pieces of cloth to give her the appearance of being swollen. Under her skirt she was wearing a pair of pants with the legs filled up with pieces of cloth also. She wore rubber boots.

The monkey, who was always played by a man, wore a tunic made out of bark cloth or an old sack. It was then covered with an *hojarasquín*, a skirt-like ensemble of palm-tree and coconut-tree leaves attached with a cord. He was barefoot, and the skin of his arms and legs was uncovered. His face was hidden by a mask made out of half a calabash in which three holes (for the eyes and the mouth) had been carved. Usually, he moved around, often running and emitting incomprehensible sounds, holding a big bag in which he kept the products of his house raids. Unlike in la Tola, the Santo Domingeño monkey never used a cord or a whip.

As had been the case the day before, the quest began around 9:00 A.M. in the upper part of barrio "Quito." The groups of cucuruchos and other disguised actors moved down toward barrio "Guayaquil," sometimes stopping in front of a house to get some money from its owner. When they arrived in front of the communal house, the cortège stopped for a longer while near the stock for adults where most of the performance of the reyeras took place. Their voices were raucous and exhausted from the two previous days of playing.

The kids were disguised in a house of barrio "Quito," with the Chachi woman. It is in the house next door that some of the reyeras became black men and women. Those who remained white left their houses half disguised, holding their masks and other objects in their hands, and went to another house. Those who were going to become black did not want to disclose their disguises before beginning their parading in the village.

Some male adolescents and young men played percussion (bombo and cununo) at the head of the parading party. They either accompanied the songs of the "Cayapas" or, at other occasions, the songs of the negritos. The negritos' songs were the same as the songs that were sung the day before. The disguised actors regrouped by "racial" identity: the Chachi children around their "queen," the blacks, and the whites all made separate groups. On January 8, the cucuruchos representing whites were usually the youngest ones, or the women who were more discreet and shy. Their roles in the activities of that day were much more peripheral than they had been in the previous two days. The hardcore players were now disguised mostly as blacks.

One of the objectives of this "multiracial" cortège was to get some coins from the nondisguised population who were solicited to give money when the cucuruchos from either one of the racial performance groups stopped in front of their houses to perform a trick or a dance. The begging for money, which in fact constituted only one rather peripheral aspect of the activities, did not hinder the performance. Most of the activities of the reyeras were not planned to obtain monetary gain.

The Chachi performers were the first to go down to barrio "Guayaquil." They sang songs that were also sung the day before, intersected with songs reserved for the Chachi kids:

> *Chichirichi Chimirichimirichimiricha* (which is repeated several times), *la mitad, ocho por ocho, la mitad, ocho por ocho, la mitad* . . . ("half of it, eight by eight, half of it, eight by eight, half of it . . .": this refers to an Afro-Esmeraldian cynical gaze on the Chachi who are seen by many in the Northern sector of the province as uneducated and who were often called in the past *chachi salvajes*)
> *De los hijos de mi padre yo soy el mejor*
> *Aquí hay pero no me dan* ("Here they have but they don't give anything").

This last verse is traditionally reserved for the group of Chachi children. In the past they stopped from house to house singing that verse. They then received various foodstuff (plantains, salted fish, plantain flour). At the end of the parading, they all got together and cooked the food they had received. In 1990, the search and begging for food continued, but the Cayapas did not get together to cook and eat. They gave what they received to the committee of reyeras for the preparation of the meal of the marimberos.

The blacks or negritos followed the Cayapas. One of them, a "man," manipulated a saw and mockingly attempted to saw the piles of guayacán wood at various houses. People in attendance were then alerting the owner of each house to what was happening, with screams of excitement. The owner then rushed outside, if he or she wasn't already there, to give a coin or a glass of aguardiente to the reyera so that she would stop sawing the pile. The "black man" then continued on to the next house, and so on. Another fiestera was disguised as an Afro-Esmeraldian male hunter. "He" was wandering alongside his black companions, mimicking a hunt. He had a rifle on his shoulder and held in his other hand a (very small) hunting dog on a leash made of vegetal fibers. The size of the dog added to the irony of the scene. He was said to be looking for paca, peccary, and other forest animals. He had on his back a traditional basket used by both men and women to transport produce from their garden or from a hunting trip.

Two other fiesteras, also dressed as men, were fishermen. One of them was going down the main walkway of barrio Quito toward barrio "Guayaquil," pretending to walk in shallow water in the river looking for river

Figure 9. A black "man hunter" with his "hunting" dog. (Photograph by Jean Muteba Rahier)

Figure 10. A "fisherman" throwing an atarraya. (Photograph by Jean Muteba Rahier)

shrimps, which he then tried to catch with an *armazón* (a long metallic fishing tool that looks like a long metallic stick ending in a trident). The second fisherman was focused on getting fish. He was moving around casting his atarraya (the round net used in the forest to get freshwater fish).

Another black woman represented a woman working alluvial river gravel to pan for gold. The curves of her body—specifically the buttocks and the breasts—had been artificially increased in ironic proportions because, they said, repeating the usual stereotype one can hear in the cities of Esmeraldas, Quito, or Guayaquil, *las mujeres negras tienen hartas tetas y tremendas nalgas* ("black women in reality have big breasts and tremendous buttocks"). She was called *la nalgona* ("the woman with a big behind") and was walking around with a batea, which she manipulated to indicate that she was panning for gold. She spent most of the time bending over, like the women who are panning for gold in the region of the Pacific lowlands of Colombia (West 1952; Taussig 2004), of which Esmeraldas constitutes the southern extremity. That position revealed even more her augmented buttocks to the audience, who were laughing as they watched her. Two men who tried to caress her voluminous behind were arrested and locked up in the stocks.

There was also a couple, man and woman, of old Afro-Esmeraldians. The man was limping because, as the story "he" was sharing with the audience goes, years ago he had had an accident in the forest. They were said to be the parents of the other black people, who consequently were all brothers and sisters.

Figure 11. La nalgona. (Photograph by Jean Muteba Rahier)

The swollen woman, who was also a black woman despite the fact that on January 8, 1990, the piece of cloth that surrounded her head was white, was said to have been the victim of sorcery that had been initiated at the request of the wife of the man with whom she had had adulterous sex. The fact that she had been bewitched was made obvious by the swollen aspect of her face and body. After a series of vicissitudes, she was cured by the "doctor," who was still around with his nurse.

The whites and the damas walked together and followed the blacks. They were much less energetic than in the past two days (the most enthusiastic reyeras were now blacks). They were primarily in charge of arresting the male villagers who tried to touch the buttocks of the gold panner and the nalgona (big-butt) black woman, and who wanted to take the hunting dog away from the hunter. They put them in the stocks and collected the liberation fees.

One of the reyeras who was not disguised was following the groups and was serving aguardiente to improve the ambiance because many were already tired for playing almost nonstop for two days.

January 8, the Act of the Brothers and Sisters, the Swollen Woman, and the Parridora

Once in front of the communal house, the "Chachi" went on the soccer field, sang a few songs, and then left the field available to the blacks, who right away began the act of the brothers and sisters. One of the black women complained to the hunter that she had not received her part of a paca that he had killed. After a series of screams and negotiations, during which accusations that one of the brothers had taken her share away were made, the disagreement was solved and the brother agreed to give her something else in exchange. All of this took place in the middle of a laughing and ecstatic audience who intervened in the dialogue to help ease the conflict.

In the meantime, the gold panner was trying to sell the "gold" she had found when two men came by commenting upon the generosity of her buttocks while trying to touch and squeeze them. All the reyeras interrupted what they were doing and ran after the two men, whom they ended up arresting. The ambiance was at its apex when the act of the brothers and sisters picked up again. The songs of the blacks and of the Chachi could be heard in the background.

The act of the brothers and sisters is difficult to summarize. Many different interventions and reversals of situations targeted numerous things: the construction of masculinity, gender relations, women's sexual agency. In this act, the cucuruchos openly ridicule Afro-Esmeraldian men, making fun of the hunting and fishing stories they tell with pride, emphasizing the money they sometimes stupidly waste to purchase aguardiente instead of taking care of their families. They ridicule as well unequal gender relations, infidelity, and children made out of "wedlock" or out of the established consensual relationships they engage in. It is mostly in this act (and in the act of the woman who gives birth) that they humiliate their men with the greatest precision. Here is a passage of one of their dialogues, which sometimes takes the appearance of an animated fistfight, to the great pleasure of the people in the audience. What is interesting in this passage is that the scene is being set up for the affirmation of women's sexual agency that is at the center of the act of the woman who gives birth, which took place not far away from the communal house:

> THE MOTHER: I am so unlucky! And my man who doesn't help me. I have to take care of my children alone. He's gone for days. What a despicable guy. He always goes to waste his money to buy alcohol.
>
> THE LIMPING FATHER: And my woman who goes around saying that I don't help her, that I don't love my children. . . . Look [and he takes a small bottle out of his pocket], I had gone to Borbón to buy medicine for my younger son. She has such a bad mouth!
>
> THE MOTHER CONTINUES: And what did you do with the money you got from selling the tree trunks in Borbón? Don't tell me that you used it all to buy this small bottle of medicine!

The audience laughed, and someone suggested that he had gone to visit a woman named Doña Jasmina in Borbón, who is known to be promiscuous with men.

> THE MOTHER: You're such a liar! You see, you went to waste the money from the logs to drink and have a good time with another woman. There are people who saw you.

At this point, some of the couple's children took part and began defending their father, while others defended their mother. The whole discussion ends up in a tumultuous, multidirectional exchange, during which some of the protagonists rolled in the dust, screaming: "Don't accuse my dad, he has done nothing wrong, he only was preoccupied by the health of my younger brother," or "My dad never helps my mom, he is such a bad person!" The exchanges went on for periods of twenty to thirty minutes, and the act was interrupted numerous times by the arrest of a man, or the necessity to take care of a child, or because the audience who initially surrounded the cucuruchos involved decided to shift their attention to the swollen woman.

The swollen woman was initially sitting on a chair near the door outside of the communal house. When someone touched her, she screamed in pain, shaking as if she were overwhelmed by her condition. She sometimes suddenly stood up and made some directionless steps, scaring the nondisguised people standing around her, who then ran away screaming and gesticulating. Some commentaries about her were exchanged:

> This woman is like that, bewitched, because she had sex with a man who wasn't hers. Tell her to stop her dirty tricks.
>
> She is bewitched; she is losing her intestines. All of her body is swollen. They really got her. She loses her intestines through her behind. She took a man who wasn't hers, that's because of her tricks that she is like that. Poor woman, and she got a huge behind . . . and she has skinny legs underneath it all.

The doctor arrived and began taking care of her. He took some pieces of cloth from underneath her clothes. He sucked her to try to extract the illness, acting like a shaman. The commentaries continued:

> The doctor cured her.
>
> THE DOCTOR: This woman was very bad, because any man who wanted her could have sex with her. It is a lady who did this to her because she took her husband away. She was a nymphomaniac, which is why she was bewitched.

The doctor asked for 200,000 sucres for his services. Everyone laughed at the huge amount of money that this represented. The doctor added that if he were not paid soon, "I'll make sure that the spell comes back."

A little before the end of the act of the swollen woman, a young Chachi girl was kidnapped by a man who took her on the soccer field. The man ran away carrying her in his arms. The reyeras got together and began a pursuit. The nondisguised kids of the village followed them screaming with excitement. The kidnapper was finally arrested and locked up in the stocks. The "lawyer" came to his rescue, of course, and began negotiating his release with the reyeras.

The parridora, who was in fact the mother from the act of the brothers and sisters, got close to Fabián Saltos—one of the two white-mestizo students from the PUCE-Quito who were my research assistants. Fabián was standing outside the communal house, near the door. He was watching what was going on inside (the doctor and his nurse were taking care of a "patient"). The parridora was obviously pregnant (a ball made out of pieces of cloth had been placed under her shirt) and proclaimed to everyone around that the baby she had in her belly was from Don Fabián. He was the only white-mestizo man in the village in January 1990. Everyone around burst into laughter. Fabián, as a stranger to the village, was treated with respect, which is why he was called "Don Fabián." The fact that the reyera who played the role of parridora involved him in the act created a special attraction for everyone. They were in fact curious to see how Fabián was going to react, how he was going to enter in the liminality of the act and follow the logic of the Play.

The parridora confirmed:

> I'm telling you the truth, the baby will not be born black, he will be colored (that is to say, mixed race).

She then had her first contractions. She called her children and her husband (the other black characters who were active in the act of the brothers and sisters) and said:

> I'm going to tell you the truth. This little one that I have in me, to whom I'm about to give birth, husband don't kill me, but I have to say it to you, this baby is not yours, he or she is from Don Fabián.

The husband, limping, responded:

> I'm going to forgive you, because this is the first time. I love you so much. That's for you that I broke my leg.

The parridora continued:

> I'm telling the truth. The baby will not be born black but colored.
> THE HUSBAND: Yes, but I will not support him.
> THE PARRIDORA: No husband, no, because as soon as I get it out, I'll send it to Colombia.
> ONE OF THE "SONS" INTERVENED: Absolutely, if this is not the child of my dad, he has no reason to give him or her support.

During that time, the two monkeys—there were two monkeys in January 1990—were wandering in the village gesticulating in all directions and running around. They stole whatever they desired, and no one could stop them. To get back one of the things the monkeys had stolen, one had to give them some money or another good in exchange. They kept what they stole in a big sack. They sometimes suddenly got into houses to lay hands on the first things they could find. When they saw a monkey coming, people tried to close their doors and windows as quickly as possible. Sometimes one of them rolled in the dust, uttering strange and incomprehensible sounds, as if he were going through an epileptic seizure. The role of the monkeys was limited to doing just those things.

Then the dialogue of the blacks continued. The focus of the discussion was on the legitimacy of the parridora's child to be:

THE PARRIDORA: Please, realize how black my husband is. Both of us are black. But you will see, the child that I will give birth to. Just like Fabián, he is colored.

ONE OF THE SONS: It's better to get a white brother or sister.

Then, the parridora explained that in the past, the limping old man had abandoned her several times and that she had had to take care of the children alone. Her husband had given all his attention to another woman. She added that she had promised herself never to have children except with one man, but since that man wasn't there, she had not been able to deal with the loneliness. (Laughter of the public.)

THE PARRIDORA: Please my husband, don't abandon me. Don't you see that you and I don't have small children.

ONE OF THE SONS: Listen, Don Fabián, my dad will take care of your child, but you are the one who has to find a midwife.

The parridora sat again, overwhelmed by the pain of the contractions. People in the public laughed. The parridora found the strength to add:

I am saying the truth, today January 8. My husband went away with another woman, and I said "I'll do the same."

One of the nondisguised partakers spontaneously took the role of midwife. She entered in a negotiation with Fabián for the price of her services. She wanted 1,500 sucres right away, before the birth. The doctor got involved in the group and asked Fabián if he was the father. Fabián responded negatively. That's when the parridora got angry. She swore in front of the audience that Fabián gave her, as a present, five pieces of cloth and that this present is the obvious proof of their intimate relationship. She shouted to Fabián that if he is ashamed of her, the cucuruchos would lock him up in the stock. People in the public interjected that everyone should all wait to see what the skin color of the baby would be, that if the baby is mixed race (*colorado*), then Fabián would have to be locked in the stocks because of this evidence of his paternity, since he is the only white person in the village. A woman went away to get a batea to place the child in once he or she was born. The pain of the contractions came back. The parridora was then installed under a small tent of red plastic mounted near the communal house. She was helped both by the midwife and the doctor, while she screamed her lungs out under the pain.

Figure 12. La parridora giving birth under the tent. (Photograph by Jean Muteba Rahier)

The child is born: he is white (a white and blond doll). Fabián had to recognize his paternity. Everybody congratulated him. The child was baptized. The other student of the PUCE-Quito, Marisol, and I became the godparents. The baptism ceremony was very short. Marisol held the child in her arms while I poured water on her head saying: *Te bautizo al nombre del Padre, del Hijo, y del Espíritu Santo.* Everyone responded: ¡Amen! (Laughter.) The child is called Fabiancito Saltos, to evoke his father. As a new father, Fabián was asked to buy some aguardiente so that everyone could celebrate the birth in a proper way. The parridora gave the child to Fabián, who took him in his arms. Everyone around exclaimed how much they looked alike. (Laughter). The doctor demanded his money from Fabián, who said he had none left. The lawyer intervened and said to Fabián that the parridora's husband wants to get his wife back, but that he does not want to know anything about the child. Fabián was arrested and locked up in the stocks for having taken the wife of another man. (Laughter.) The lawyer insisted to Fabián:

> The old man is going to kill his wife if you don't take the child with you, when you go back to Quito.

Spontaneously, the lawyer decided to try to get alimony for the parridora. People around burst out in laughter. Someone suggested that Fabián loves black women.

While Fabián was still in the stocks, the mother took her child back in her arms and went inside the communal house. Strident screams could suddenly be heard coming out of the communal house. The child has died. Fabián is freed. The reyeras began a chigualo (funeral ceremony for deceased children) right away in the communal house. The cununos, bombos, and guasás were played to accompany the arrullos sung by most of the women present in the room. Games were performed around the small corpse. The lawyer got inside the house and demanded that an autopsy be performed:

> *Quiero una autoksia, quiero una autoksia* (I want an autopsy, I want an autopsy)—he was saying.

Figure 13. Fabián in the stocks. (Photograph by Jean Muteba Rahier)

He justified his demand by saying that it appeared strange to him that the mother could be playing and dancing in such a way just after the death of her child. The true reasons for the death had to be discovered. The gold panner came nearby and commented:

> It is better that he died because he was white and everybody else here is black. If he had not died, Fabián would have had to take him away.

The brothers and sisters recaptured the attention of everyone. They were fighting among themselves: some were defending their father while others were in favor of the mother, who had been caught in an adulterous relationship with another man. They all rolled in the dust, simulating a general fight. The last marimba dance began right after the last song of the ritual of *Buen Viaje* ("Have a good trip"), which is performed at the closing of every chigualo.

The last afternoon of the Play was not the most agitated. There were almost no men arrested. The entire village was exhausted: many had only slept a few hours since January 6. The last dance ended around 6:00 P.M.

Conclusions

The Afro-Esmeraldian Play of the Cowls makes a series of commentaries on Afro-Esmeraldians' daily lives. In that sense, it manifests what Victor Turner called "public reflexivity" (1977, 33).

This moment of public reflexivity is, obviously, in existence within a liminal time, a time that is not controlled by the clock, an enchanted time within which anything could happen. It is a time that is always clearly framed.

The temporal frame of the Play of the Cowls is unmistakably marked on December 28, when the reyeras obtain the permit to play, as well as on January 8, with the last marimba dance. The space of the village that cucuruchos spontaneously occupy when playing automatically acquires a particular quality: children must stay away and not bother the playing adults. If they do, they will be punished and locked up in the stocks specially constructed for boys and placed, unlike the stocks constructed for men, away from the central space where the performances of the Play take place.

The large, public, carnivalesque festivals that provide liminal time and space often contain satires, jokes, comedies, and parodies. They tend to insist on the equality of all, even if this implies a reversal of status and roles. Their principal objective is to caricaturize the power in place, its wealth and its authority (see Turner 1977, 36).

Indeed, large public festivals, and particularly "plays" among them, can be highly subversive. As Don Handelman puts it,

> [E]vents that re-present the lived-in world do work of comparison and contrast in relation to social realities. This kind of event re-presents lived-in worlds by offering propositions and counter-propositions, within itself, about the nature of these realities. Whether through the juxtaposition and conflict of contraries, through the neutralization of accepted distinctions, or through their inversion, the more hidden or controversial implications of the propositional character of the world are exposed. These implications may pose alternatives to the ordering of social realities. They may offer a grab bag of options. They may thrust towards relationships of thesis and antithesis. But, at the bare minimum, they work through contrast and comparison within the event itself. In turn, such work may raise possibilities, questions, perhaps doubts, about the legitimacy or the validity of social forms, as these are constituted in the lived-in world. Events that re-present are like multiple or magic mirrors that play with forms of order—that refract multiple visions of the possible, from among whose uncertainties there re-emerge probabilities. (1990, 49)

Natalie Davis, a historian who studied European festivities of the Middle Ages, also seemed to have been writing about the Afro Esmeraldian Festival of the Kings when she indicated that the sexual inversions—women dressing up as men and vice versa—that often occur during carnivals express nothing but the "liminal quintessence" of festive or carnivalesque time, because women, who are usually oppressed individuals in the profane world, see their prerogatives reinforced. The women's undiscipline marks the "ultraliminality" of the festival and indicates that anything could happen. The power of the weak to insult and to criticize puts limits to the power of the dominant to restrain and command (1975, 147).

The concepts of "repetition," "representation," and "improvisations" of performance-studies scholars allow for the appreciation of the prerogative to create and to innovate shared by the characters involved in the Play's acts; and this is an essential attribute of the actors of rituals and "representations" in general (Schechner 1985, 120).

When discussing the concept of "repetition," Thompson Drewal identified the error that consists in conceiving "repetition" in an exclusively structuralist perspective: "A fundamental problem with the study of ritual has been our understanding of the nature of repetition, which has heretofore been seen as structurally restrictive or—at the very least—confining" (1992, 1). Repetition is by definition a "re-presentation" and therefore a "representation."

What is repeated is always a previous temporality, which was itself already a repetition. And it is because they represent preceding periods that repetitions incarnate creativity, at the very same time that they give some illusion of return, of recurrence. But one should not be mistaken. A manifestation never has the same value twice.

Linda Hutcheon's understanding of "parody" is also useful here: parody is not a particular form of satire but instead is a singular genre of repetition, a repetition with a "critical distance." Parody—I paraphrase her—often allows for the ironic signaling of a difference at the very heart of the similarity at the same time as it also indicates, paradoxically, cultural continuity and change, transgression, and authority (1985). As this chapter has shown, the concept of "improvisation" is fundamental to making sense of the Afro-Esmeraldian Festival of the Kings. Improvisation is the art of maneuvering based on "in-body" techniques so that one can realize an effect or a particular style of performance. Drewal states: "In improvisation, each move is contingent on a previous move and in some measure influences the one that follows. Improvisation requires a mastery of the logic of action and in-body codes together with the skill to intervene in them and transform them. Each performance, each time, is generated anew" (1992, 7).

Each day of the Festival, acts of various duration were performed by disguised characters in the communal joy of the local public, not disguised, who nevertheless intervened spontaneously in the dialogues without in any way provoking the irritation of the disguised actors or of the rest of the local audience, who stood around the specific place where the act was unfolding. When such an intervention occurred, the "interrupted" actions continued as if the last intervention had been made by a disguised actor: the audience was not reduced to silence; its (informed) participation was invited. The spontaneous intervention was completely integrated within the act and had some influence on its development. From one year to the next, some of the people involved in the performances often decided to change one of the aspects of their disguises or to include in the dialogues themes that had not been dealt with the previous year. These thematic additions had often to do with one of the major events that had an influence, during the year, on the population of the village.

"Improvisation" allows for the appreciation of performances in their reality, their movement and change. In the case of the Play of the Cowls in Santo Domingo, improvisations constitute a relatively sure way to provoke laughter and guarantee the general joy. The principal objective of the Play of the Cowls was "derision," and also to comment on the experiences of daily life; and it was often the most ingenious and mischievous improvisations that allowed that to happen.

Linda Hutcheon's notion of "semiotic competence" (1985, 84–89) helps to explain some aspects of the Play. The relation between encoders and decoders implies the sharing of a mutual and necessary code that gives existence to the phenomenon (joke, parody, and satire) that is looked for. To make sense of the irony of a particular text, the decoder must be able to appreciate what is meant, as well as what is actually said, written, played, or painted. Without this necessary knowledge, without the indispensable references (the codes, the sociocultural and political contexts), no one would have been able to make sense of the acts of the Play, the reason(s) for the smiles and laughter, what the target of the parodies and satires were. All the adults involved in the Play, in both Santo Domingo and La Tola, were then both encoders and decoders, independent of whether they were disguised or not.

The objective is not to reject the concept of "structure" altogether, but instead to emphasize the "structuring" properties, by indicating how the actors and other participants use them. In such an optic, structure and "traditions" appear as "resources" for action, and the "acquired in-body techniques" do not constitute necessarily structures or systems of reproduction but are instead body techniques that are as many means used by educated agents in the negotiations at work in the performance.

This in fact coincides well with what David Guss calls the "multivocality" of festivals: the fact that there is no such thing as a festival that does not involve permanent negotiations, following, among other things, the agency of the various actors involved (2000).

The semiotic competence, or rather the "semiotic incompetence," explains the exclusion of the children from the Play of the Cowls. It is a play for adults, and when the participation of disguised children was required for a particular act, its duration was limited and they were always under the strict control of the fiesteras. The smallest children were usually afraid of the cucuruchos, whom they followed from afar during the three days of the Play. Intellectually, because of their lack of life experiences, they were not really able to understand the sense of most acts, their numerous inversions. Their uncontrolled participation would have limited the degree or the range of the satires, the parodies, the irony, and the laughter.

4

The Festival of the Kings in La Tola

The situation, the population, and the history of the village of La Tola differ quite strikingly from those of Santo Domingo. These differences explain, in final analysis, the singularities of the Play in each one of the two villages. In the following pages, I underline the characteristics of La Tola that are indispensable for the interpretation of the Toleño Play and for its comparison to that of the Santo Domingeños. If I am more brief than I have been when writing about the characteristics of Santo Domingo, it is because the lesser intensity of the Play in La Tola makes its interpretation somewhat easier. Additionally, some of the previous ethnographic information about the Santo Domingeño context is also valid for the village of La Tola.

The village is located at the mouth of the Santiago River and is the head village of the parish of La Tola, which was created by a decree in 1828. It is one of the oldest Esmeraldian parishes. The actual village of La Tola, however, was founded by Pedro Vicente Maldonado in the early eighteenth century as an attempt of the elites of the Sierra to establish a road from Quito to a coastal port closer to Panama that would give them independence from the southern Ecuadorian port of Guayaquil, which was under the control of competing costeño elites (Rueda Novoa 1990). La Tola constitutes a regional center for the smaller surrounding villages, particularly Olmedo, La Barca, Cuerval, and La Tolita Pampa de Oro. A road, which was mostly dirt at the end of the 1980s and in the early 1990s, links La Tola to the capital of the province, the city of Esmeraldas.

During the dry season, the trip to Esmeraldas lasts around four hours. The same trip during the rainy season could last more than six hours as a result of the numerous and relatively deep mud pools. La Tola is therefore much more accessible to the influences of the "national Ecuadorian society" (institutions of the state, the Church, international organizations, absentee elite). Two cooperatives of public transportation—*La Costeñita* and *La Co-operativa del Pacífico*—transport peoples and goods to and from Esmeraldas. Between 6:30 A.M. and 3:30 P.M. there is an hourly departure of a bus from La Tola. A cooperative of lanchas transport passengers and goods from La Tola to Limones and San Lorenzo. They make four to five round trips per day (the number varies according to the season and the goodwill of the lanchas' pilots-owners). La Tola constitutes an obligatory transit point for many passengers and goods. During the dry season, many of the passengers are European and North American backpack tourists who have taken the *ferrocarril* (a bus mounted on railroad wheels) from Ibarra, the capital of the Andean Province of Imbabura, to San Lorenzo. Many of the passengers are also inhabitants of the villages of the northern coastal area (around La Tola, Limones, and San Lorenzo) who are going to or coming back from Esmeraldas and beyond. Three Toleños own lodging facilities, two owned bar-restaurants, and various Toleño men were luggage carriers who help passengers and traveling salesmen to carry their luggage and packages from the lanchas to the buses, or vice versa. There are therefore more numerous and varied salaried jobs in La Tola than in Santo Domingo. In a more general way, Toleños are much more dependent on the cash economy for their survival than Santo Domingeños are.

The population of La Tola is also more numerous than that of Santo Domingo. In December 1989–January 1990, there were 1,016 inhabitants; 55 percent of them were between 0 and 20 years old, 27 percent between 21 and 40, 11 percent between 41 and 60, and 7 percent were older than 60. Moreover, La Tola's population is multiracial. I established three categories of racial identity, all based on local usage: the Esmeraldian white-mestizos and mulattos, the non-Esmeraldian white-mestizos, and the Afro-Esmeraldians; 20.8 percent of the head of households fell within the first category, 7 percent in the second, and 72.2 percent in the third.

The Esmeraldian white-mestizos were the individuals who had physical traits that could unambiguously be associated with Europe, although their skin was rather brown: they had light colored eyes, straight hair, pointed noses. They were all born in La Tola, and many were the descendants of the first white and white-mestizo families that founded La Tola under the leadership of the Spaniard Pedro Vicente Maldonado in the early eighteenth century. Their ancestors were mostly white and white-mestizos and secondarily black. That is why I have added "mulattos" in parenthesis. This group corresponds quite well to what Norman Whitten has called "light Costeños" (1965, 1974).

The non-Esmeraldian white-mestizos are the in-migrants who were not born in the province of Esmeraldas. Most of them were born in another coastal province. Thirty people are entered in that category; they almost all came from the neighboring province of Manabí. Only five were born in an Andean province.

The category of Afro-Esmeraldians is composed of all the black people who reside in the village. It includes Toleño blacks as well as the Afro-Esmeraldians who migrated from another Afro-Esmeraldian village, as well as some Colombians. In 1989, there were forty-one Colombians in La Tola (thirty-eight were black): fourteen men and twenty-seven women, who for the most part came from Tumaco and Barbacoas.

The geographic situation of the village allows for an easy access to different economically exploitable ecosystems: the river, the ocean, the inland area, and the mangroves.

A Glimpse at La Tola's Socioeconomic Sectors

While I distinguished only two community sectors in Santo Domingo, the "poor peasants" and the "leaders," in La Tola the intracommunity differentiation is more complex and follows "racial identities" rather closely. My experience of the village brought me to set apart several sectors: the peasant-fishermen, the poor proletariat, the fishermen of the cooperative Buena Esperanza, the proletariat-employees, the small local entrepreneurs, the local entrepreneurs, the local Afro-Esmeraldian professionals, and the absentee elite. La Tola has a greater racial and socioeconomic diversity than Santo Domingo. There are sometimes tensions between the different sectors, which diminish the extent of the communal life and the strength of the Afro-Esmeraldian cultural traditions (arrullos, chigualos, the Festival of the Kings, the *Décimas*). The latter are often looked at as expressions of nonmodernity.

Almost all Afro-Esmeraldians were peasant-fishermen. There were among them some Esmeraldian white-mestizos, but no non-Esmeraldian white-mestizos. Peasant-fishermen are certainly the group with the least economic power. They are mostly subsistence fishermen. Their precarious economic means does not allow them to acquire the necessary equipment to fish in high seas. They fish primarily in the river and its tributaries, and the techniques they use are rather rudimentary: atarraya, catanga, *trasmayo* (a long net of around fifteen meters used to fish in the river, which requires the collaboration of three or four men). The product of their fishing is usually not destined for the market but for their households. If they sometimes produce a small surplus, its sale brings them small amounts of money. They sometimes also own one or two small gardens inland near the village, on which they cultivate by slash-mulch the same products that Santo Domingeños cultivate. The harvests are mostly for household use, and the small surplus only brings in small amounts of cash. The youngest among them try to get menial jobs in the small businesses of the village or as day workers in surrounding haciendas. Around 50 percent of the heads of households are in this category. They live in a permanent situation of economic insecurity. Their women and children sometimes bring in a small income by fishing in the river with rudimentary techniques. During the dry season, when the water level in the river is lower, women sometimes collect small black mussels called *conchas* in the mud banks in the middle of the river. These are then sold to intermediaries who bring them to the markets of the city of Esmeraldas or of Andean cities.

The poor proletariat is also mostly composed of Afro-Esmeraldians, although some Esmeraldian white-mestizos are included in this category. The latter are chiefly male in-migrants from other villages of the province or from Colombia. They usually do not have family responsibility in La Tola and live off only the small remunerations they get from unstable jobs for their subsistence. They do not own a garden, canoe, or fishnet and usually live alone in an abandoned house or in the house of one of the peasant-fishermen, for a small contribution toward the cost of food. Their economic insecurity is even more precarious than for the poor peasant-fishermen, and their total dependency on the cash economy makes them the first victims of the periods of bust. They carry the luggage and other packages of the passengers of the lanchas and buses. They work as day laborers in the surrounding haciendas at harvest. They help the owners of the lodgings with whatever task their services are needed for. Their survival strategy consists of keeping in touch with as many people from the other sectors as possible, so that they can secure a small job as soon as the opportunity presents itself.

The individuals of these two categories, who represent around 70 percent of the household heads, are those who have a lifestyle that is close to that of the Santo Domingeños. Their education is rather limited (they usually did not complete primary school). They prepare their meals on *fogones* (charcoal cooking fire) and not on gas stoves. They sometimes hunt, although much more rarely than in Santo Domingo: beef and other kinds of meat are much more available in La Tola, and fresh fish is abundant. They continue to share Afro-Esmeraldian cultural traditions and beliefs.

The fishermen from the cooperative Buena Esperanza must be differentiated from the poor peasant-fishermen. At the beginning of the 1980s, the Afro-Esmeraldian intellectual, Juan García Salazar, who was born in Cuerval, obtained funding from the Inter-American Foundation (IAF) to help the economic development of the small fishermen of the area around La Tola. Under his leadership, cooperatives were created in each one of the villages. La Tola's cooperative Buena Esperanza was also in charge of the commercialization of the fish caught by the fishermen of all cooperatives, so that they could break the abusive power of the intermediaries who arbitrarily fixed the prices to their advantage. The small fishermen who were the founding members of the cooperative were between twenty and thirty years old when the cooperative was created. They each received, thanks to the funds from the IAF, an outboard engine and nets to fish in the ocean. Each cooperative received an initial small budget that allowed them to begin functioning. The cooperative Buena Esperanza also received, because of its commercialization goals, a cold-storage room in which to keep frozen fish. Each cooperative member was supposed to reimburse his respective cooperative the cost of the motor he received. This money would have helped the cooperatives to reinvest in another aspect of the fishing activities, or to purchase new equipment. None of these cooperatives ever functioned as they were supposed to. The cost of the motors was never reimbursed, and the leaders of each cooperative (president, vice president, treasurer) did not really respect the bylaws that asked for regular elections.

Instead of allowing economic development for the benefit of all small fishermen, the funds allocated by the IAF led to the emergence of a group of privileged fishermen within each community. These privileged fishermen were the members of the cooperatives who had access to the IAF funds that allowed them to purchase the technical means to fish in the ocean and in that way to secure more stable and higher incomes than the other fishermen who were not members of the cooperatives. They did not really identify either with the long-term goals of the cooperative as stated in the bylaws or with the preoccupations of the peasant-fishermen. In 1990, a single plentiful sea-fishing trip could bring one fisherman up to 30,000 sucres (about US$40.00 at the time). Usually, they did not work on the surrounding haciendas as day laborers. Without being "rich," their income was sufficient to provide for the immediate needs of their families. After a good fishing day, it was not rare to see them relax for a few days.

My visits to the village allowed me to witness the transformation of some of the members of the cooperative Buena Esperanza at a managerial level. The cooperative was affiliated with the National Association of Cooperatives, which offered seminars rather regularly to the leaders of the member cooperatives. These seminars were usually held in a city such as Quito or Guayaquil, or the capital of another province. To go there, the leaders of the Buena Esperanza used the funds allocated by the IAF to give themselves a per diem. In 1990, some of them had the opportunity to attend an international seminar for black minorities of Latin America, organized in the United States and funded by U.S. black organizations. The delegates from Buena Esperanza came back from that trip—extraordinary at the time for an Afro-Esmeraldian fisherman—admirers of the progress and life conditions of the middle-class

> MIGUEL: Don Jean, for me, what was the most fascinating about the Johnny (the United States) was to see that over there, even if one is black, one can own a lot of things, a nice car, a beautiful house, go to the university. Over there, it's just normal to go to the university. The blacks from over there are more advanced than us. I would like to go back. Hopefully to stay. (Fragment of a conversation recorded in La Tola in 1991)

The peasant-fishermen had profound resentment against the fishermen of the cooperative, whom they sometimes found pretentious and arrogant. They often expressed a snarling jealousy toward them. As well, the members of the cooperative did not really participate anymore in "traditional activities," which they looked at as vestiges of the past. And I am convinced that many of them never really understood my passionate interest in the Festival of the Kings.

Those included in the category "proletariat-employees" are all non-Esmeraldian white-mestizos. They are the worker-fishermen employed by Don Rafael Arboleda, and also the workers of the *camaronera* (shrimp farm) that was installed in Cuerval. I separate them from the poor proletariat for three reasons: they are not Afro-Esmeraldians, their remunerations are higher and more stable, and, finally, they do not really consider themselves as true residents of La Tola, to which they travel for the duration of their employment. They do not invest any of their income in the local economy.

The small local entrepreneurs are those who own, in addition to a garden eventually larger than the gardens of most peasant-fishermen, a small shop with limited stock (wherein they sell few articles and buy only a relatively minor part of the surplus of small peasants and fishermen) or a small restaurant to serve meals to passengers, or a small store in which they sell clothes. They do not own a small truck, nor do they have sufficient capital to impose themselves as important intermediaries. They are mostly Esmeraldian white-mestizos, and rarely non-Esmeraldian white-mestizos.

Those whom I call "local entrepreneurs" correspond quite well to Norm Whitten's definition: they are the intermediaries for the local commerce and the farmers of which production is entirely destined to the regional and national markets. Their economic means are much greater than those of the small local entrepreneurs. They are able to engage in new business ventures and take some risks instead of limiting themselves to live off of a small stock of merchandise and a relatively small garden. They are predominantly non-Esmeraldian white-mestizos, although one Afro-Esmeraldian was entered in that category when we conducted the census. They all own a private pickup truck, which is indispensable for their commercial activities. They usually maintain a commercial relationship with relatives in the province of Manabí or in the Andes. They buy the fish, shrimp, and conchas from the fishermen of the villages of the area to sell them to these relatives, who in turn sell them in the markets of Quito, Ibarra, and other cities. Their small shops are the largest in the village. They are the richest individuals of the village and usually do not participate in Afro-Esmeraldian traditional activities. They look at local blacks as "people who have no culture": *Son vagos que no quieren trabajar. Y luego, vienen a mendigar* ("They are lazy and don't want to work. And then, they come to beg for things").

One of them, Rafael Arboleda, could constitute a category by himself. He is probably the man who manipulated the largest amount of cash in the region. He is a Colombian white-mestizo who immigrated to the village in the early 1980s. There are rumors that he escaped the Colombian justice system. He arrived in the village with enough cash to buy big lanchas and outboard motors for navigation in the deep sea, nets, a generator for electricity, and a huge freezer twice the size of the one owned by the Cooperative Buena Esperanza. He also funded the construction of a private wooden deck and hired a series of salaried workers who fish in the sea for him. During the five working days of the week, a medium-size truck comes from Quito to pick up his fish and shellfish. He is said to have big business connections with members of the national elite in Quito. He has refused my invitation to be interviewed.

He has installed a small store in which he sells a great diversity of products. He does not participate in village life, from which he is completely independent. The Afro-Esmeraldian poor peasant-fishermen and poor proletariat often complain about the fact that he is only hiring strangers to the village community: his salaried workers are all Colombian or Ecuadorian (from Manabí) white-mestizos who work for periods of three weeks without interruption. They then take a weeklong vacation, which they use to go back to their place of origin. They are all single young men in their twenties.

The absentee elite is "present" in the parish through the shrimp farm installed in Cuerval. It was constructed in 1986, thanks to investments from a company based in Quito of which an ex–vice president of Ecuador, Blasco Peñaherrera, owned some stocks. The making of the pools, with big machinery, and the construction of three buildings in wood and cement were accomplished with white-mestizo laborers from Quito. The personnel (workers and guards) of the shrimp farm are all white-mestizos.

The arrival of the shrimp farm on the bank of the Santiago River, just behind the village of Cuerval, accelerated the disappearance of that small village. On one side, the river was eroding the land at the rhythm of the successive tides, and on the other, the barbed wire of the shrimp farm prohibited expansion. Most of the inhabitants of Cuerval migrated to La Tola, Esmeraldas, and even Guayaquil.

Strong tensions sometimes exist between the fishermen of the cooperative Buena Esperanza and the small fishermen on one side, and the employees of the shrimp farm on the other. In periods of shrimp reproduction in the brackish water of the sea-river merger in the mangrove, the shrimp-farm workers installed lamps near the water to attract shrimp larvae during the night near the big tubes they used for sucking in river water for their pools. In that way, they took away—for free—a large portion of the future shrimp population that was supposed to be available for everyone's fishing. I have witnessed several fistfights between Toleño fishermen and shrimp-farm workers. The guards of the shrimp farm also prohibit inhabitants of Cuerval from using a small trail they have walked on for decades to access their inland gardens. They argue that now the trail is on private property and that therefore the residents of the community are prohibited from using it.

To these seven sectors, I must add an eighth one: the schoolteachers, the school administrators, the employees of the transportation cooperatives, the employees of the phone company, and the nurses. They number around twenty in total, mostly women. They are all Afro-Esmeraldians from the area around the city of Esmeraldas (with the exception of the employees of the transport cooperatives), and their salaries are lower than the salary of the medical doctor who sometimes spends a week or two in the village (he is most often a male student intern spending his year of *medicina rural* prior to obtaining his diploma). Most of the people included in this last category are not involved in the economic life of the area, and they take the first opportunity they have to stay in Esmeraldas or in their village or town of origin and not come to La Tola.

Outmigration from La Tola

The data about outmigration gathered in La Tola have similar characteristics as those from the census in Santo Domingo. They only concern the outmigrants who had at least one parent (head of household) living in the village at the time of the census. The following numbers are therefore underestimations of reality. In January 1990, there were 278 outmigrants, all children of inhabitants of the village. They represented 27.4 percent of the population of inhabitants, 7 percent less than in Santo Domingo. Twenty-two migrated to another village of the Eloy Alfaro Canton; 124 (44.6 percent of outmigrants) went to live in the rest of the province (principally in the city of Esmeraldas [97] and in San Lorenzo [12]); 80 (28.8 percent) went to Guayaquil, 45 (16.2 percent) preferred the rest of the country, six emigrated to Colombia, and one left for the United States.

The 45 outmigrants who went to the rest of the country can be subdivided as follows: 12 in Santo Domingo de los Tsachilas; 6 to the *Oriente*; 20 to the province of Manabí; 3 to Quito; 1 to Loja; and 3 to Latacunga. They were proportionally more important than in Santo Domingo de Ónzole because the non-Esmeraldian white-mestizo in-migrants tend to send their children to high schools in their city or village of origin, or at least in their province of origin. Of these 45 migrants, many are therefore students.

The Toleños who outmigrated to another village in the rest of the parish were all Afro-Esmeraldians. They continue to be peasant-fishermen for the men and housekeepers for the women. The rest of the canton did not attract that many people, when compared with the 177 people (respectively 97 and 80), that is to say 63.7 percent of the population of outmigrants, who were living in Esmeraldas and Guayaquil, where they were primarily workers (poor proletariat) and cooks (for the women) in Guayaquil, and workers, cooks, domestic employees, and students (secondary education) in Esmeraldas. Those who migrated to another country were mostly workers and domestic employees.

The outmigration from La Tola must be explained by reference to two principal factors: negative conjunctural conditions and the progressive replacement of La Tola by Borbón as the commercial center of that area of the northern sector of the province.

In the 1960s, when the ferrocarril Ibarra-San Lorenzo was completed, the provincial authorities funded the construction of the road and of the numerous necessary bridges between the city of Esmeraldas and the northern cantons. Two destinations were chosen: La Tola and Borbón. The labor for the construction of the road was constituted by men from the villages served by the road, in the form of minga, the communal form of work. The provincial council provided the materials and fed the workers. The Toleños participated enthusiastically in the making of the road. However, the road accelerated the decline of their village as regional center for the commerce of forest products brought by the poor peasants who lived upriver on the Santiago, the Cayapas, and their numerous tributaries. Before the road existed, all commerce and communication between the provincial capital and the northern sector had to transit by La Tola. The "Y"—as the inhabitants of the region call the division of the road from Esmeraldas in two stretches, one going to La Tola and the other to Borbón—did not exist, and no road arrived at Borbón, which was nothing but a small village. To go from La Tola to Esmeraldas, people traveled by foot, by horseback on the beach, or by boat in a sea voyage. Don Luguerio Montaño, who was born March 27, 1903, shared the following about this "golden age" of La Tola:

> Here, in the past, small ships came to carry away wood and things. The products from our forest were brought here on the backs of men, because we didn't have horses. Horses were for the people of the big haciendas. They brought the wood using the current of the river. This was the major parish of the region. La Tola is an old parish. On National Day, August 10, people came from Colombia and from other places of the province. They even organized bullfights. The village filled with visitors. (Recorded in La Tola in January 1990)

The completion of the road and the "Y" favored the development of Borbón as commercial center for the forest products coming from the gardens of poor (Afro-Esmeraldian and Chachi) peasants living in the villages on the banks of the Santiago, Cayapas, and Ónzole Rivers and their tributaries at the same time that they were detrimental to La Tola, which had played that role of commercial center for decades before. The volume of the commercial exchanges in La Tola has diminished greatly, replaced by a flux of passengers in transition who rarely spend the night: they do so only if their bus arrives late and if they miss their lancha to Limones or San Lorenzo.

The Geography of the Village

The map of La Tola shows the importance of the Santiago River for the Toleños. The elders remember that in their youth, the village was located farther north, in an area that is now part of the riverbed. There were two wooden

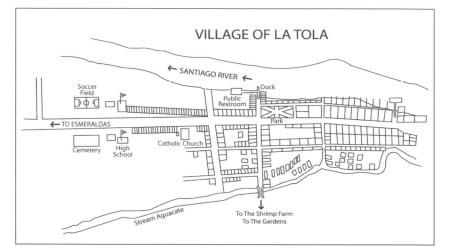

Figure 14. Map of La Tola. (Map by Florida International University Web Services Enterprise)

docks: the older one was situated at the east, with the public toilets. It was renovated in 1990 with funding from the canton of Eloy Alfaro Council.

The road from Esmeraldas ends in the principal street of the village, which is called Pedro Vicente Maldonado, from the name of the village's founder. The second most important street is the 14 de Abril (April 14), which is the date at which La Tola became a parish. All the small businesses that belong to the two categories of local entrepreneurs are either in the Pedro Vicente Maldonado or in the 14 de Abril, near the intersection with the Pedro Vicente. The other neighborhoods are mostly residential, and the houses located near the small waterway Aguacate are the most rustic. They are all inhabited by Afro-Esmeraldian peasant-fishermen, some of whom also live in the Pedro Vicente and in the 14 de Abril.

La Tola's high school (*Colegio Agropecuario*) was fifteen years old in 1990. The building also housed the state primary school (*escuela fiscal*), which is older than the high school.

The cooperative Buena Esperanza also has its own primary school, with two teachers. It was called the *Escuela Particular Nueva Esperanza*.

A roof maintained by four piles protects the village's electric generator. Until the end of the 1980s, the generator produced the energy necessary to provide electric lights to the entire village every night from 6:30 P.M. through 6:30 A.M. It unfortunately broke down and was replaced by a smaller generator that then only illuminated the eastern part of the village on even days, and the western part on the odd days.

In the early 1980s, a fire destroyed eight houses in the village. As a result, a politician who was candidate for the position of president of the canton council funded the construction of a house for firefighters. He got the votes and only paid for the construction of the building, which was made out of wood and bamboo, with a roof of zinc. He never purchased the manual pumps that he had promised, and in the early 1990s the big one-room construction was usually completely empty. It was sometimes used as a dance hall.

A similar story explains the presence of the water tower. The provincial council, which is based in Esmeraldas, offered (with great publicity, and before an election) the construction of a drinking-water distribution system in La Tola. In 1987, the vice prefect came to make a speech, accompanied by journalists and cameramen from the Esmeraldian Channel 6 television station to announce the immediate arrival of drinking water in La Tola. The water tower was constructed with general enthusiasm, then the work suddenly stopped for mysterious budget limitations. The dry water tower is still there, alone, as if it were suspended above the roofs of the village.

The Preparation Period of the Play

From conversations with elders, it seems that in the past (before 1980), the preparation period in La Tola was quite similar to what had been happening in Santo Domingo: a committee of women got a permit to play reyes from the lieutenant, and they locked up men in stocks until the men had paid the fine requested. In the late 1980s and early 1990s, however, nothing special happened between December 28 and January 5. The group of women who either set up or were directly involved in the few performances were not really organized into a committee. They did not request a permit from their political lieutenant. There was no stock, there was no formal hierarchy of ranks among them, and the few cucuruchos who were active between December 28 and January 5 limited their activities to stopping the vehicles that came and went on the dirt road from and to Esmeraldas. Many drivers refused to pay them anything. The cucuruchos had no means to force them. Most of the men of the village refused to pay the taxes that the cucuruchos wanted to levy. The men justified their refusal by saying that the women would use the money collected on themselves rather than to put it aside for the organization of the Play. I could observe at the time that this was indeed the case. At the end of the 1980s and the beginning of the 1990s, none of the women who had white-collar jobs participated in the preparation of the Play from December 28 through January 4 at all. Some of them, however, as I reveal below, were disguised during the performance of the Play in January 1990.

In January 1987 and 1988, the organization of a competition between the villages of La Tola, Cuerval, Olmedo and La Tolita Pampa de Oro by Juan García Salazar discouraged the formation of a committee of fiesteras, as the objective shifted away from actually preparing the Festival and Play with the rest of the village community toward, instead, participating in the competition and try to win the first prize. Juan García's stated objective with the organization of the Festival of the Kings competition among the local villages was to revive a tradition that he saw as threatened by disappearance as the intensity of playing had been greatly diminishing over the years.

The Play in La Tola in the 1970s

Various Toleño elders shared with me their memories of the Festival as it was played in the 1970s and before.

January 6 was called the day of the white race, *día de la raza blanca*. In the morning, between 8:00 and 9:00, three young boys of around age fifteen were disguised as the three kings, who represented the three races, *disfrazados a su manera y demostrando sus colores* ("disguised in a particular way, and showing their colors"). They were Gaspar, the black king, Melchior, the indigenous king, and Balthazar, the white king.

The kings dressed up in the same house where the cucuruchos had gotten together to don costumes. A parade, which was headed by the three kings, began from that house and went to the church or to the house where the *arrullo al Niño Dios* (the Afro-Esmeraldian ritual performed to celebrate the birth of Jesus Christ) had been celebrated on Christmas Eve. The crib was still there, which allowed the kings to place their offerings to Christ in front of it. Their offerings consisted of fruits, a chicken, a duck, and other objects. After the singing of a few arrullos (arrullos also refers to the songs that are sung during the ritual) by the *cantadoras* (women singers), the kings returned to their houses and their role was completed. The president of the committee of reyeras was physically present near the kings when they installed their gifts near the Christmas crib. She was holding the national flag. Her face was not masked, and she was not the most important character of the first act, as is the case in Santo Domingo.

The activities of the white cucuruchos began in the afternoon. Some of them had already accompanied the kings in the morning for the gift offerings. Back then, January 6 was the calmest day of the Festival. The cucuruchos walked around in couple (a man and a woman) in the village in a "well-educated manner," *de manera bien educada*—"like white people sometimes walk in reality," as the elders indicated. They walked holding hands, or the women holding the arm of their "husbands." Their dances were less animated than the dances of the following two days. Men cross-dressed as women and vice versa. They did their best not to be recognized. They always walked in groups throughout the village, stopping in front of most houses to dance to the sounds of an accordion and a guitar (instruments directly associated with "white music"). They usually received a glass of aguardiente or a small amount of money from the house's owners. The white cucuruchos reached the end of the afternoon somewhat drunk. They then joined the other Toleños in the evening to dance in the dance party of the whites, always animated by guitars and accordions.

The three kings wore long dresses and capes with crowns made out of golden paper on their heads. The dresses and capes varied from one king to the other, but they were always entirely white for Balthazar, the white king. They always wore boots. The skin of Balthazar had been colored in white with white chalk, the skin of Melchior in red with achiote, and the skin of Gaspar in black with charcoal.

The white cucuruchos were disguised in a similar fashion as the whites in Santo Domingo, with the only difference being that in La Tola the clothes of the whites seem to have been somewhat more "sophisticated." They never used leaves or added packs of cigarettes or pieces of aluminum foil to their disguises. Their masks, or "cucuruchos" (cowls) in white cotton had three holes, for the eyes and the mouth. They had been cut and fashioned with a pointed nose above the mouth. These cowls, on which two red cheeks had been drawn, were sufficiently oblong to cover the neck. The "white men" were played by women. They were dressed in white or light-colored shirts. Their hands were covered in white gloves or white socks. Their breasts were hidden as much as possible. They wore pants, and shoes or boots. They tried to find a cane or an umbrella to walk with distinction. The "white women" (played by men) had masks identical to the masks of the "white men." They sometimes had fake braids or flowered hats, and they wore feminine shirts. Their hands were, just like the "men's," covered in white gloves or socks. To indicate the presence of breasts, they wore bras filled with pieces of cloth. They also wore pants under their skirts or dresses. The white men and women walked around without rifles but did carry wooden machetes. The "women" fanned their faces with fans made of vegetal fiber (*abanico*). All parts of the skin of the white cucuruchos were covered.

Although January 7 was the *día de la raza india*, day of the "Indian race," various white cucuruchos were still disguised and behaved in a way similar to the day before. The "Indians" were divided in two groups. The first was composed of adults who parodied activities they interpreted as typical of Chachi activities. They mostly fabricated hats and baskets with vegetal fibers, as this was interpreted as a specifically Chachi activity. They also danced in front of the houses of the village to the sounds of what they interpreted as "Indian music," which for the most part consisted of the sounds of the cununos and bombo. They received aguardiente or money from the houses' owners for their performances. Some adults in costume as "Indians" walked around with wooden bowls in which they had placed a variety of herbs that evoked those that Chachi shamans manipulate when they cure an illness. The second group was composed of young kids who followed the queen of the "Indians" (played by an Afro-Esmeraldian woman) and played games with her. They also tried to gather food from the houses where they stopped. Just as in Santo Domingo, at the end of the day they usually cooked the food they had received. A dance with marimba music, bombo, and cununo was organized on that night. In the northern sector of the province of Esmeraldas, marimba music is associated both with Chachi and with Afro-Esmeraldians.

The black women impersonating "Indian women" were dressed with single swaths of cotton rolled around their bodies from their breasts down to their ankles, while the men were topless and wore shorts. The legs and feet of the men were not covered, but the visible areas of their skin had been decorated with small crosses and drawings in annatto. The "Indian" kids were dressed like the adults. They had flowers, feathers, and leaves in their hair. The queen was dressed like the other women except that she was wearing a long cape. The "Indians" did not cross-dress.

January 8, the day of the black race, was in fact the day of the three "racial groups." All the elders who provided me with information about "the Festival in the past," *la fiesta de antes*, agreed that it was a very animated day—in fact the most animated of the three days of the Festival.

As in preceding days, the activities usually began in early afternoon. The blacks moved around in groups just as the others did. They went from house to house, parodying the activities that black folks "usually do." Their songs were accompanied by the bombo and cununos, and their dances were much more lively and rhythmic than the dances of the other groups. Their hip movements were also much more pronounced.

Various black women wandered around with wooden bowls mimicking the gravel gold panning in the rivers. They were surrounded by a large group of young kids and could suddenly begin cooking with the pans and other kitchen tools they carried with them. One of them, the parridora, unexpectedly gave birth to a white baby while she was "looking for gold." Among the joyful screams of those in attendance, a white or lighter-skinned man was arrested and accused of being the father. He was then, just as Fabián Saltos was in Santo Domingo after the act of the parridora, locked up in the stocks for having taken the wife of another man.

The disguised characters representing black men mimicked hunting activities in the forest, shooting their rifles into the air, or miming the activity of gathering forest products, which they mockingly placed in the baskets that they carried on their backs.

The third and final day of the Festival always ended with the frenetic marimba dance of the blacks, which was much more animated than the dance of the night before.

The blacks in La Tola were dressed with the same kind of old clothes as in Santo Domingo. Their skin had been blackened with charcoal. They wore boots, "like us, the black folks, when we go in the forest," (*como nosotros los negros cuando vamos al monte*). Various black women placed half calabashes under their skirts and dresses to augment the volume of their buttocks, as did the "gold-panner" woman in Santo Domingo.

The monkey was dressed like the monkeys in Santo Domingo. His role in La Tola seems to have been slightly different than in Santo Domingo. He protected the disguised actors of the Play against the eventual lack of respect of the nondisguised population. He did not allow people to touch the calabashes under the women's skirts and dresses or to pull the braids of the "women." He was a kind of security guard who made sure that the playing unfolded without incident. With his whip, he punished the people who wanted to intervene in the Play of the disguised actors and eventually tied them up to a nearby tree. As in Santo Domingo, he could suddenly enter in a house and steal whatever he found. He returned what he had stolen when he was offered a few coins or a glass of aguardiente. He did not talk but only emitted incomprehensible sounds. Unlike in Santo Domingo, the monkeys in La Tola were present during all three days of the Play.

There is a fundamental difference between the Play in La Tola and the Play in Santo Domingo: in Santo Domingo, the audience's or partakers' interventions are welcomed during the performance of the acts, even though when men intervene in an unfolding act, they run the risk of being arrested or locked up in stocks. In La Tola, by contrast, if we follow the elders' descriptions, the separation between masked actors and the audience was much more clearly marked, and the audience's participation in the actual act performed and within the relations between masked actors was not sought after—hence the security guard role of the Toleño monkeys who had to maintain the separation between masked actors and audience.

The Play of January 1990

In January 1990, I was in Santo Domingo. Two research assistants linked to the PUCE-Quito, Rocío Rueda and Hernán Chico, participated in the Play in La Tola at that time. The following interpretive descriptions are made using their fieldwork reports, as well as my own numerous fieldwork experiences in La Tola and surrounding area.

On January 6, around 4:30 P.M., the three kings briefly walked around the village accompanied by young men playing a cununo, a bombo, and maracas, and by a few adult women and other nondisguised youth. They stopped to dance in front of the houses of the people who had more financial means: small shop owners and pension houses. Once these visits were completed, the small group of about fifteen people went to the church where the kings offered their presents and some cantadoras sang arrullos. These activities, during which the kings were the only disguised individuals and which involved only a few people, ended around 6:00 P.M.

The white king, a boy with light skin and light-colored eyes, was dressed in a white skirt, a white cape, and a white crown. He wore pink earrings, and the visible parts of his skin had been whitened with chalk. He carried a small box covered with white paper that symbolized his present to Baby Jesus. The "Indian" king, a boy who was identified by many as a zambo, wore a pair of white shorts, a blue cape, and a crown decorated with chicken feathers. His lips and his face had been painted red with achiote. The black king had all visible parts of his skin painted black with charcoal and was wearing a sleeveless dress and a light blue cape. His lips had been painted red, and he had a golden crown on his head.

Around 9:00 P.M., some white cucuruchos appeared and regrouped in the village's park. They went as a group to the salón *La Lambada*, where the white-mestizo owner denied them entrance. They then decided to go to the salón *El Beso*, where they danced for fifteen minutes. In that group of white cucuruchos, only three were adults, and they were cross-dressed men. Among the youth, the girls and boys were also cross-dressed. While they were still in the salón El Beso, a monkey suddenly came on the dance floor. He was not traditionally dressed; instead, he wore a plastic mask (probably bought in the city of Esmeraldas) representing the face of a wolf-man. He took great pleasure in frightening the children who stood around El Beso.

Figure 15. Three kids representing the Magi kings in La Tola. (Photograph by Jean Muteba Rahier)

The whole group then decided to go to another salón located at the entrance of the village, where they danced for twenty minutes before everyone went back home. They used the money they had been able to gather here and there during their short wandering in the village to buy some drinks in the small bars (*salones*).

On January 7, the activities of the Play began at around 5:00 P.M. The cucuruchos wandered in the village as they had day before, with the objective of collecting some money so that they could buy some drinks. There was a group of blacks—two adult women and a few kids. They first danced in front of the houses of the "wealthier" Toleños and then mimicked—in a way that somewhat recalled the activities of the blacks in Santo Domingo—the sweeping of the village's streets and the ironing of clothes, as if they were domestic employees. Others manipulated a wooden bowl to evoke gold-panning

Figure 16. A couple of white cucuruchos in La Tola. (Photograph by Jean Muteba Rahier)

activities, or parodied hunting and fishing. A group of white cucuruchos who had been dancing separately in the streets joined the blacks. One of them, who wore a pair of glasses above his cowl and who was dressed elegantly, was saying that he was originally from the United States. He publicly indicated that he did not want to get too close to the blacks because they smelled bad. During the street dances, which were animated with music coming from a battery-powered tape recorder, a third black adult joined the group of blacks and played the role of husband to one of the two black women. As soon as he arrived, he began commenting loudly, as if to make sure that everyone present would hear him (he was somewhat drunk):

> White folks are like weed. White folks don't want to hang out with blacks. I would never marry a white woman, don't even ask me to do that. Any white person who comes this way, we'll make him or her black. Come here, black woman, don't you see that white folks push you away. Whites don't dance with blacks.

The rest of the evening looked very much like the prior evening. The cucuruchos visited some of the village's small bars before ending their activities around 9:00 P.M. The previous dialogue excerpt, and La Tola's interactions between white and black cucuruchos in general, contrast meaningfully with the focus on gender that characterizes the Play in Santo Domingo (the sketches of "the woman who gives birth" and of "the brothers and sisters," for example). In La Tola, intraracial solidarity and interracial animosity are the major issues played out in the streets during what was then, already, a disappearing festival.

On January 8, the Play began around 4:00 P.M. with the installation of the marimba in the park and with the arrival of the group of cucuruchos from Cuerval. They entered the park while dancing to the sound of a cumbia from a portable cassette player. The group of white cucuruchos from La Tola quickly joined them.

In the group from Cuerval there were a couple of blacks played by two women. The woman who represented a black man was pretty much dressed like blacks used to dress in the Play of Santo Domingo, with old clothes, rubber boots, a rifle on her shoulder, and a basket on her back. The woman who represented a black woman wore an old dress and also had a basket on her back. They both had their skin blackened with charcoal. Within the framework of the Play, a fight began between the real political lieutenant (an Afro-Esmeraldian man) and the black "man." They both rolled on the floor. The reason for the altercation was the "attempt" by the teniente to seduce the black woman. Then, the lieutenant interrupted the brief act to offer aguardiente to everyone present. Later, he also gave away some *cebiche de camarones* (marinated, quickly boiled shrimps) that he had asked a woman to prepare with some of the shrimp he had confiscated from a fisherman who had not respected the period of interdiction to fish shrimp in January (*ley de veda del camarón*). Then the act continued with the black woman saying to her companion:

> Well, I don't want a black man, I don't want a black man, I want a white,
>   I want a white.
> THE BLACK MAN: Ah, my black woman, my black woman.
> THE BLACK WOMAN: Hurray for January 8! Hurray for the last day of
>   the Festival!

At that point, two new characters emerged: a black woman widow (a cross-dressed man) who called "herself" *la viuda* (the widow), and a white doctor (also played by a man). The black man exclaimed:

> The black woman is going to give birth! Call the doctor, call the doctor!

The widow, who had the volume of her behind augmented by two half calabashes, feigned pregnancy. When she had her first contractions, the black man became alarmed and called the doctor, who arrived without delay. In the middle of a tumult the widow gave birth to two white twins, represented by two white dolls, a boy and a girl. The newborns were placed in a wooden bowl, and then the mother looked for people who could be godparents for the performance of the baptism, which took place with aguardiente instead of water. Then the widow immediately went back to dance, which provoked the following reaction of the women in attendance:

> She just gave birth and now she is dancing, that's not right. She's gonna get a hemorrhage, you'll see.

After the birth, two black women arrived in the park. Although their skin had been darkened with charcoal like the skin of the other blacks, their clothes were much more refined than the typical old clothes of the black characters. They were each holding a purse, had nice straw hats decorated with flowers, and wore rather elegant dresses or skirts. One of them, ostensibly wearing an expensive watch, had a flashy new red belt on top of her dress. She was proclaiming to anyone who could hear that she wanted to marry a white man. In the group of cucuruchos of Cuerval, there was also a young girl, of around age twelve, who represented a young black girl. Her skin had been blackened with coal, but she wore a nice and flowery dress, on top of which they had placed

Figure 17. Two "black" women evoking modernity in La Tola. (Photograph by Jean Muteba Rahier)

a red band with the name of the Red Cross. This is the kind of band that is used in white-mestizo festivities and for the winner of beauty contests. These last representations of black women are clearly, in this particular context of the Play in La Tola, used to associate the black women with the white-mestizo world and modernity, as opposed to the usual association of black people with the "backward" and nonmodern life of the people who live in the forest.

There were also youth of both sexes who portrayed Chachi and whose disguises were quite similar to what has already been described.

The Play ended with the marimba dance party that had been organized in the school of the Cooperative Buena Esperanza. The party did not last beyond 9:00 P.M. The musicians declared they were too tired to continue playing. None of the members of the Cooperative Buena Esperanza were really involved in the Play.

Conclusions

The particularities of the village of La Tola itself are directly expressed in the performances of the Play there and account for the major differences it has with the Play in Santo Domingo de Ónzole.

La Tola has a multiracial population that is also economically diverse. Afro-Esmeraldians have generally been occupying the lowest echelons of the socioeconomic ladder. The village is connected to the electrical grid and is closer to urban centers, thanks to the road coming from the city of Esmeraldas. Until the construction of a road segment connecting Esmeraldas to Borbón, La Tola was the local center for the area, through which all goods and passengers traveling between the northern sector of the province and the city of Esmeraldas had to transit. The road to Borbón displaced La Tola's role as regional center.

From conversations with elders we know that the Play in La Tola has for a long time involved specific performances of racial identities, where whites were associated with a certain type of music and with specific behaviors that showed social respectability (they walk around in a well-educated manner—*de manera bien educada*). The very fact that the disguised whites always managed to be in a (cross-dressed) couple denotes the intention to associate them with respectable and civil behaviors, as they are opposed to blacks who did not walk around in couples, who went about hunting and fishing, and whose gender relations were associated with sexual promiscuity and infidelity and—in general—vulgarity.

It must be noted that indigenous peoples, who do not live in the vicinity of La Tola, have mostly been represented off to one side of the main opposition between whites and blacks: walking about the village in a way that evoked what was perceived as the indigenous way, fabricating baskets and other objects.

The intraracial solidarity and interracial (black-white) animosity that characterize the most recent performances of the Play in La Tola must be linked to the earlier performances of the Play there, when clear differences between black and white disguised actors were markedly in existence. Unlike the Santo Domingeño Play I have previously described and in which the differences between blacks and whites slide away from the field of meaning of race and race relations and must be understood with references to other fields of meaning (insiders versus outsiders, and sexuality and gender relations), the Play in La Tola has provided a space where racial differences have been historically emphasized. It should therefore not be a surprise to see that more recent performances of the Play in La Tola have represented strong animosity and even straightforward tension between racial groups. As I have explained earlier, these representations must be directly related to the actual socioeconomic context of the village.

It is noteworthy to underscore the fact that the recent presence in the Play of La Tola of black women disguised as educated and respectable black women moving about the village wearing dresses and objects associated with urban civility and modernity fits well within this tradition of the Play in La Tola to provide a space where racial differences can be expressed and discussed. The disguised respectable black women's presence in the Play is nothing but the expression of Afro-Esmeraldian women's resistance against the claims of white-mestizo superiority that have been circulating in the village with the arrival of new white-mestizo in-migrants.

It is worthwhile as well to contrast the level of participation of the nondisguised audience in the recent performances of the Play in both villages. While in Santo Domingo that participation has been very high and has virtually involved the entire village population along with the population of surrounding villages, it has been much lower in La Tola, where many simply refuse to be bothered by what they see as Afro-Esmeraldian traditions of another age.

5

Race, Sexuality, and Gender as They Relate to the Festival of the Kings

As the descriptive interpretations of chapters 2, 3, and 4 have shown, race and race relations, as well as sexuality and gender relations, constitute major fields of meaning for the interpretation of the Afro-Esmeraldian Festival of the Kings in Santo Domingo de Ónzole and in La Tola.

According to elders, sexual dichotomy is one of the foundational principles of the *Juego de los Cucuruchos* in both villages. As my ethnographic observations show, it is however in Santo Domingo de Ónzole that the importance of sexual dichotomy as a field of meaning appears more clearly and directly to make sense of both ordinary life and the time of the Play. The people who organize the Play are never male! Women organize and prepare the Festival. In a typical carnivalesque inversion, they rule its liminal time from December 28 until January 8. The liminal time of the Play is clearly marked by women's request of the official permit to play the Kings from the always-male political lieutenant of their parish. In Santo Domingo, race appears as much more peripheral than it is in La Tola. The birth of a white baby during the act of the woman who gives birth, to which they actually refer with the expression *colorado*, which stands for "mixed race" or "lighter brown," should not be misinterpreted by invoking the wrong field of meaning: race relations, instead of sexual dichotomy and gender relations. The mixed-raced-ness of the baby, or his filiation to a white or lighter-skinned father, is there only to make sure that there is no doubt possible that the mother has engaged in "adulterous" sexual intercourse, following the adulterous behavior of her male companion (chapter 3).

Comparatively, in La Tola, as shown by my ethnographic interpretative descriptions, sexual dichotomy and gender relations are relegated to a backstage position by the centrality of race relations. This is the case certainly in both everyday life and in the liminal time of the Play. In La Tola, a village that has been more open to influences from urban Ecuador, women have achieved a level of independence that they have not achieved in Santo Domingo, where they remain more dependent on their husbands or companions.

In this chapter, I'd like to explore a bit more the socioeconomic and political realities that make the contexts of the Play in both villages by paying special attention to these two fields of meaning: race and racial relations, and sexual dichotomy, gender relations, and sexual role reversal. These explorations should provide additional evidence in support of my interpretations of the Play in the two villages while also shedding some light on the Play's acts.

Glimpses of Afro-Esmeraldian Sexuality, "Matrifocality," and Gender Relations

There are significant similarities between Afro-Esmeraldian and Circum-Caribbean gender relations (Smith 1956; Smith 1962; Freilich 1961; Gonzalez 1965, 1970; Wilson 1969, 1973; Safa 1995, 2009; Herlihy 2007; Wilson 1989). One of these similarities is certainly the importance of consensual unions, called *unión libre* in Esmeraldas, as opposed to legal marriages (civil or ecclesiastic). The lack of enthusiasm for legal marriages is common throughout the Pacific lowlands (see, among others, Whitten 1965; Pavy 1967, 1968; Friedemann and Arango 1995). In Santo Domingo, at the time of our census, there were seventy-five inhabited houses or residential units. Of these, 75 percent had for household head a man who was part of a pair of individuals who lived together consensually; 12 percent had for household head a man who was a partner in a couple married legally (either civilly or ecclesiastically); and 13 percent had a household head who was an isolated woman, following the death of her partner during a consensual relationship or the separation from a partner with whom she had been engaged in a consensual relationship. These numbers indicate an unambiguous aversion for legalized unions. The men I questioned about it justified their choice with their preoccupation to remain *libres*, free from real commitment, so that they could decide to take off whenever they felt like it. For that reason, they preferred to be *pegaditos no más, juntados,* or *unidos* (all expressions meaning "not legally married"). Most women, by contrast, would have preferred to get married with their partners. They complained about the lack of true commitment on the part of most men.[1]

I first naively thought that this high proportion of consensual unions was due to the geographic removal of Santo Domingo from urban centers and to the fact that there had never been an official responsible for the civil register in the parish since its creation, someone who could perform civil marriages. However, the data I gathered from La Tola do not allow for such a conclusion; indeed, in La Tola there has been such an official for a long time, and missionaries, Catholic priests, and nuns, who routinely perform marriages, visit more frequently than in the villages removed in the forest. Of the 325 residential units reporting in La Tola, 67 percent had for household head a man who was partner in a couple involved in a consensual union; 13 percent had a man who was partner in a couple married legally (2 percent civilly and 11 percent ecclesiastically); and the rest, 20 percent of residential units, had an isolated woman as head of household, as the result of a separation from a consensual union, a divorce from a legal marriage, or the death of the partner or spouse. The rate of consensual unions remained quite elevated despite the greater access to civil and/or ecclesiastical marriages.

Whitten explained Afro-Esmeraldian men's lack of enthusiasm for marriages with what he called "serial polygyny," which implies a series of norms and values:

> Serial polygyny refers to the expected behavior pattern of male movement from one spouse to another. In San Lorenzo a man is expected to have a series of wives in his lifetime. Societal norms, expressed in conversation and marimba songs, make the change of mate a male prerogative. Actually, of course, the woman, too, has a series of men. But she is relatively more spatially restricted, and she plays a less active role in any change. (1965, 122)

For Whitten, there would be two kinds of serial polygyny: one which is monogamic, when the man lives with one single woman at a time; and another which is polygynous, when a man lives and shares economic responsibilities with more than one woman at a time (Whitten 1965, 122–23). The relatively separated spaces of men and women are not ruled by similar norms and values. In different ways, Afro-Esmeraldian men usually enjoy greater prerogatives than women.

To continue borrowing from Caribbeanist literature, I use the concepts of "reputation" and "respectability" proposed by Peter Wilson (Wilson 1969, 1973) to discuss the traditional Afro-Esmeraldian sexual dichotomy. The

separation between reputation and respectability is predicated on the acknowledgment of a double standard of sexual morality: "Males are esteemed
for their virility and are granted a freedom which they are expected to exploit. Females are, ideally, constrained in their sexual activities before and
after marriage, and are expected to observe these constraints and other allied
modes of behavior (such as modesty and obedience)" (1969, 71). For Wilson,
reputation is chiefly associated with men, respectability with women.

Traditionally, Afro-Esmeraldian men's sexuality has been less socially controlled than women's. In fact, men must be able to demonstrate their virility.
A good way to manifest it publicly is to have several women, simultaneously
or successively, and a high number of children. I was able to observe, both in
La Tola and in Santo Domingo, that men are proud to indicate that the son
or daughter of a woman in the village who is not their actual companion is
also their child. Moreover, I was told more than once by several of them, in
both villages, that they were having an affair with another woman who was
actually "isolated," legally married or engaged in a consensual union with
another man.

Sexual mobility is a prerogative that men valorize a great deal. In the case
of "adultery," it is usually the woman more than the man who is blamed by
the male concubine or spouse. It is not rare to see a man who has two or
three families simultaneously, or who has one or more lovers in the same
village, or in another part of the province.

In both villages, around 70 percent of the women interviewed had had
children outside of the relationship they were involved in at the moment of
the census, with one or more men. Sexual mobility, which usually takes place
at men's initiative, is therefore a characteristic of Afro-Esmeraldian gender relations. To evoke it in male conversations allows for the confirmation of one's
virility and machismo, and provides—to use Peter Wilson's vocabulary—a
good "reputation."

David Pavy has shown that there was a correlation between the age of
adults and the rate of legal marriages (civil or ecclesiastic): the probability of
marriages augments with age (Pavy 1968, 343+). That is what I could observe
in both villages as well. The people who are married were all more than forty
years old on the day of their marriage. And many nonmarried men indicated
that they preferred to marry late so that they could continue to enjoy freedom
and varied sexual experiences: *andar y conocer*, to travel in far away lands and
meet women, so that one can show having a knowledge of the world, a strong
virility, in order to build up a good reputation. Geographic mobility is an

important source of prestige. Indeed, unlike the Chachi who, until relatively recently, tried to avoid as much as possible any contact with modern society by moving away into removed areas deep into the forest, Afro-Esmeraldians valorize a great deal traveling in unknown regions and meeting new people. Afro-Esmeraldian society has been much more open to outside influences than the Chachi communities. Many Décimas, always recited by men, make numerous references to far away places, in foreign countries, which serve to reinforce the *decimero*'s ego (see García Salazar 1979, 1984; Rahier 1987, 1999a).

A real man, *un hombre de verdad*, is one who knows how to be respected and who eventually responds aggressively to any questioning of his *hombría*, his masculinity and virility. The most aggressive insults are stylistic questioning of the fidelity of one's wife or companion, or even of one's mother toward one's father. What Wilson wrote about the Caribbean is also true for the northern sector of the province of Esmeraldas: "Such insults are not only a reflection of the expectancy of fidelity and modesty in wives; for a man who is unable to keep his wife satisfied cannot be considered *macho* and whoever lures his wife away is more *macho*. Similar expectancies among spouses are reported throughout the Caribbean—husbands are expected to be unfaithful to some extent, and wives are expected to be faithful and modest" (1969, 72).

Women try their best to keep their husbands and companions. The material stability of their matri-central cells depends upon their ability to do so. Men, by contrast, "value the ability to hold a woman's attentions until they tire of her, and the ability to find a replacement for her quickly" (Whitten 1965, 123).

Reputation and the Prevalence of the Sexuality and Gender Relations Field of Meaning in Santo Domingo de Ónzole

The preceding section provides general information about sexuality and gender relations among Afro-Esmeraldians. In the context of my discussion of the prevalence of sexuality and gender relations as a field of meaning to interpret the Play of the Cowls in Santo Domingo, I have to insist on the distinction that must be established between the two villages in focus of this book. Indeed, the proximity to urban centers, the almost permanent availability of electricity and the use of radios and televisions that this permits, and the daily departure and arrival of peoples and goods to and from bigger towns and cities makes of La Tola, along with its ethnic or racial diversity, a very different place than Santo Domingo de Ónzole. As suggested by the data provided by the census conducted in the early 1990s, and as a result of the relative economic importance of the village in the region, women were already occupying at that time job positions (mostly bus cooperative employees and teachers) that would simply be impossible to imagine for women in Santo Domingo. Urban Ecuadorian and global values about gender relations are reaching its inhabitants daily through the assiduous watching of telenovelas, daily reading of newspapers, and easier outmigration or short travel to urban centers. To this must be added the presence of a high school, in which both boys and girls are being educated.

By contrast, Santo Domingo de Ónzole is very much isolated in an area upriver of the Ónzole, where the only way to travel *is* the river, which is rather shallow during the dry season. Electricity is scarce in the village, where there is no high school. No one watches telenovelas or read newspapers, as these cannot reach the village. It can be safely stated that in Santo Domingo, women have no real option to be independent from men. The only way to reach such independence is to migrate to a city, which many have. As shown by my previous ethnographic descriptions, the more traditional gender relations that one can find in Santo Domingo traverse all domains of ordinary life. What follows in this section will provide a good idea of the oppressive reality experienced by women in this more traditional context.

A male elder in Santo Domingo, whom I call here Don Alberto Morcu Medina to protect his identity, once told me how he got a second "wife" in 1985.

After the definitive departure of her companion for the favors of another woman who lives in another village, a Santo Domingeña woman (Doña Susana) of around age thirty at the time found herself alone with her three children. She was therefore in a very perilous economic situation. Don Alberto, who was already paired to his first "wife," Doña Tomasa, began having an affair, publicly, with Doña Susana, who progressively became socially recognized as his second female companion or "wife." Doña Susana continued living in the house she occupied before the relationship began, and Don Alberto supported her financially and sometimes spent the night with her. At first, Doña Tomasa did not accept Don Alberto's new companion at all. She continuously attacked her rival with great violence. Don Alberto evoked that period with the words: *Doña Tomasa se ponía como una fiera. Pegaba a mi nueva mujer sin parar. Era fregada.* (Doña Tomasa was infuriated. She was constantly hitting my new woman. She was out of control.) That's when, he told me, he had the idea to install another small shop; he already had one in Santo Domingo, which he was running with the help of Doña Tomasa, in the village of Colón, half an hour to forty-five minutes by canoe upriver from Santo Domingo. By opening this new small shop in Colón and having Doña Susana move there to take care of it, he could avoid the fights between his two female companions and by the same account augment the profitability of his trips downriver to the town of Borbón to buy for two small shops. He was going to Colón once every ten days for two to three days to visit "his second family" and supervise the functioning of his other store.

When she was upset, Doña Tomasa never took it out on Don Alberto. The target of her frustration and anger was always her female rival. As she explained to me in a conversation, she did not really blame Don Alberto—who after all "was only a man," as she said. She instead held the other woman as responsible "because she was trying to take away from her and from her children some of the economic stability they had been enjoying." A man with virility is also a man "who knows how to maintain calm and order in his household and how to have his female mate or wife obey," as Don Alberto told me, and this he finally did by imposing his second woman on Doña Tomasa. In fact, as Don Childo explained to me, political lieutenants in the area, who are the judges of lower level in their parishes, respect a rule that is not written in any of the codes that they are supposed to follow when solving problems between conflicting parties: domestic disputes must be solved by the individuals and families involved. The lieutenant does not intervene, even if a man physically brutalizes his female partner.

On another occasion, during the three days of the 1990 Play in Santo Domingo, an altercation between a young man and his female companion began at the end of one afternoon. She had gotten close to the communal house where a marimba dance was underway and looked inside through one of the windows. She remained outside with other young people: her male companion had prohibited her to come near the communal house where all dances for the Festival were taking place. Her companion was an extremely jealous young man who actually feared that she could be invited to dance by another man. He was himself inside the communal house, dancing with someone else, when he saw her. He rushed outside, where he engaged in an altercation with her. He publicly insulted her, stating that she was nothing but a slut, a prostitute, an easy woman! She grabbed a small mirror she had with her (she was doing her hair before going to the communal house) and threw it at him, slightly wounding his right ear. He then became infuriated and went to pick up his machete. Using the side of the blade, he hit her once or twice slightly wounding her on the right arm before being restrained by other men, who were relatives of his.

The fight provoked a major commotion, and the marimba dance was interrupted for about twenty minutes. The couple separated for a few days: her parents took her back into their house until the matter was solved amicably with the young man's family. He apologized to her, in the house of her parents, and they went back to live together, in their own house. The lieutenant never intervened directly and instead encouraged both families to deal with the conflict. During a conversation I had with the young man once the conflict was over, he explained that once he had been wounded at the ear, he could not have remained passive, he had to demonstrate that he was going to be respected by his woman (his reputation was at stake). In the conversations that took place in the village after the fight, many were arguing in his favor, saying that although he was a jealous freak, she should not have thrown the mirror at him, despite his strong insults. A man "who wants to be re-spected" cannot be physically threatened by a woman just like that. Many Afro-Esmeraldian men are convinced of the inferiority of their women, on the back of whom they build their machoist reputations.

Reputation also has economic aspects. In Santo Domingo, and in similar small villages in the Esmeraldian forest, men are in charge of subsistence agriculture and of the sale of their surplus to buyers in the towns of Borbón and Limones, or in one of the small shops of the village. They are the owners of the gardens, which pass down from father to son(s). In La Tola, men pos-sess gardens; they are also involved in fishing, and they try to obtain a small salary in one of the small businesses of the village. Men are therefore those who handle the cash and decide how it should be spent. Their reputations also denote their eventual economic success, or lack thereof. Relative economic success is another expression of virility. A man who is able to support his household(s) without too many difficulties, thanks to his "entrepreneurship" and to his work, is more respected than if he were in constant need of help. Sexuality and relative economic success are related. A man who enjoys a good reputation has more success with women than if he were in financial need. The former is often involved with more than one woman, while the latter will have difficulty retaining one woman. Men who maintain more than one family are always among those who have accumulated more "wealth."

Similarly, the outmigrants do not miss the occasion to suggest relative eco-nomic success when they occasionally visit their village. It was always remark-able for me to see young people who have rather unstable jobs in Guayaquil or Quito come back to the village in the humid forest for a few days wearing a thick coat (anorak) with bright colors that Europeans and North Americans use to go skiing. They wore it at their arrival and then eventually offered it to a relative before going back to the city. They also came back with presents for close relatives, and during their stay they wore the best pieces of clothes they had managed to buy before the trip, sometimes showing off with plated gold jewelry which they had borrowed from a friend in the city for the occasion of their visit. They also walked around in relatively expensive urban shoes, which are quite out of place in the often-muddy village paths. Some tried to take advantage of these signs of prestige to seduce a young woman before going back to the city. These trips back home represent expensive journeys for the outmigrants.

The consumption of aguardiente is also a way to expose one's virility. Only real men can drink a lot (*solo hombres de verdad saben divertirse*). In various villages of the Eloy Alfaro canton, older men evoke the festivities of the past, which could last for an entire week, and during which many remained drunk. It is when they drink that men are more inclined to fight. Male gatherings in the villages at the end of the afternoon are often accompanied by aguardiente drinking and with stories about hunting, fishing, and traveling experiences aimed at asserting virility and hombría. Fights emerge when one man questions the honor of another. Reputation constitutes therefore an ensemble of values that govern the relations among men and between men and women, and that posit masculine power as one of the fundamental principles of the Afro-Esmeraldian social system.

Afro-Esmeraldian Matrifocality

As is the case in rural areas of the Caribbean, women assure the stability of the households and of the kinship networks in the northern sector of the province. During the day, because men leave the villages to go to their gardens, to fish, to hunt, or to sell their surplus in the towns of the area, women are often the only ones left from 7 or 8 A.M. to 3 or 4 P.M. They are often the first ones up and the last to go to bed. They prepare the meals, wash the clothes at the river, and keep an eye on their small children. Occasionally, they also help their mates or spouses in the gardens. They depend entirely on their mates or spouses for the daily domestic expenses and for access to cash in general. The relations they have with their children—the matri-central cells (Smith 1956, Fortes 1958)—are fundamental.

If we follow the definition proposed by Nancie González (1970) (see also Wilson 1989; Safa 1995, 2009; Herlihy 2007), the Afro-Esmeraldian kinship networks can be qualified as "matrifocal" because:

1. In the domestic context, it is rare to observe a multiple or shifting loyalty of women with different households or family groups. On the

contrary, women who occupy the role of mother tend to be the more stable figure in the households, and other family members regroup around them.

2. When members of the expanded family and kindred live in a household, they are usually relatives of the mother and less so relatives of the father or of the man who is in the position of "husband-father."

3. The personal contacts with the matrilateral kin are more frequent than with the patrilateral kin.

4. In the domestic context, women enjoy a relative autonomy, although the man, when there is one present, is always involved in the most important decisions. Men are usually the disciplinary figures for the children.

The relation of a mother with her children offers the most stable basis for Afro-Esmeraldian domestic groups. Fortes called this relationship the "matri-central cell": a woman and her young children (1958). González preferred the expression "mother-child dyad," which underlines the close links between a mother and her children (1970, 233). For Afro-Esmeraldians, the solidarity between a mother and her children is of the utmost importance. All other relations within the kin group tend to be defined in relation to this original mother-child kernel. In the context of men's sexual mobility, the mother is central to child rearing. And although a child will receive the family name of his or her biological father, independently of his presence or absence in the household, it is generally with matrilateral brothers that one has the closest links. Usually, uterine brothers share a same residential unit. Patrilateral brothers, on the other hand, tend to live in different households, in the same village or not. An Afro-Esmeraldian proverb says: *Hermanos de madre, hermanos verdaderos, hermanos de padre, nunca se sabe* ("uterine brothers are true brothers, patrilateral brothers, you never know").

Afro-Esmeraldian women share a system of values, more related to respectability, which valorize men who have a sense of commitment to their female partners and to their children, and who do their best to maintain the stability of their household. Before I reached the village in December 2002–January 2003, while in the town of Borbón before getting in the lancha of a Santo Domingeño man who was going back to the village, I learned during a conversation with a woman from the village that Don Alberto had become completely blind, and that his strong reputation was now a thing of the past. When I spontaneously expressed my sadness for his blindness, the woman began arguing that he had been paid for all his bad behaviors, that he did not deserve my sadness—and she made reference to, among other things, the way he had treated Doña Tomasa, whom, she added, was now spending most of her time in Guayaquil, with one of her daughters. Don Alberto had become the shadow of his past, well-reputed self, and he lived alone in the village, depending on the generosity of his two children still living there with their own families.

While gender relations in both villages are comparable and are based on the same sets of sociocultural and moral norms and values, there exists nonetheless a major difference between the two villages. Both adult men and women tend to be less formally educated (less time spent in school) in Santo Domingo than in La Tola; usually men are more educated than women in Santo Domingo. The daughters of Don Chama, one of Santo Domingo's "leaders," Dagnis Neyra and Daneyis are somewhat of an exception. They not only have completed their primary education, which is already a big achievement when compared to most Santo Domingeñas, but have gone to teachers' school (*escuela normal*) in the city of Esmeraldas after completing a high school degree.

In La Tola, by contrast, a larger proportion of both sexes have gone to high school (La Tola had a state high school), and some women have taken advantage of these opportunities for education to gain access to a stable income and enjoy a relative independence from men. Various teachers in the two primary schools and in the high school of La Tola are women, and women also occupy white-collar jobs as employees in the cooperatives of transport; two or three are employees of the local office of the national phone company, which was at the time called the *Instituto Ecuatoriano de Telecomunicaciones* (IETEL); some are nuns officiating masses at specific dates during the year (mostly Christmas and Easter), and others are nurses for the medical doctor who is running the local office of the Provincial Direction of Health. Other women, who are usually less formally educated, have also created (under the impulse of Juan García) a cooperative that deals with issues directly related to women's well-being, such as healthcare for them and their families, the bulk purchase of food, and selling the *conchas* that women (called *concheras*) gather in the sand banks in the middle of the river when the tide is low to intermediaries for the national market. In La Tola, with a good antenna, a television can sometimes receive programs from Colombia and Esmeraldas. The programs people like the most are Spanish translations of Brazilian as well as Mexican and Colombian telenovelas. These television programs, along with the newspapers that arrive in the village daily, bring along values and ideals of gender relations that are rather opposite to the ones described above, in that they show possibilities for independence from men and portray women pursuing professional careers, which more than one young women I talked to found encouraging. In the case of a conflict with a man or parent, it is relatively easy to decide to leave the village. The trip to Esmeraldas is relatively cheap and easy from La Tola. Eight to ten buses leave La Tola every day for Esmeraldas.

In general, there is a lower level of female dependency on men in La Tola than in Santo Domingo. I argue that this situation of differential gender statuses explains why the Play in La Tola is less focused on gender issues than it is in Santo Domingo. As I have shown in previous chapters, the level of racial tensions among the various socioeconomic sectors of the village population is the major focus of the Play in La Tola. Such tensions, by contrast, are completely absent from the Play in Santo Domingo, even though representations of racial identities are performed.

To fully appreciate the performances of the Play's acts and other activities, it is necessary to spend some time discussing northern Afro-Esmeraldians' relations with whites or white-mestizos and with indigenous Chachi.

Blacks, Whites, and Indigenous People in Northern Esmeraldas: The Prevalence of the Racial Relations Field of Meaning in La Tola

The interracial relations differ greatly in La Tola and Santo Domingo de Ónzole. There is no Chachi community living in the parish of La Tola. Toleños know of the Chachi, but only as people who live far away, upriver on the Cayapas and Ónzole Rivers. They rarely have the opportunity to actually meet Chachi, unless they go to Borbón, where Chachi also come regularly to sell their surplus and buy the products they need, or to the city of Esmeraldas, where the *Federación Chachi*, the official Chachi organization which is affiliated to the CONAIE (*Confederación de Nacionalidades Indígenas del Ecuador*), has its offices, and where one can sometimes see and meet Chachi in the streets.

La Tola also contrasts with Santo Domingo in the sense that there is no real "community" there, the village population being divided into eight sectors, which I have identified earlier: The peasant-fishermen (mostly Afro-Esmeraldians); the poor proletariat (mostly Afro-Esmeraldians who worked for the hacienda of Tambaco, owned by a family of Esmeraldian white-mestizos); the fishermen from the cooperative (Afro-Esmeraldians); the workers of Don Rafael and of the local industrial shrimp cultivation in the village of Cuerval (non-Esmeraldian white-mestizos); the local middle-class or white-collar workers (Afro-Esmeraldian and Esmeraldian white-mestizo women); the middle-class professionals (white and white-mestizos); the local entrepreneurs (non-Esmeraldian white-mestizos, Esmeraldian white-mestizos, and Afro-Esmeraldians); and the absentee elite (non-Esmeraldian white-mestizos). The daily interactions among these various sectors are often characterized by tension that seems to be racially based. The white-mestizo workers who work for the Colombian Don Rafael (who has put together an operation of deep-sea fishing with motorized lanchas, and also Cuerval's shrimp farm), as well as Don Rafael himself, are absolutely adamant about not being confused with native Toleños, Afro-Esmeraldians or not, whom they look down upon as being culturally retarded and backward people. They clearly identify as white-mestizo urban citizens who are present in the village for a while, to make quick money, and who are not interested in investing any money or time in the village or in activities that are not directly related to their own specific work. They do not want to be bothered by Afro-Esmeraldian traditions and would have reacted violently if, as was the case in Santo Domingo for example, Afro-Esmeraldian women had tried to lock them up in the stocks. In fact, because of this situation of social interactions in La Tola, Afro-Esmeraldian fiesteras would never think about such a possibility.

Non-Esmeraldian white-mestizos basically live among themselves. They spend their leisure time together, either in the house of Don Rafael, in the houses of the camaronera workers, or in local bars. When they get together in one of the bars of the village, they sometimes hire the services of traveling sexual workers (of a variety of racial backgrounds). They are not interested in having romances with local women. When conflicts erupt between individuals from different sectors, racial identity very quickly becomes an issue, with Afro-Esmeraldians usually ending up insulted with racial slurs. La Tola's political lieutenant, an Afro-Esmeraldian at the time of the late 1980s and early 1990s research, who had two or three rural police officers (*policía rural*, a special brigade of the Ecuadorian national police) at his disposal, was very much aware of the political influence of the managers of the shrimp farm and always did his best not to sanction its employees. By contrast, the Colombian Don Rafael was also involved in more or less legal commercial activities with partners in Colombia, and always made sure to have the teniente on his side. This arrangement protected Don Rafael's workers in the event they got into a fight with a local Afro-Esmeraldian man. In many different ways, Afro-Esmeraldians in La Tola had progressively been displaced—despite the fact that they represented a demographic majority of the local population—by non-Esmeraldian white-mestizos.

The situation of Santo Domingo is very different. There exists indeed an ideological-cultural community that could be represented by the opposition Santo Domingeños–Afro-Esmeraldians versus the others. The first term of this opposition is based on racial-cultural identity. Indeed, unlike La Tola and, generally, the other Esmeraldian villages of the coastal area, the entire village community of Santo Domingo and the other Afro-Esmeraldian villages of the forest area are entirely black. The others, the second term of the opposition, are the Chachi indigenous people and the white-mestizos, two groups that were clearly differentiated by Afro-Esmeraldians, each of whom maintained a particular kind of relation with Afro-Esmeraldians. The Afro-Esmeraldian racial-cultural unity of the village community is included in a larger, translocal ensemble that comprised the black population of the entire province. In fact, Santo Domingeños could migrate to another Afro-Esmeraldian village of the forest without running the risk of being rejected as a stranger. Some Santo Domingeños also marry or enter consensual unions with Afro-Esmeraldians from other villages who come to live in Santo Domingo. In such cases, they integrate into the village community and are allowed to utilize a piece of land in the surrounding forest for a swidden garden. The other villagers do not interpret their in-migration as an invasion by strangers. This is not the case when white-mestizo in-migrants try to establish themselves in the parish. They are looked at as potentially aggressive invaders against whom the community must organize. Afro-Esmeraldian in-migrants get involved in a mating relationship with Santo Domingeño(a)s, and have children with them. White-mestizo in-migrants never take a woman in the village (they usually come with their own wives or partners) and have rather negative feelings toward Afro-Esmeraldians. They reproduce stereotypical representations of blacks that widely circulate in Ecuador (black people are uneducated and lazy, they only think about having fun) and feel somewhat superior to them (see Rahier 1999a, 1999b, 2003b). They never intend to build a house within the inhabited perimeter of the village. When first arriving in the area, they usually do not seek the permission of the village community to build a house in a location of their choosing in the forest, which they interpret as being mostly unoccupied land, *tierra baldía*.

This feeling of belonging to a translocal group of black Esmeraldians is also grounded in networks of kinship that link together the Afro-Esmeraldian villages of the upper Ónzole and beyond to all local black communities of the province. Many Santo Domingeños have relatives as well as compadres and comadres in the villages of Zancudo and Colón, for example. The inhabitants of Zancudo do not have a cemetery. They bury their dead in Santo Domingo's cemetery, and when attending a funeral ritual in one of the villages of the parish of Santo Domingo, one always meets people from different villages of the parish, and even sometimes from villages of other cantons. At the end of the 1980s and at the beginning of the 1990s, the Afro-Esmeraldian identity in the parish was mostly emulated through the activities of an organization with the objective to defend black ownership of the parish's lands menaced by white-mestizo in-migrants. Some Santo Domingeños called it *la invasión manaba*, "the invasion by people from the province of Manabí," although some of these white-mestizo in-migrants also came from other Ecuadorian provinces (Loja and El Oro, among others). This migration constituted a recent phenomenon in the history of the parish, which was until the mid-1980s only populated by Afro-Esmeraldians and Chachi. This organization was called *la Junta Pro-Defensa de las Tierras de Santo Domingo*. Its president, the Santo Domingeño Trífilo Corozo, told me in 1990:

This committee was founded on January 25, 1988. The committee was put together because we saw a series of abuses of our land: there was the risk of invasion. A guy came from Esmeraldas; he was the president of the committee *Pro-Defensa de las Tierras de Esmeraldas*. He came to organize us here. At the same time, he was the secretary of an organization called the UOC (*Unión de las Organizaciones Campesinas*). And that's how we created our committee. What happened is that through time this committee was in process of not existing anymore, until the threat of invasion came back. Then we organized again. We have already reached some of our objectives. We were able to get some invaders expelled from our land, and we went several times as a commission to Esmeraldas, Borbón, and San Lorenzo. We got involved with the OCAME (*Organización de Campesinos de Esmeraldas*) of Borbón and with another organization in Esmeraldas.

We have a central organization based here in Santo Domingo. But we also have a community committee in Zancudo and in Colón [I have attended several times the meetings of the Committee of Colón]. These two committees have the support of the central committee of Santo Domingo.

Our objective is to defend our land, because we have been threatened by great invading powers, like the Manaba and the people who also come from other provinces. We know that these people are dangerous, that wherever they go, they provoke violence, and we cannot allow this to happen, because we cannot allow the peace that we have lived for so long be interrupted by violence. That's why we have organized.

At first, we were not organized like the Chachi. And that, I know very well because I'm a friend of all the Chachi. They are even organized as a tribe. We, the black people, we live more individually. Each one of us lives in his own corner. That's only now that we are getting organized so that we can reach our important objectives, which is to defend our land.

We have been ignored by the agencies of the national government. They don't even know that there are black people living here. But, I've been in delegation, alone, to Quito, to have a meeting with the director of the IERAC (*Instituto Ecuatoriano de la Reforma Agraria y Colonización*) to ask for, and demand, that they recognize our land as *asentamiento tradicional* just like they did for the Chachi. Because if there is a good reason to recognize the land of the Chachi, then the same reason must be applied for us. The government says that the Chachi are the natural owners of these lands, but the Chachi also came from other places. Before they didn't live here. Before they lived closer to the coast. That's because of the Concha war that they escaped and came here. Black folks also came from other places, although maybe a bit later. Some came from Colombia. Some others came from the Santiago. They first went to the area on the Santiago River, in Playa de Oro, Selva Alegre, and then they came here. We have the same rights as the Chachi.

The in-migration of Manabitas and of other white-mestizos is principally the result of drought and of the high cost of land in their regions of origin. At the time of my earlier fieldwork, the Chachi were the only ones, with a few individual Afro-Esmeraldians, to have their lands legally registered in the Upper Ónzole. The national government gave to their community organizations a title of ownership called *propiedad tradicional* (traditional property), which protects them against any land invasion. The remaining land of the parish, with the exception of the lands that some individual Santo Domingeños had officially registered by employees of the San Lorenzo branch of the IERAC—and who paid, individually, the cost of such legalization—are legally "unoccupied," although they are either used by Afro-Esmeraldians or are considered by them as land in reserve for their children and grandchildren. However, legally speaking, they are available for colonization. Afro-Esmeraldian lands in the Upper Ónzole are therefore really menaced by the Manaba invasion, even though some rules and regulations of the IERAC recognize some rights to already established "peasant communities."

The refusal of Santo Domingeños to accept new white-mestizo in-migrants was the result of various factors: the Manabitas consider themselves superior to Afro-Esmeraldians, and what is looked at by Afro-Esmeraldians as their arrogant attitudes cannot but provoke frictions and rejection. When, in the past, some Manabas obtained the authorization from Santo Domingeños to exploit a piece of land for agriculture, their cultivation techniques were highly disliked by Afro-Esmeraldians and Chachi. They cut down all vegetation, burned it on the ground, and then planted two or three products that they planned to sell on the local or national market. Only a small part of the land they exploited was reserved for their subsistence.

Of all the Manabas I met in the northern sector of the province of Esmeraldas, in Santo Domingo or elsewhere, none had been able to secure an income significantly higher than the income of Afro-Esmeraldians (with the exception, of course, of the local entrepreneurs of Borbón, Limones, La Tola, and San Lorenzo, and of the owners of sawmills near Borbón). Their ambition was to one day be able to produce for the international market, which could, as they said, "bring some progress to these backward regions of the country." They tended to try to expand their control of lands above and beyond the limits that were given to them initially. They looked down on the production techniques of Afro-Esmeraldians and Chachi—slash-mulch swidden cultivation and agroforestry—which are less aggressive with the forest ecology, and which they sometimes qualified as rustic remnants of another age. For Afro-Esmeraldians, Manabas did not do anything but destroy their forest. In fact, they made references to the Manabas' agriculture techniques as an additional argument to obtain official ownership of their land: "We know, unlike them, how to protect our forest."

Manabas also had the reputation of violence. In the mid-1980s, various families of Manabitas decided to establish themselves in a forest location thirty minutes' walking distance from the village, on the banks of the small waterway called Piquígua, which is an affluent of the Ónzole River. They had previously received the authorization from various men in the village. A short time before the beginning of my fieldwork in Santo Domingo in 1989, as the result of fights among themselves, two of the Manabas were shot dead. Santo Domingeños, who were concerned with this violence, said that the best way to put an end to it was not to allow any new arrival of Manabas. And it is with this preoccupation in mind that they created the *Junta Pro-Defensa de las Tierras de Santo Domingo*, which aimed at obtaining formal recognition of their lands by the Ecuadorian state as *territorios comunales*, "communal lands."

> DON TRÍFILO: In a concrete way, our objective was to create a commune (*una comuna*), because we thought that this was the best way

to defend our land, and to protect ourselves from the Manaba invasion and from the terrible situation we were in. A commune is an
organization that, when it is recognized legally, is owner of its land.
In our commune, all of us who live within the established perimeter,
we must be *comuneros*. But that commune must have very subtle
rules and regulations. In the area of the commune, I cannot even
sell you a piece of land. Nobody can sell any land to anyone. If you
don't want to live here anymore, you must leave the land to the commune. In the commune, there is a committee, with a president, a vice
president, a secretary, and a treasurer. There are also members who
participate in the meetings. People get elected according to the rules
and regulations. For us, this commune begins in Zancudo and goes
up to reach Colón, up to the river of the Chachi. That's the commune
of the parish of Santo Domingo de Ónzole. The villages included are
Zancudo, Baquería, Baquerita, Santo Domingo, and Colón. (Conversation recorded in 1990)

Another factor that pushed Santo Domingeños to organize is the support that the "Manaba invaders" seemed to have received from the regional
authorities of the San Lorenzo branch of the IERAC. The employees of that
branch had the prerogative to give land titles to any peasant who came to
request access to "unoccupied lands," who filled the appropriate forms, and
who paid the necessary fees. The bureaucrats of IERAC in San Lorenzo, who
were all white-mestizos, tended to support the colonization project of the
Manabas. One of the reasons for this support had to do with the fact that
the Manabas, who had sold everything they owned in their places of origin
in the province of Manabí, and who therefore had a small capital in hand,
could give the necessary kickbacks to the often-corrupt IERAC bureaucrats
to "facilitate" and speed up the whole process.

To this day, Santo Domingeños have been successful in resisting in migration of Manabas into their parish. Their land was recognized as communal
land in 2008.

Before the beginning of the Manaba migration in the parish, the population
of Santo Domingo had only brief relations with white-mestizos. The white-
mestizos who episodically visited the village were mostly Catholic priests and
missionaries, medical doctors, and eventually some traveling salesmen. The
tense relationship with white-mestizo in-migrants was in fact a novelty. The
relative protection that Santo Domingeños enjoyed as "already established
peasant communities" with the IERAC did not allow for the emergence of the

Manaba as a real threat. And in the early 1990s, despite the Santo Domingeños' determination to resist the Manaba invasion, they did not feel displaced by white-mestizos as the Afro-Esmeraldians from La Tola did. The interactions they had with the Manabas were taking place in such a way that Afro-Esmeraldians were in a position of force. Their daily interactions with the Manabas living nearby at Piquígua were not characterized by racial tension, as were the daily interactions between Afro-Esmeraldians and white-mestizos in La Tola. This, I contend, is the reason why the Play in Santo Domingo, unlike La Tola's, does not express a major concern with race and is more focused instead on gender relations.

The history of the relations between Santo Domingeños and Chachi is different. Chachi and Afro-Esmeraldians have been sharing the forest in the area that became the parish of Santo Domingo for more than a century. In the past, their interactions had sometimes been problematic, but since the official recognition by the Ecuadorian state of the lands used by the Chachi as "traditional land," and since the beginning of the Afro-Esmeraldian process to get their land in the parish recognized as "communal land," the situation has been simplified. Their respective land ownership cannot anymore be the object of conflict. Respect now characterizes the relations they have with each other, although each group continues to entertain a feeling of superiority vis à vis the other.

Since the beginning of the Spanish conquest, the Chachi adopted a strategy of resistance that consisted in moving away from any possibility of contact in removed regions nearer the sources of the rivers in the Esmeraldian forest. They—as a matter of policy—have been avoiding interracial mating with Afro-Esmeraldians and have only allowed for limited cultural exchanges. This strategy was in reality quite successful: of all the indigenous groups who were living in the province in the sixteenth century, the Chachi are the only ones who survived the processes of colonial "integration." After the arrival of the Illescas (see chapter 1), and following their domination of the central area of the province, the Chachi retreated toward the north. In the nineteenth century, at the beginning of the processes of economic integration of the province within the rest of the country and the world economy—the tagua boom—and the immigration of Colombian blacks, they further retreated toward the source of the Cayapas River, on lands that were unoccupied at the time. Later, during the Concha revolt (1912–16) (see Estupiñan Tello 1977; Chávez Gonzalez 1971), they escaped from the Conchista commissions (which conscripted by force poor peasants as soldiers) and colonized lands in the Upper Ónzole, where a population of Afro-Esmeraldians had also began occupying the land and had founded the villages of Zancudo, Santo Domingo, and Colón.

Before the official recognition of Chachi territory, the two groups some-times competed for the control of land. In such cases, Chachi were usually the victims of abuses and thefts by Afro-Esmeraldians, who treated them as uncivilized and savage, and who did not think twice before stealing things from them. Chachi, by contrast, made reference to blacks with the expres-sion *juyungo*, which means "devil," "bad," or "monkey" in Tsapalachi.[2] They looked at Afro-Esmeraldians as being lazy thieves (Barrett 1925).

Milton Altschuler provides similar information: "They must spend a lot of time away from their properties, which opens the way for black people to illegally harvest their products or plant their own seeds on the land owned by the Cayapas" (author's translation; Altschuler 1965, 440). Eulalia Carrasco reported the following conversations with Chachi:

> Black folks abuse Indigenous people, they steal plantains and wood. We have already established the limits of our land, but they do not respect them. The Political Lieutenant has received letters from San Lorenzo and from the Of-fice of the Governor of Esmeraldas, but he doesn't do anything to stop them. Blacks threaten to kill us.
>
> [. . .]
>
> Not long ago, a black guy from Pintor asked me for permission to cut 300 trees on our land. He said that he would pay 1,000 sucres. I did not respond anything. Now, they entered on our land with up to 10 teams of men and they took 100 trees of Guayacán, and 90 other trees, and they sold them to the companies without giving us anything in exchange. I asked them to give us some money so that we can pay the cost of having our land recognized legally, but they didn't even pay any attention to me. (Carrasco 1983, 124)

Various Chachi cultural norms and behaviors were cited by Afro-Esmer-aldians as justifications for their disdain. The Chachi have maintained an indigenous language of the Barbacoan family—Chapalache—that Afro-Es-meraldians, for the most part, do not understand. Until relatively recently, because of their distance from urban centers and their limited interactions with the "national society," most Chachi could not speak Spanish very well. They consequently had difficulties communicating with white-mestizos and blacks alike when they traveled to sell their surplus and purchase what they needed in Borbón or Limones. Their limited knowledge of the Spanish lan-guage was often cited by Afro-Esmeraldians as one of the reasons they con-sidered them to be "savages." They sometimes imitated the Chapalache, in which the sounds "chi," "che," "chechereche," and "cha" are often pronounced with the mocking expression "chichirichi." And I have heard several times statements such as "Don Roberto (a Chachi man) is a civilized Cayapo [*sic*]. He can speak Spanish properly," or *Hay Chachis que no pueden hablar cristiano; son como indios salvajes* ("There are Chachi who cannot speak like Christians; they are like savage Indians"), or *Hay cayapas montuvios y cayapas castellanos, es decir civilizados* ("There are uneducated Cayapas and Cayapas who speak Spanish; that is to say, some are civilized").

Some Afro-Esmeraldians learned to speak Chapalache. This was the case of Don Gilberto, who was born and grew up in the village of Telembí, on the Cayapas River. He was one of the marimberos who came to play marimba during the Play of January 1990 in Santo Domingo. During a conversation I had in Santo Domingo with a Chachi man, Don Alberto, during the 1990 Play, I asked if he had heard Don Gilberto talk in Chapalache, and if he did, what did he think about it? Don Alberto responded,

> Yes, I heard him talk. He speaks well, but I personally don't like to hear my language spoken by a black or white person. I listened to what he was saying, but I did not respond. In Spanish I can talk with him, but not in my language. It even infuriates me, I hate it; it's like if he had stolen something from me (the other Chachi present during the conversation agreed with him). (author's translation)

As a consequence of moving away from national society, Chachi of the most removed communities began going to schools later than Afro-Esmeraldians. When they had an economic transaction with an Afro-Esmeraldian, they were often taken advantage of. This situation changed in the 1980s, when various Chachi began getting an education in the Catholic missionary schools of Santa María de los Cayapas and of San Miguel, two missions located near Borbón. Later on, some of the students of these missionary schools went to Esmeraldas, where they enrolled in high schools and even obtained a degree in the escuela normal (teachers' school) of Esmeraldas. After graduating, many of them went back to their community of origin, where they now teach in a national program of bilingual education, in Spanish and Chapalache. Afro-Esmeraldians commented on this change of situation with expressions such as: *Ahora, hasta hay chachi licenciados* (Today, there are even Chachi with a bachelor's degree). The emergence of teachers in Chachi communities transformed the traditional structure of power. They entered into competition with their governors, or *uñis* (see Carrasco 1983).

Despite the feeling of superiority of Afro-Esmeraldians and the negative images that Chachi had about blacks (interracial marriages with blacks or white-mestizos have been traditionally forbidden by the Chachi leadership and the Chachi Federation), individuals of both groups entered into a relation of alliance through compadrazgo. A black godfather and godmother were chosen by Chachi to baptize their children, and vice versa. This relation of alliance can be very precious to Afro-Esmeraldians when they hunt deep in the forest, closer to the source of the rivers, where Chachi have established their villages. They receive help if a problem arises, and they can sleep in Chachi houses and share their food. Compadrazgo assures support to Chachi when they travel downriver to Borbón to sell their surplus and buy the products they need. They can spend the night in the house of their compadre or comadre and leave their packages safely in their houses if they need to go somewhere else before going back to their villages.

The additional ethnographic information this chapter has provided should contribute to a better appreciation of my interpretation of the Play in La Tola and Santo Domingo de Ónzole using different fields of meaning to make sense of the content of their respective performances.

6

Performances and Contexts of the Play in January 2003

       This chapter provides ethnographic information about the Play in both villages at the beginning of the twenty-first century.

    In December 2002, after having decided to go back to my work on the Festival with the purpose of eventually publishing it, I traveled to the province of Esmeraldas, where I spent four weeks doing some fieldwork. My objective was to find out how the Play was being performed since I last visited. Once back home in Miami, I revised my diary in order to develop my initial analyses. I also inserted transcriptions of fragments of interviews I conducted while in the field. I have decided to keep the diary format in this chapter, hoping that this approach would be a better way to share with the reader my progressive reconnection with the Festival and the two villages.

December 24, 2002, 2:00 P.M.

I just arrived in Santo Domingo, more or less half an hour ago, with Childo, Jenny (a woman from the village who was in Borbón when we organized the trip in lancha and who took advantage of it to come back), Liliana (Childo's older daughter), and other Santo Domingeños we picked up along the way. We left Borbón this morning around 9:30 A.M.

    I have been lucky so far. Indeed, when I arrived in Esmeraldas from Quito, in the afternoon of December 20, I immediately tried to make contact with Santo Domingeños I knew were living there, in the neighborhood called *El Pampón*. I wanted to get some news about the village, how things had evolved since my last visit in 1991. I also wanted to know who would be traveling in the next few days to Santo Domingo for the end-of-year celebrations, so that I could accompany him, her, or them. When I arrived in the street where the small shop of Chamita, the son of Don Chama, is, I saw a group of Afro-Esmeraldian youth standing near the door of the house where I was going. The shop was closed, and I asked whether they knew where Chamita was. They responded that he was traveling, and that they did not think that he would be back soon. I explained that in fact I was looking for news from Santo Domingo, and that I wanted to travel there and hoped to arrive in the village before the celebration of the Niño Dios. Intrigued by the fact that I was a foreigner but that at the same time I knew about arrullos to be sung for the Child Christ, they asked me why I wanted to go there and who I was. I explained that I had been going to the village quite frequently at the end of the 1980s and early 1990s, some twelve years before. I explained that I had been very much interested in Santo Domingo's Fiesta de los Reyes, and that at each one of my visits I had been staying in the house of Childo Corrozo, who was then the political lieutenant.

One of the young women in the group exclaimed: "That's my dad. I'm Childo's daughter!" I could not believe my luck; I gave my name, and asked for hers. She said that she remembered me from a picture that her parents had kept. She was Liliana, was eighteen years old, the older daughter of Childo and Neyra. She said that she was planning to go to Borbón before Christmas, where her mother now lives, and where I could possibly find her father, who was dividing his time between Santo Domingo and Borbón. She added that I could perhaps convince her father to bring me from Borbón to the village. She said that we could actually call her mother's house in Borbón because she had a phone, which we attempted to do. We went to the phone company's main office a few blocks away and called. Nobody was home. Liliana then promised to contact me the next morning after she talked with her mother that same evening. I took the phone number of the house where she lived in Esmeraldas and went back to my hotel. By the following morning, everything was arranged. Liliana had talked to her mother, who was curious and pleased to hear that I was around again. Liliana added that her father was in Borbón. We were to leave Esmeraldas together the morning of December 22 for Borbón, where we were to go to Childo's and Neyra's house. We traveled by bus and arrived in Borbón in the early afternoon. Childo, Neyra, and their other kids were pleased to see me and welcomed me into their house. They were surprised to see how much heavier I was (¡*Que gordo se puso, Don Jean!*). We also very quickly made plans to go to Santo Domingo on December 24. I offered to pay for the gasoline.

When we arrived at the shore of Santo Domingo's barrio "Guayaquil," I immediately realized that the wooden stairs that Childo and other men had built were gone. "They were taken away by a heavy flood," someone said. Various people recognized me right away and wondered why I had come back. I recognized the faces of all the people I had met in the past. I only remembered some of the names.

We carried the packages that we brought to the houses of Childo and of Don Chama and Doña Ermelina, Neyra's parents. Liliana was to stay there, and I would sleep in Childo's house, with Childo. Don Chama had died a few years before. Childo's house was only a pale memory of what it had been. One could clearly see that no one was living regularly in this house. Some wooden boards had not been replaced both on the floor and in the walls. This meant that during the night mosquitoes and rats could roam about the house as they liked. I felt lucky to have a mosquito net. I wondered when Neyra had been in this house last. Obviously, Childo was only spending a few days per month in Santo Domingo. His chainsaw had broken and he had not repaired it for months. I'm going to have to get used to rather uncomfortable sleeping conditions again. It seemed easier to do when I was younger.

I walked around the village and chatted with all the people I met. I learned that there would be no *balsa* raft this year, for Christmas, as they used to have in the past, although I was assured that there would be an arrullo for the Christ Child that same night.

My conversations with the women I met were enlightening about what had been going on, or not, with the Play of the Cowls along the years. The village had not played Reyes for the last two years. The reason: each time, someone had died a few days before January 6; the first year, it was a very active reyera, and the second year a man. Many of the women I remembered for being among the most active reyeras told me that they hoped that this year they would get animated and that they would play Reyes. I shared with them the fact that I was curious to see what they would do.

Don Alberto is still around. He is blind. I will go visit him tonight.

I saw Tana, who is nicknamed Luciola, at the river. She was washing some clothes when we arrived. She first acted as if she had not seen me. We were good friends in the past, to the point that some among the villagers thought that we would end up having a more engaged relationship, of the *unión libre* kind. I remember finding all these small rumors somewhat unpleasant, although also enlightening about man-woman relationships, and the ease with which both relationships and rumors could eventually begin and end. Childo made sure that I realized she was there. We hugged. She had now four children with a Santo Domingeño who was living in Guayaquil when I was visiting the village in the late 1980s and early 1990s. He was not in the village at the time of my 2002–03 visit: he was traveling.

Most people who had not seen me for twelve years told me how heavy I looked, adding: *Entonces, tiene Buena vida en la Johnny, Don Jean, hu?* (You apparently have a good life in the U.S., Don Jean?). I hated it. They also complained about their financial difficulties. In fact, Neyra and Childo are rather well off when their situation is compared to that of many in the village.

December 25, 2002

It is around 10:00 A.M. What happened last night is quite edifying, although somewhat depressing. There was no arrullo to the Baby Jesus. It seemed to me that the two new evangelical churches each organized a competing cult to celebrate the birth of Christ. One of the churches was built near the clinic, while the other was in barrio "Guayaquil" also, but near the path going up to barrio "Quito." The spread of the evangelical faith in the village has direct consequences on the performance of what has been considered Afro-Esmeraldian "traditions": the arrullo to Baby Jesus and to the saints, the Festival of the Kings, and the funerals. There seems to be a competition between the two evangelical churches, and between the evangelists on one side, and the Catholics on the other.

Childo and most of his brothers are either evangelist sympathizers or even, for one of them, an evangelist missionary. According to Neyra's mother, Doña Ermelina, who often cooks for Childo and me, this would be due to the fact that Childo's father was an assiduous evangelist. She also said that most of them, despite their evangelical tendencies, like to drink their aguardiente. She sees that as a contradiction, as do most people in the village. One of the major differences between a Catholic and a Protestant is that the first drinks—sometimes abundantly—while the second doesn't (supposedly).

The villager, Adalberto Padilla, who is in charge of the evangelical church near barrio "Cuenca" and the clinic, is very active and ambitious. I had an encounter with him this afternoon while I was sitting with some of the young men of the village chatting near the cement stairs. I had just purchased a bottle of aguardiente, and the single glass we were using was passing from one of us to the next. Adalberto came into the group, recognized me (someone had probably already informed him of my arrival), hugged me warmly, and began criticizing—in a friendly and respectful manner—the fact that I had purchased a bottle of aguardiente. During his monologue filled with barely disguised condemnation I looked around in our group to see the facial re-actions of the young men. There was a thick tension: everyone just listened to his speech. I wondered how this was going to end up. Adalberto finally left. The ambiance relaxed. I could not help it, of course, and asked questions about him. One of the young men said that he did not like the fact that evangelists, such as Adalberto, took the right to meddle in the private lives of others in an authoritarian way to tell them what they could and couldn't do. He added that he was a member of no church and that he could therefore do whatever he liked. And he ended shouting: *Y ahora, me da la santa gana de tomar aguardiente, ¡Carajo!* ("And now, I have the desire to drink aguardiente, damn it!"), which provoked from the rest of us a burst of laughter.

About the Play: it seems that my presence might animate them to celebrate. I am closely associated with the Festival of the Kings in the memory of the village. They did not play Reyes for two years because of the death of two people, among whom was Doña Florencia, a very active reyera. In fact, she was the reyera playing the tunda during the 1990 Play.

I talked to Don Alberto last night. He is now blind. It is sad to see someone who was so proud in such a situation of dependency. He depends on others for almost everything.

The family of Don Chama is definitely still the most ambitious and entre-preneurial family of the village, even though Don Chama died. They own a generator, most of their children are teachers or nurses, they own a series of material objects that set them apart, they are fervent Catholics, and they are adamantly opposed to the evangelists.

We might go to Arenales this afternoon.

December 26, 2002

They know that I am going to go to Esmeraldas and then will come back to the village before the beginning of the Play on January 6, so here is the list of things I have to buy:

- Don Alberto asked for an injection or dosis of Dipropan, for his con-dition, which he calls "Reumo."
- Hair extension for two girls in the village: 3 meters of black hair, 3 meters of brown hair. I included these items on the list because they were for two female adolescents whom I was close to when they were little girls in 1990.
- Don Segundo wants a watch.

- The reyeras want six bottles of aguardiente Frontera, one gallon of aguardiente Juan del Monte, cigarettes, cassettes of marimba music, and batteries for the cassette player. I also donated $10 to buy some gunpowder.

December 27, 2002

I am now back at the Hotel Estuario in the city of Esmeraldas. I arrived today. I think that this first brief trip to Santo Domingo was rather positive. In Santo Domingo, where I spent the night of Christmas eve to see what Santo Domingeños were going to organize for the arrullo al Baby Jesus, Childo asked me in a rather preoccupied way—he was slowly realizing that perhaps no arrullo would take place—if I wanted to go to Colón or Arenales (two neighboring villages) where there would most certainly be an arrullo. I had to explain to him that my interest was much less to attend an arrullo at any cost than to participate in what would happen, or not, in Santo Domingo. I told him that I had attended many arrullos in the past and that my interest now was on the sociocultural reality of the village. He understood my explanations and felt more at ease.

I also photographed the two churches. Back in the house of Doña Ermelina for my meal, I commented that it was quite interesting to see that twelve years ago, when there were very few converted evangelists in the village, there were arrullos. This year, on the contrary, there was no arrullo, but there had been two evangelical services to celebrate Christmas. I think that she interpreted my comments as the expression of a profound deception. She then took it upon herself to make sure that the rest of my stay would not add to what she saw as my sorrow: she went to talk to all the women known to be reyeras to make sure that they would play Reyes. In the afternoon of December 25, a dozen women, accompanied by Don Aquiles, came to see me at Doña Ermelina's to talk to me about the preparation for the Play. After a moment of hesitation, one of them began talking. She explained that they would need help to make sure that the Play would be a success (see the previous list of items they wanted). At one point during the conversation, Don Aquiles and a woman asked me to buy plastic masks in Borbón or Esmeraldas. I spontaneously responded that I would do anything I could to help, but that I would not purchase plastic masks for them to play Reyes. I tried to explain that I could not participate in what I saw as a cultural innovation in such an active way. I added that in the past reyeras never asked me to buy plastic masks and that I did not want to have the responsibility to choose the masks. The proposal was dropped by everyone. I still wonder if I was successful in explaining my position. Their idea with the masks was to give more strength to the fire/Play.

Later in the evening, Doña Ermelina approached me with a similar proposition: she wanted to add to the acts of January 6 the performance of the adoration scene by the three Kings. (It is interesting to note that she only remembered the name of Gaspar and had forgotten the two others.) She wanted to construct, near the entrance of the Catholic church, a crib with the animals, which she called *bestias*—the cow and the donkey/horse. Three youth disguised as the three Kings would come to the crib and give their presents to Christ. She wanted to know if I could buy masks in Esmeraldas: one with the face of a black man, one with the face of a white man, and the third with the face of an indigenous man. She explained that the idea had come to her when listening to a radio program during which the scene was described. Since she was there when I responded to Don Aquiles that afternoon, it was not difficult to argue that I did not really want to do that either, that I knew by experience and following my long conversations with reyeras in the past when I was around at the end of the 1980s and early 1990s, that in Santo Domingo nobody remembered the participation of characters representing the kings in the Festival. I added that if someone wanted to do that transformation or addition, he or she would have to do it without asking for my complicity, particularly if that entailed my selecting and purchasing the masks by myself in Esmeraldas. I then provided a safe way out. I explained that in La Tola, unlike in Santo Domingo, they always played Reyes with brief representations of the kings, and that there they did not use plastic masks but red, white and black dyes to paint the face of the three boys. She said that she would do the same. She nevertheless asked me to bring some sheets of cardboard and some markers, which I promised to do.

This preoccupation of Doña Ermela (as she is also called with affection) with the adoration scene should be related to the fact that she is the mother of many "successful" young adults, of which three are teachers. As wife of Don Chama, she was always very proud to think of herself as *mejor preparada* (better educated) than the other women of the village. She is a fervent Catholic and is proud to resist the evangelical pressure for change in the village. She told me that she had refused to attend their meetings despite persistent invitations from members of both Protestant churches. She also said that when they come to teach her about the content of the Bible, she tells them that she can read just like they can and that she can also interpret it on her own. She was very proud to tell me that she had told them that, for example, in the Bible there is no Jehova, but only Yavé.

The evangelist leaders do not want women to participate in the Festival or in the arrullo. Various women who were very animated reyeras in the past told me that they could not participate anymore. I asked why. They said: *Nos entregamos al Evangelio, ¡Don Jean!* (We converted to Protestantism, Don Jean!) The adding of the Kings adoration scene allows Doña Ermelina to give an orthodox face to the Festival, which, as she said, is called *de los Reyes* (of the Kings), even though there is no representation of the kings. Obviously, Doña Ermelina's insistence on a greater Catholic orthodoxy in the performance of the Play must be understood in light of the evangelical presence in the village.

Monday, December 30, 2002

This morning I will buy the stuff for the Play in Santo Domingo.

Yesterday, I went to La Tola. It was a long and slow trip. Uncomfortable! I expected that the trip would not be longer than the trip to Borbón (it's more or less the same distance). In fact, it was longer. The road to Borbón is entirely asphalted between Esmeraldas and Borbón. The road to La Tola is not asphalted after the "Y." The state of the road to La Tola denotes the secondary status that La Tola now has for the local and provincial politicians and decision makers and for the economic life of the northern sector of the province. The road that now exists between Esmeraldas and San Lorenzo pushed La Tola in the periphery of the movement of passengers and goods between San Lorenzo and Esmeraldas. Before, the commerce and transportation of passengers between San Lorenzo and Esmeraldas had to transit by La Tola (in lanchas); it is now done by bus or truck and by road, without passing by La Tola but by Borbón. The buses that go to La Tola continue to transport passengers and goods to Limones. No road goes to Limones. Inhabitants of La Tola told me that in fact the "economic and political elite" of Borbón is very much involved in discussions with the provincial authorities and with the national congress to try to create Borbón canton. Borbón would become the new canton's head town, and the parish of La Tola would be part of this new canton. The past importance of La Tola has been replaced by the current growth of Borbón. Many Toleños feel that they live in a declining village. In the past, until about fifteen years ago, the inhabitants of Borbón who wanted to travel to Esmeraldas had to go first to La Tola, in canoe or in a lancha; from there, they took the bus to Esmeraldas. The road La Tola–Esmeraldas was completed in the early 1960s. The portion of the road between the "Y" and Borbón was finalized about fifteen years ago. The rainy season often made it unusable. The most secure way to reach Borbón was then through La Tola.

Outmigration from La Tola continued, even accelerated. Now, the school does not offer more than the third grade. There are only three teachers. The cooperative Buena Esperanza no longer exists. The members sold the material and equipment and shared the product of these sales among themselves. La Tola has a desolate aspect now that it did not have before. The decline of the commercial transit through the village killed a series of small businesses. The local economy is declining. People continue to fish, and many are still peasant-fishermen. Fishing is more complicated than before, they say, because many areas are over-fished and the fish and conchas were not allowed to reproduce, and also because the shrimp farmers steal shrimp larvae from the river and otherwise contaminate it. The *jaíba* (a crab of great commercial value that was abundant at the mouth of the Santiago River in the past) is now threatened by extinction. As one fisherman told me: *Ahora, las jaíbas que se coje son pequeñas no mas, y ya no se vende por pieza sino por libra* (The jaibas that we get today are small, and we don't sell them individually anymore, but by the pound). Local agriculture has almost completely disappeared. Most of the land around La Tola was sold to big companies that own shrimp farms. They employ a labor force from the Sierra, the province of Manabí, and elsewhere. An employee of a shrimp farm told me that the local population was not sufficiently educated to get these jobs. The arrival of shrimp farmers in the region had only negative impacts. They did not create jobs, nor did they improve the local economy.

I was rather surprised by the emergence of tourism in the region. Olmedo now has a series of *cabañas* (small cabins) for rent as well as a small hotel, which was founded by Japanese investors interested in developing a site of ecological tourism in the mangrove regions. An association of women from Olmedo now manages the hotel.

During conversations with people I knew, it appears that the Reyes will not be played this year. They told me that in the past years very few people disguised themselves as cucuruchos. Those who did wandered around in the village for a while, trying to get some money from people to purchase drinks in the local bars.

There are more Manabas than before. Many people whom I knew died or migrated.

There is now a system of phone lines in La Tola. Some villagers even have a private phone, which was completely unthinkable at the beginning of the 1990s, when there was only one single phone line for the entire village.

When buses arrive in La Tola, they are usually empty. The buses are now primarily used by the local inhabitants. They no longer carry any passengers going to or coming from Limones or San Lorenzo.

Jairo, a Toleño, told me that he would be in Esmeraldas when I came back from Santo Domingo. He will then tell me if people have played Reyes or not.

Friday, January 3, 2003 (11:05 A.M.)

I arrived in Santo Domingo yesterday around 5:15 P.M. with Childo. I am again staying in his dilapidated house. Last night, after a dinner of *arroz con queso* (rice with cheese) at Doña Ermelina's with Childo, he disappeared in the now completely dark paths of the village. Evenings in Santo Domingo are different. The soundscape is for the most part occupied by the songs of the two competing evangelical services. The church near the dispensario owns a generator, which makes a lot of noise.

After the services, village life progressively fades away. One can see the lights of oil lamps through the windows for about an hour. Then the village falls asleep, in a silence sometimes interrupted by barking dogs and cats in heat.

After Childo left, two young men came by to talk to me about life in the United States and to ask what I thought about it. They also asked if it was different than in Belgium. They seem fascinated by the United States. In some ways, they also admire Osama Bin Laden. They commented: *Don Jean, es extraordinario que un solo tipo pude hacer esto, lo de las torres, a un país potente así como los Estados Unidos. ¡Y todavía no le han cojido!* (Don Jean, it's extraordinary that one single guy could do the thing of the towers to a country so powerful like the United States. And they did not get him yet!)

There are about ten prisoners in the village prison. They are all from Colón. They apparently stole some food . . . I must find out what's going on.

This morning I had a conversation with Don Alberto. With a question, I invited him to talk about women in general, and their relationship to men. He also talked about the two women he once had. He quickly noted that today there is equality between men and women in many ways, particularly in the services and agencies of provincial and national governments. Before, men dominated women, he said, but now there are new laws that demand women's presence in political parties, and that protect women's rights. He added: "In the past, if you would see a woman that you liked by simply looking at her, after talking to her, you could arrange things for you to enjoy a relationship with her even if you already had another woman. Now, it's not possible anymore, you can't do it anymore, it's economically or financially impossible. You have to remain firmly involved with only one woman."

The reyeras seemed to be disappointed last night. I'm pretty sure that they thought the container with aguardiente (I had decided to empty the bottles in a container I bought, to make the trip and transportation easier) should have been fuller. They also deplored the fact that I had not been able to find aguardiente Juan del Monte. That kind of aguardiente is not found easily in the city of Esmeraldas since it is usually produced in rural areas by someone who distills cane alcohol.

The reyeras have the permit. They went to Zancudo on December 28 and to Colón on December 31. There were about ten of them during these trips.

I talked to Pedro Caicedo, the current political lieutenant. The prisoners stole food that had been stocked in the reserves of the provincial government for the breakfast of the kids of Zancudo and Colón. They will have to remain imprisoned until the accusers arrive so that the teniente can make a ruling.

Childo told me that the political lieutenant receives a salary of U.S.$200 per month. He can also keep the money he gets from the fines he imposes. He also said that following the elections that took place recently, he will probably become lieutenant again soon. They already called him to come to Esmeraldas to fill the forms. The lieutenant is chosen by the provincial authorities, usually the office of the governor, according to his/her political affinities. I have never heard of a female lieutenant in Esmeraldas.

People are broke in Santo Domingo in a way that they were not in the late 1980s and early 1990s. The reyeras were not active at all today. The two stocks have already been assembled: one for the kids and one for the adults.

Saturday January 4, 2003

I just had my breakfast, coffee with milk and *patacones* (fried plantains). I also bathed in the back of Doña Ermelina's house: she has a big container in which she collects rainwater. The neighbor is going to wash my clothes.

Peter, Neyra's brother, has a dog he calls Reynolds, like the brand of aluminum foil. I went to visit Peter after breakfast.

An interesting scene this morning while I was coming back from Peter's house: When I passed in front of the house where the day before I had seen the abogado (Childo's brother) at the window, I asked if he was in. Catalina, the woman I thought was his wife, responded that he wasn't there, that he would be back in the afternoon. A boy laughed and told me that he was in his other house, and began shouting: *¡Abogado! ¡Abogado!*—showing me the house with his right hand. Catalina added: *¡Si, pero esa no es su mujer!* (Yes, but that one is not his wife/woman!). The boy laughed again. The abogado showed up at the window of the other house and said hi. I asked if he would be available later to talk to me, after his day of work. He accepted and said that he would look for me once he got back.

The village gets busy by 6:00 A.M. Around 9:00 A.M., calm returns, when everyone who had to go into the forest has departed.

Today I'll try to interview Sixto, the protestant missionary who is also the leader of one of the two evangelical churches, and Livio, who is his right-hand man and one of Childo's brothers.

This morning, the reyeras and some men extracted the juice of some sugar cane to make guarapo. I took photographs.

Sunday, January 5, 2003

This is the day before the beginning of the Play. I saw some reyeras with their caps with a piece of paper indicating their grades: *policía, guardia del estanco, intendente general de policía, capitán de mar y tierra, teniente político.*

It is 10:15 A.M. I had my breakfast at Doña Ermelina's as has been the case since I arrived here (I gave her some money to cook for me). This morning, my ear infection is worse than yesterday. The abogado is a health worker also; he received some training for that. He gave me an antibiotic and some drops. I hope to heal that before my Esmeraldas–Quito flight. Yesterday I interviewed Sixto, the leader of the evangelist church called *Iglesia Evangélica Cristiana*. He is the one who convinced Livio Corozo to become an evangelist missionary too. In the evening, from 7:45 through 9:00 P.M. I also interviewed Livio. I took some notes (the batteries of my recorder are gone; I don't have that many left).

The beginning of the conversation with Sixto was recorded without problem. Sixto is arrogant. He talks with the assurance of someone who is convinced that he has seen the light and who talks to others who are still in the dark. The conversation began with his questions, after I had explained to him what the objectives of my visit were (the Festival of the Kings, the changes the village went through since 1991). He asked rather suddenly about my religious faith. He qualified his first question by asking another one: "Who is Jesus Christ for you, Don Jean?" His facial expression was very serious and inquisitive, like when a demanding schoolmaster wants to make sure that a pupil has studied his or her lesson and looks at him or her very severely.

I responded that as an anthropologist, I had great respect for all religious faiths. I attempted to make a short pause to think about something to say that would appease him when he interrupted my thoughts and added: "Yes, but I'm talking about you, personally, as an individual. Work is one thing, but your individuality is another!" I responded that for me, as for many anthropologists I know, work cannot be easily separated from personal life. This kind of "work," for lack of a better word, is very different from the work of a carpenter, for instance, which is done in a particular place (a shop, a house), and that begins and ends at a particular time.

My "work," I continued, is an integral part of my everyday life, of my worldview, and I could not simply put it aside, just like that. In order to say all that, I had to insist that he let me answer his question the way I choose. I added that really for me, all religious faiths—Christianity, Islam, Voodoo, Candomblé, Buddhism—were all respectable, all important aspects of human cultures, and that none of them was superior to another. He insisted: "Yes but what does Jesus Christ represent for you?" I responded that all religions are centered around the worship of one or more supernatural figures, and that Jesus Christ was one of them, particularly associated with Christian religions. Although I know that he didn't really like my response, he nevertheless authorized me to turn my recorder on. I did not want to say that I mostly consider myself to be an atheist. If I had, he would have engaged in a rhetorical fight with me, and I did not want that to happen.

One of the themes of our conversation seemed particularly important to Sixto: the private school. There is no public school in the village anymore, just a private school financed by the organization that employs Sixto. He said that because he had not had the opportunity to get an education beyond the third year of primary school, when he got back to the village from Argentina, where he had attended a four-year-long religious seminar, one of his first preoccupations was to find the necessary funding to open a private school, which was finally done, he insisted, thanks to God's mercy.

He also talked against the use of religious images by Catholics. It is wrong, he said, to represent Jesus as a baby. "Jesus is not a baby anymore!"

He asked me to keep Santo Domingo in my mind when I got back to the states, so that I could eventually help with funding for one project or another.

I had another conversation with Livio Corozo, Childo's brother. He is a very active Evangelist who works with, and is calmer than Sixto. He left Santo Domingo when he was thirteen years old. In 1972 or 1973, he began living with a woman, with whom he had two children. Later, he had a girl with another woman from Guayaquil. His first two children are now living in Esmeraldas.

When he was living in Guayaquil, he drank a lot and loved going to parties and such. Around 1992–93 he didn't want to live in the city anymore and decided to come back to the village, where he met Sixto, who was getting ready to go to Argentina. Sixto presented him to Carl Wilson, an American evangelist missionary (who had already enrolled Sixto for missionary work), and the abogado for training to become a "rural nurse" (*promotor de salud*). After meeting Carl Wilson, he began reading the Bible more closely.

Livio thinks that the Festival of the Kings and the Holy Week (see Rahier 1999d) are examples of traditions celebrated by Afro-Esmeraldians who are ignorant because they don't really know what they are celebrating, they don't know the profound meaning of what they are doing.

One day Carl Wilson suggested to him that he should go to Argentina as well. He accepted and went two years after Sixto, in April 1995, to participate in a four-year program of study organized by the *Instituto Bíblico Palabra Vida*. During his studies, he also took part—in Argentina—in meetings with three hundred students from all over the world. These meetings were organized by the *Unión Misionera Estudiantil*. The students coming from all regions of the world were regrouped by the organizers by country of origin. He was designated to be the leader of the group of students who came from Equatorial Guinea (the only Spanish-speaking country of sub-Saharan Africa). He liked his role as leader of that group a lot.

When he came back to Ecuador in 1999, the missionary-funded school Gastón Figueira already functioned at the initiative of Sixto. The school was, and still is, financed by the evangelical mission for which he works and which is called *Ecuador Para Cristo*. The organization *Compasión Internacional*, which is dedicated to the promotion of education and "physical and spiritual health," funds the school. Similar schools were also opened in Zancudo and Arenales. The state-funded school in which Neyra worked disappeared in 1991.

Ecuador Para Cristo was first active in the province of Pastaza (in the Oriente), where they opened thirty-five schools and perhaps twenty high schools.

When I asked him if the founding of the school had given evangelists the power to change Santo Domingo's traditions, he responded that Santo Domingeños walk away from their traditions of their own will, not because they obey orders from his church.

The teachers of the schools are supervised by Sixto and Livio, who are in charge of supervising the Christian education in all three schools. Peter, who is Neyra's brother and Doña Ermelina's son, is the director of the school.

This afternoon, there was a meeting of the reyeras on the path outside Doña Ermelina's house. Doña Ermelina was of course leading the conversation. We waited for a while until all the reyeras who had been called were present. The meeting began when about fifteen of them had gathered. Doña Ermela began explaining that she had seen in a flyer she got from a course on catechism that the meaning of the Festival of the Kings—to which she referred with the expression *la Santa Epifanía* (the Holy Epiphany)—was the celebration of the adoration of Baby Jesus by the three kings: Melchior, Gaspar, and Balthazar. She said that she wanted to add an act to the Play this year. She wanted to disguise three kids as kings (one "Indian," one "white," and one "black"). Each one of them would mount a bestia, and they would follow a star to the place where Jesus Christ had been born. She wanted the cortège to begin on the soccer field, near the extremity of the field, downriver, and to progress toward the higher side of barrio "Quito," near the Catholic Church. She wanted people to build a big crib where they would install an image of Jesus as baby, on the side of which would be a woman representing Mary, Christ's mother, and a man representing Joseph, Mary's husband. On several occasions during her presentation, Doña Ermela turned toward me and asked: *No cierto, ¿Don Jean?* (Isn't it, Don Jean?) Every time, I responded that I was in no way the ultimate authority to which she should turn to get a final approval. I was not the one who should decide what would happen in this year's Festival. She ended up proposing that when the cortège reached the church, women would sing some arrullos. She then turned towards me and asked, *"Don Jean, ¿usted tiene con que grabar los arrullos?"* (Don Jean, do you have a recorder to tape the arrullos?) I responded, a bit irritated perhaps, that they should decide to do anything or to not do it on their own. She then added, to let me know that she had understood, and as if she wanted to translate what I had said: *Don Jean está aquí solamente como observador* ("Don Jean is only here as an observer").

Before she opened up the floor for any other proposition, she said that these were only her ideas and that she was open to any proposal from anyone. Nobody had anything to say. One person asked where the cucuruchos would be during the cortège. Someone answered that the cucuruchos would have to be disguised already and would have to accompany the cortège and the kings to the church. I asked if the act of the visit of the president would be played. Ermelina responded that the president would have to come from Esmeraldas. Another reyera said that the president would have to come to the village before the kings go to the church. Everyone accepted. I asked if they had already decided who would be the president this year, and if the president had already chosen a name. She said that a woman named Rosa was about to arrive in the village from Guayaquil (a visiting outmigrant), and that if she indeed arrived, she would be the president.

Once the meeting was over, Ermelina invited me to come inside her house. She proceeded to ask me if I knew how to make the crowns for the kings. I gave her an idea of how to do it, although I again tried to make her understand that I did not really want to decide how the crowns should be made. It progressively appeared clear to me that Doña Ermela wanted to put the eventual respectability I might have in the village on her side, in her resistance against what could be called an evangelist hegemony. The fact that I am passionately interested by the Festival of the Kings, one of the traditions "condemned" by the evangelists, puts me "naturally" in the camp of the "Catholics." She asked me for a donation to construct a cement floor in the church. I gave U.S.$60, which probably helps her think that way.

Monday, January 6, 2003 (8:30 A.M.)

The Play has not begun yet. I just finished my breakfast (coffee with milk, fried fish, and *verdes*, or boiled plantains). Doña Ermelina is preparing the disguises of the kings. I took a photograph. While going to Ermela's house to have my breakfast, I talked to one of the older women of the village. I told her that years ago, at this time, the Play had already begun (I wanted to get her reaction). She said that the death of various women who were among the most dedicated reyeras had deprived the Play of energy. The other women must be preparing themselves and taking care of the breakfast for their families. "Don't worry!" she said, "I'm sure that around ten o'clock the Play will be in progress." We'll see.

Aquiles will probably not play. His wife has been sick for days now. This morning, he killed one of his young cows, to get the necessary money to bring her to see a doctor in Borbón. He sells his meat at U.S.$1 per pound. Most Santo Domingeños have been buying meat since early this morning.

For Ermela, the act of the kings is definitely the most important.

During the last few days, most people have harvested their cacao. There is cacao drying under the sun everywhere in the village, particularly on the soccer field. They hurry early in the morning to expose it to the sun, before the fall of the first rain in the early afternoon.

Something important happened yesterday, when there was an animated discussion about the following question: Should the reyeras bring a Chachi marimbero from the village of Pambíl, located a bit more than one hour upriver by canoe? The final decision was to not do that because of the lack of funds. The dance party will therefore be animated with cassettes of marimba music.

(3:00 P.M.)

The activities of the reyeras stopped. This is what happened this morning: Around 9:00 A.M. Doña Ermela went downriver with a lot of stuff in her hands to the extremity of the village to prepare the three kings. A lot of kids were following her and got together around the horses and the place where the preparation of the Play was underway. Various reyeras were there too. They were busy decorating the horses with flowers and leaves, while others colored the faces and arms of the three young boys who were going to represent Gaspar, Melchior, and Balthazar (respectively in black, red, and white).

The reyeras began to get agitated. I asked: "And what about the act of the visit of the president?" Ermela did not acknowledge my question, as if she thought, for herself, that the most important act that will be played on that day was the adoration of Christ by the kings. Other reyeras decided to take the initiative and went downriver by canoe to Baquería, to put on their disguises before coming back to the village. About 10:00 A.M., the bombo announced

Figure 18. The three Magi kings in Santo Domingo de Ónzole in 2003. (Photograph by Jean Muteba Rahier)

their arrival. Once they were about to reach the village, one of them shot her shotgun in the air, which provoked strident screams from the children. Many children fear the cucuruchos (which they often pronounce "cuculuchas"). Instructions to debark by using the cement stairs were shouted to the reyeras in the canoe. A group composed of the cucuruchos who had stayed in the village, the three kings on their horses, and various women, youth, and young men began to move slowly toward the cement stairs. A shotgun discharged once or twice, provoking screams and emotions. The kings were accompanied by a bombo as well. There was no presidential chair, and the act of the president basically did not take place.

The president—who had adopted the name of Lucio Guttierrez (the then-sitting president of Ecuador)—debarked with his entourage and walked up the cement stairs. A shotgun was shot. The president joined the three kings who were waiting on their horses on top of the stairs. Some women began shouting, *¡Que viva la llegada del presidente!*

I forgot to write that before the arrival of the president, some of the reyeras sang songs that were already associated with the "whites" in the Play of the late 1980s and early 1990s.

The two groups merged and went toward the upper part of barrio "Guayaquil," where the church is, and where the crib still stood. In the crib, a girl represented Mary, and a boy Joseph. A white doll stood for Jesus. The president was the first to pay his respects to the Niño Dios. The white king followed with a sack symbolizing his present. Then came the "Indian" and "black" Kings.

After that scene, the group went toward barrio "Cuenca," crossed the small bridge above the small waterway, traveled on down to barrio Guayaquil, and entered the soccer field. There, after ending the singing that accompanied the movement, various young men were pursued, arrested, and placed in the stocks. To be freed, each had to pay U.S.$0.25. I was also arrested and locked in the stocks.

I must add that various women who were reyeras in the past and who did not put on disguises this year because they were now Protestants nevertheless accompanied the group. And the nondisguised women were among the most active to arrest men and lock them up in the stock.

About 11:00 A.M., a marimba dance party began, slowly, in the communal house, with music coming from cassettes. The bombo was also played. The dancing stopped about 1:00 P.M. Today, it did not rain. It was very hot and humid. I've been sweating a lot.

The dancing continues on tonight.

Tuesday, January 7, 2003 (8:45 A.M.)

There is no reyera activity yet. Many left for the forest, as if it were a regular day. I just had my breakfast (coffee with milk and bread; Doña Ermela made some bread using her brick oven). Last night, the dance began again around 8:00 P.M. It's interesting to see that they still actually prefer to dance with marimba music, even if it is coming from a cassette player. Once in a while, a man played the bombo. Around 11:00 P.M., they switched to cassettes of salsa music. The party ended at around midnight. Many people came to dance. The reyeras had purchased gasoline to feed the generator so that we could have power in the communal house.

Wednesday, January 8, 2003

Yesterday, the activities of the cucuruchos began around 10:30 A.M. They began their progression in the village in barrio "Cuenca," went down to barrio "Guayaquil," then proceeded to arrest young men and lock them up in the stocks. For their arrests, they sometimes had to get into houses. The duration of the acts was rather short. They spent more time involved in arresting men than in performing acts. As was the case many years ago, the nondisguised women have an automatic solidarity with the cucuruchos.

About 11:00 A.M., Doña Ermelina sent a Chachi who had come down to the village with his family, to pick up a marimba in his village of Pambil. He came back in the afternoon with other Chachi men. The dance was particularly animated and lasted all night. Chachi and Afro-Esmeraldians played marimba together. I've taken some pictures. Chachi women danced with black women. Chachi men danced with black women. But no Chachi women danced with black men. The Chachi man who went to fetch the marimba had asked that no Afro-Esmeraldian man fail to respect Chachi women (no black man could invite a Chachi woman to dance). This was his condition for bringing the Chachi marimba and musicians to play for the dance.

Friday, January 10, 2003

On Wednesday, the reyeras did not really have energy in comparison to the intensity of January 8, 1990. That is when I wondered whether they were dressing up as "negritos" and "cayapitos" just to satisfy me, as if they felt obligated to do so. About six reyeras disguised as "negritos." None of the

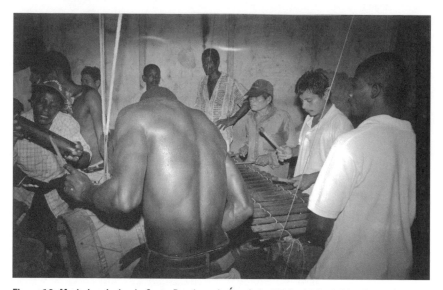

Figure 19. Marimba playing in Santo Domingo de Ónzole in 2003 with both Afro-Esmeraldian and Chachi musicians. (Photograph by Jean Muteba Rahier)

Chachi women present in the village for the Play agreed to play the role of the Chachi queen. A young Santo Domingeña played that part. She was accompanied by three Santo Domingeño boys and three Chachi girls. All were covered with red colorant and sang *Chichirichi . . ., Aqui hay pero no me dan.*

The group of "negritos" and "cayapitos" began their cortège in barrio "Cuenca" and went to the upper part of barrio "Quito," and on down to "Guayaquil," where the parridora gave birth to a little white girl.

The act of the brothers and sisters began with the old man saying that the child was not his. I was pointed to as the guilty party of this "obvious adulterous relationship." Since there were Chachi in the village, as well as a young mestizo teacher (from the Oriente) who had just arrived to teach in the village school, I defended myself and said that I was way too dark to be the father of such a white baby. I pointed toward a Chachi man who was in the group of people that surrounded the place where the exchange was unfolding. The reyeras accepted my argument and went to the Chachi man and told him that it was shameful that he could have done such a thing. However, they did not arrest him, nor did they lock him up in the stocks.

Symbolically, the child died, as in the act of the parridora in the past. A chigualo was performed in the communal house. The activities ended at the end of the chigualo. The whole act lasted less than one hour.

Figure 20. A reyera playfully pointing a rifle at "arrested" men locked up in the stock in Santo Domingo de Ónzole, January 2003. (Photograph by Jean Muteba Rahier)

It was the time of the school morning recess when the cucuruchos were walking around the village. It was somewhat odd to see all these kids in uniform mixing with the cucuruchos. In 1990, there was no school during the Festival. Obviously, the fact that the ownership of the school is in the hands of evangelists explains why the school didn't close for the Fiesta de los Reyes this year.

During the trip back, by canoe downriver to Borbón, and then by bus to Esmeraldas, I couldn't stop thinking about the impact evangelists were having on the cultural life of Santo Domingo, and how much things had changed in both villages.

Once back in Esmeraldas, a few days later, I saw Jairo. There was no Play at all in La Tola in 2003.

Conclusion
From the Centrality of Place in Esmeraldian Ethnography to Theoretical and Methodological Considerations for the Study of Festivities

The work of Isidoro Moreno (1985; 1997; 1999) leaves no doubt about the European and Catholic origin of the Afro-Esmeraldian Festival of the Kings, which was certainly introduced to the forefathers of today's Afro-Esmeraldians by Catholic missionaries. It would be interesting to consult, if they exist, Catholic missionaries' reports and other relevant documents in the archives of the various religious orders that have been active in the region of the Pacific lowlands to see what information they provide about the organization or "invention" of festivities.

For Moreno, this invention of festivities by missionaries in the Americas was very much inspired by the experiences of black Andalusians in southern Spain in the sixteenth, seventeenth, and eighteenth centuries. These festivities continued an association of evangelized African slaves and their descendants with the folklore of the three kings. As indicated in chapter one, the folklore of the Catholic Epiphany has provided the Catholic Church with a tool to celebrate the Catholic deity in a universalistic perspective by somehow incorporating communities of people of "different races and colors" into the masses of faithful Catholics. Fundamentally, the departure point of the Afro-Esmeraldian Festival of the Kings is the acknowledgment of the presence of the three "races" that had in fact populated not only the province of Esmeraldas but also all the ex-colonies of Spain and Portugal in the Americas: whites, "Indians," and blacks. Although separated in daily life by their different social statuses, they are all united in Christ through the presence in the sacred realm of Catholic legends of a king of their race.

We must recognize that the folklore of the three kings is profoundly diverse wherever it can be found around the globe, among communities of the African diaspora in the Americas or in any other cultural community. As this book has illustrated, festivities are never limited to reproducing faithfully a "traditional" scenario or narrative structure. In the European contexts, to take an example strikingly different from what I have described in the preceding chapters, some of the festivities associated with January 6 do not involve or are not based on any representation of racial differences among the Kings. That is how in France and in Belgium, for example, where I grew up, January 6—which is called in French *la Fête de l'Epiphanie* (the Celebration of Epiphany), *la Fête des Rois* (the Festival of the Kings), and also *la chandeleur*—comes with the preparation of a pie in which a bean has been hidden. When the pie is sliced and its pieces distributed, the lucky one who gets the piece with the bean receives a crown and becomes king or queen for the day. He or she can choose his queen or her king by bestowing a crown. The couple then "rules" until midnight, being able to express and impose upon others their most whimsical wishes in the midst of laughter.

As indicated early on in this book, my main objective was to conduct an analysis of the parodied racial identities—"whites," "blacks," and "Indians"— performed in the Afro-Esmeraldian Festival of the Kings, and which often involves sexual cross-dressing. The fundamental theoretical premise has been that festivities are nonstatic texts that are always embedded in ever-changing or evolving sociocultural, economic, and political realities. I illustrated and emphasized that basic fact, valid for any festive reality, by looking at the Festival as it has been performed in two different contexts within one single cultural area (the province of Esmeraldas): the villages of La Tola and Santo Domingo de Ónzole. I proposed to re-locate the Festival's "texts" within the webs of social relations and social practices that constitute its "contexts." In doing so, I have underscored the importance of "place" and "space" for the study of festivities in general, and of carnivalesque festivities in particular.

Two Villages, Two Places

From what I have discussed in chapters two and three, we know that Santo Domingo de Ónzole was formed as a village or place (Cresswell 2004; Tuan 1977; Harvey 1996) at the end of the nineteenth century by Afro-Esmeraldians who migrated from villages on the banks of the Santiago River during the period that has been called the tagua boom, in a developing economy characterized by a system of gathering-export that functioned mostly with black gatherers. The products exported were collected in the forest and were not produced on plantations. This was an economic system in which invest- ment of capital for new infrastructure was very limited or nonexistent. Vil- lages were founded with the communal work (*minga*) of villagers, and the commercial companies that controlled that economic period of booms and busts only had to establish buying stations in local towns (La Tola, Borbón, Limones, and San Lorenzo). To this day, investment in infrastructure by private companies or by the national and provincial governments has been limited to the relatively recent creation of a few asphalted roads and neces- sary bridges in some areas of the northern sector of the province.

Some villages located in the upper sections of rivers, deep in the forest, have remained marginally affected by the road: this is the case of Santo Do- mingo. These villages have continued to function as patriarchal communi- ties involved in an economy of subsistence wherein kinship networks play a pivotal role and where mostly men control the revenue and income of the productive activities and the sale of products either cultivated or collected in the forest. As explained in chapters two, three, and five, Santo Domingeños have indeed erected boundaries around their village in an attempt to keep (white-mestizo) Manabas away and to preserve what they consider to be their ownership of the land they and their forefathers have been living on, and for which they recently obtained a formal communal title.

This preoccupation with the defense of communal land points to the ex- istence of what I have called an "ideological cultural community" that goes beyond the actual village to incorporate Afro-Esmeraldians from other villages of the northern sector of the province, who sometimes move into the village following a union or "marriage." That ideological community is racially based and excludes white-mestizos and Chachi, even though the latter are closer to Afro-Esmeraldians than the former in occupying the same environment, sharing cultural techniques (housing, music, hunting), and being routinely involved in ritual kinship (*compadrazgo*) with Afro-Esmeraldians. The fact that Santo Domingeños have the upper hand on their communal land over white-mestizos and Chachi is a major reason—I argue—why they do not feel the need, as Toleños do, to perform racial identities in the context of the Play in a vengeful spirit. Instead, in Santo Domingo de Ónzole gender rela- tions provide the prime sociocultural material that inspires most of the acts performed during the Play in a let-off-steam process that lasts for three days (January 6, 7, and 8) or even longer if we take as the departure point for the festivity the day when the preparation of the Festival begins (December 28).

La Tola's population is clearly divided into a number of socioeconomic sectors that very much follow racial and racialized identities (Afro-Esmeraldians, non-Esmeraldian white-mestizos, Esmeraldian white-mestizos), with all lower sectors primarily composed of Afro-Esmeraldians. Antiblack, racially based disdain—something that doesn't exist in Santo Domingo—is the stuff of everyday life in La Tola, and resentment about it surfaces in the performances of the Play.

Santo Domingo is much more of a community than La Tola, and its socioeconomic differentiation is rather limited. I predominantly identified one social category into which all Santo Domingeños fall, even though a few of them—those I call the individual leaders—stand out for being more entrepreneurial than the others and consequently for owning a few more things. This greater communal spirit is behind the humoristic decision to name the three neighborhoods of the village with the names of the three biggest cities of the country, metaphorically making of Santo Domingo a geographic entity that encompasses the entire nation, thereby making the village the nation's center, in a move that negates marginalization.

Outmigration from the village to urban centers has been important in Santo Domingo as it has been in so many other rural villages and towns across the country during the past few decades. The census I conducted measured outmigration to represent 34.6 percent of the population of inhabitants, which is quite high. Women migrate more than men, which could be explained easily by the fact that they do not inherit land from their parents (mostly their fathers) as frequently as their brothers do. Additionally, many might have chosen to escape from an environment that has been characterized by patriarchy and gender inequality, as opposed to the perceived greater gender equality in urban areas. This is the very reason why the patriarchal Afro-Esmeraldian traditions are the principal target of the ironic humor of most, if not all, the acts of the Festival in Santo Domingo and in the performances of the committee of reyeras who joyfully and arbitrarily arrest men to lock them up in the stocks during the eleven days prior to the beginning of the Festival and during the three days of its duration. Once they receive the permit, their authority must not be challenged. And it is here that we can clearly see the carnivalesque nature of the Play in Santo Domingo. Important sociopolitical rules of daily life are suspended and inverted in what could be seen as potentially subversive, but that is in fact nothing more than a let-off-steam process that reaffirms the rules' centrality in nonliminal time.

La Tola was founded under the leadership of Pedro Vicente Maldonado in the early eighteenth century. The specific history of La Tola and the social dynamics found there (explained in chapters four and five) reveal how different it is from Santo Domingo de Ónzole. La Tola's socioeconomic division explains why, in the final analysis, its Play could not have been as intensely performed as it was in Santo Domingo de Ónzole.

La Tola's population, which is larger than Santo Domingo's, is much more dependent on the cash economy than are any of the smaller all–Afro-Esmeraldian villages located in the forest area of the northern sector of the province, including Santo Domingo. In fact, until the late 1990s, many in La Tola had a source of income that was directly linked to the economic activities generated by the daily movement of people and goods. La Tola has a partially asphalted road that connects the village to Esmeraldas. Daily trips to and from Limones and San Lorenzo also bring in a number of passengers and goods.

The non-Esmeraldian white-mestizos who live in La Tola do not want to be bothered by Afro-Esmeraldian traditions. They look down on Afro-Esmeraldian inhabitants and have only negative things to say about them. The white Colombian Arboleda, some (if not all) of the teachers who usually come from the city of Esmeraldas, and also the employees of the shrimp farms are in La Tola to make a living, with no other emotional investment in the place. Additionally, the very functioning of the shrimp farms, which entails the use of river water and the removal of the native shrimp larvae, which thrive in the mangrove estuaries, to be placed in enclosed pools is at the source of conflicts between farm owners and peasant-fishermen. The latter lose because the former have the political and financial means to get the local political lieutenant and other authorities on their side.

Unlike what is going on in Santo Domingo de Ónzole, there is no ideological-cultural community that would include all inhabitants in La Tola. Afro-Esmeraldians have built resentment for the racially motivated, poor treatment they have been subjected to. This shows up clearly in the performances of racial identities in the Play of La Tola, wherein some disguised black characters complain about the racism of white-mestizos, while others feel the need to portray blacks as respectable citizens who are aware of the mores of modern and urban life. In La Tola's Play, gender relations are not emphasized as they are in Santo Domingo's.

Outmigration from La Tola is also important: the census I conducted in the early 1990s shows that 27.4 percent of the village's population migrated to an urban center. Fieldwork in the early years after 2000 indicated that the process of living in the village had continued.

Places and the Performance
of the Play of the Cucuruchos

In the case of the carnivalesque Afro-Esmeraldian Festival of the Kings, the focus of the performances and exchanges between disguised actors and between those actors and the participating audience is primarily on race relations in La Tola, while gender relations provide the main field of meaning in Santo Domingo de Ónzole.

There are nonetheless similarities in the representations performed in each village that suggest the existence some time ago, in the minds and plans of the people who are responsible for introducing or for spreading the Festival of the Kings in the region, of one initial scenario structuring the festivity.

The similarities of the Play in both villages, which leave no doubt about the fact that we are here in the presence of two different locally determined performances of the same Festival, include the idea that each "race"—"white," "Indian," and "black"—would have one dedicated day, which justifies the holding of the Festival during three days; the representations of whites as people associated with power, prestige, and respectability; the representations of blacks as poor forest people; the representations of black women as nalgonas (women with protuberant behinds) who have an active sexual appetite; the figure of the parridora or black woman who gives birth to one or two white babies who die soon after birth; the representations of monkeys (although their roles in each village slightly differ); and the representations of the Chachi.

These similarities should not eclipse the major differences that also exist between the Play in La Tola and the Play in Santo Domingo. These differences should be interpreted in light of the different local contexts and histories and suggest that the Play has had a life of its own in each one of the villages where it is performed.

The contrast between the two modes of festive participation in La Tola and in Santo Domingo reveals that the very spirit of the Play and the relations between disguised actors and the rest of their local community were fundamentally different in both villages. We have seen that in La Tola the Festival involved but a relatively marginal participation of the village's population as nondisguised audience. In Santo Domingo, by contrast, the entire village community was joyfully and spontaneously involved in the performances with the disguised actors, until the recent rise of evangelists.

In the province of Esmeraldas, the letter *j* is often pronounced as the letter *f*, and vice versa (García Salazar 1984, 1988; Hidalgo Alzamora 1982). This means that the word *juego* (play) is often pronounced *fuego* (fire). On one occasion in Santo Domingo in 1990, when the Play was over on January 8, a reyera approached me and asked: *Que tal le pareció el fuego, Don Jean?* (How did you like the fire, Don Jean?) Tired, I had to ask her to repeat the question, because I did not understand what fire she was talking about. After remembering the particularities of Afro-Esmeraldian pronunciation, I was fascinated by her spontaneous play of words, which made a quite meaningful metaphor.

The Play in Santo Domingo could indeed be compared to a fire. The frenzy of the play (fire) could be seen in the performances of the actors-reyeras, the loud singing of their songs, the drinking of aguardiente, the meeting of the actors-reyeras with the nondisguised participants that allowed for spontaneous satires and parodies, which underscored the fact that everyone and everything could be ridiculed. The conjunction of all that could be interpreted as a fire to which everyone contributed by participating in the intensity of the numerous acts, for three days. The liminal time of the festivity contrasted a great deal with the relative calm of everyday life that preceded and, most importantly, followed the three days of the Play, when everyone was exhausted, some with a bad hangover for having abused the aguardiente, and others with a painful throat for having abundantly sung and screamed during the acts and dances.

During the Play in Santo Domingo, it was expected that masked actors or spectator-partakers add a new element to their disguises, prepare in advance an intervention during one of the acts that they knew was going to take place, escape loudly if a reyera wanted to arrest them, with the objective of adding ¡*un poco de fuerza, para darle más fuerza al fuego!* (a bit of strength, to give it more strength or force to the play-fire!). *Fuerza* means in this context "force, intensity, pleasure, joy." The engagement of the talent of the masked actor-preparers and of the spectator-partakers had for its ultimate objective having fun, with intensity. The 1989, 1990, and 1991 Play of the Cowls in Santo Domingo was not conceivable without the active and collective participation of the spectator-partakers in the acts that were for the most part played and initiated by the actor-preparers. The two groups encouraged, supported, and excited one another.

In Santo Domingo, at the end of the 1980s and at the beginning of the 1990s, the Play was still very much a community event. A committee of women prepared the Play from December 28 on, after having received a formal permit to play from the teniente político. During the three days of the Play, all economic activities were interrupted and the whole village population was immersed in the enchanted time of the Juego. In La Tola, during the same period, close to nothing was happening before January 6, and there was no real committee of women. The activities of everyday life were not interrupted, and disguised actors only came out in the streets at the end of the workday.

In Santo Domingo, whites, in addition to being associated with power and prestige, were seen as strangers to the local community. This was apparent in the mock medical visits played by mock medical doctors, dentists, and their nurses, who actually parodied the visit of real doctors, dentists, and nurses who sometimes came to the villages of the Ónzole River. It was even more clearly so during the act of the visit of the president. Eduardo Baca and his entourage were all identified as white-mestizos who came from faraway lands, where they controlled the institutions of the state. Unlike the doctors and dentists, the president and his collaborators' disguises were *embasurados*: they carried above their clothes leaves and packs of cigarettes that were mostly smoked in the urban areas of the country. I suggest that the leaves (see Rahier 1999d, 44), just like the packs of cigarettes, evoke the foreign-ness of these white characters, who were, because they actually never visited the village, more foreign or distant than the doctors, dentists, and their nurses. This non–Santo Domingeño origin of whites—recalled by the fact that they arrived in the village from downriver—came along with the affirmation of Santo Domingo as a place or parish of black people, where *gente de color* (people of color—in other words, "whites") do not live.

In 1990, the act of the visit of the president began with Eduardo Baca's representing the president of Ecuador before suddenly becoming the president of Peru, while the general-president became the president of Ecuador. At no time during the "conflictive" exchanges between the reyeras and the tropa was the actual race of the characters directly referred to. The opposition between reyeras and tropa largely followed the demarcation between the categories "from here" and "not from here," between *los de acá* and *los de allá*, between Ecuador and Peru, and ultimately between young Afro-Esmeraldian men and Afro-Esmeraldian women. In fact, race was not brought into the dialogues of the acts until the end of the Play, on January 8, during the performance of the woman who gives birth, when the parridora and some people in the attendance suggested that Fabián would have to take his colorado child with him to his land of white-mestizos. Even here, though, the racial opposition between blacks and whites was only meaningful along the line of "from here" and "not from here." The Santo Domingeño Play never represented "racial tensions" between different segments of a local population as it does in La Tola's.

In La Tola, where as we know racial tensions between various segments of the village population is a thing of everyday life, whites were not automatically and definitively marked, as in Santo Domingo, as strangers to the village. As a matter of fact, I would suggest that the silence of the dialogues about a possible non-Toleño origin of the whites in La Tola meaningfully marks them, along with other characteristics, as an integral part of the local population. The dialogues between white and black cucuruchos add evidence in support of this interpretation. Indeed, the racial tensions performed in the short exchanges are reminiscent of what happens in La Tola's everyday life and illustrate quite well the workings of La Tola's socioeconomic and "racial" hierarchy.

The fact that the act of the visit of the president was performed in Santo Domingo and not in La Tola denotes the distance of Santo Domingo from regional and national centers of power. La Tola's greater proximity to these centers, which brought about the in-migration of non-Esmeraldian white-mestizos who ended up occupying upper segments of the local socioeconomic and political hierarchy, explains why Afro-Esmeraldian "traditions" could not "survive" there as they did in Santo Domingo. La Tola's village population was too segmented to allow for the performance of a rather complex act such as the visit of the president, which celebrated the identity of a local community. The performance of that act in Santo Domingo unambiguously proclaims an Ecuadorian citizenship for the local black population, despite the geographic peripherality of their village and despite their treatment as second class "citizens" or as "ultimate Others" when they go to the city of Esmeraldas, to Quito or to Guayaquil. During that act, when the general president challenges the authority of the visiting president, the local population even appears as more nationalist than anyone else in the country.

As a result of the contextual differences surrounding and shaping the Play in La Tola and in Santo Domingo, I interpret the act of the woman who gives birth differently in each village. In Santo Domingo, because of the local reversal of gender hierarchy from December 28 through January 8, and because the act of the parridora was performed as part of the longer act of the brothers and sisters, the birth of a white baby should be seen, I argue, as the manifestation of Afro-Esmeraldian women's sexual agency pitted against men's "sexual mobility." The fact that the baby was born white allowed for an unequivocal proof that the mother had indeed engaged in sexual intercourse with someone other (Fabián, a stranger who was visiting the village) than her black "husband" or companion. The dialogues among the various characters involved entirely support this interpretation, along with the fact that there was no local "racial hierarchy" dominated by whites or white-mestizos in Santo Domingo: whites were nothing more than strangers.

In La Tola, by contrast, the socioeconomic and racial hierarchy dominated by whites or white-mestizos, and the racial tension that characterized the entire Play added a dimension to the issue of Afro-Esmeraldian women's sexual agency. Indeed, the issue of interracial sex and union between white men and black women was talked about on several occasions during the Play. Unlike in Santo Domingo, Toleña black women expressed their desire to have sex with or even marry white men, instead of choosing black men. La Tola's act of the parridora evoked to me the process of blanqueamiento discussed in chapter one. This was particularly the case when, at the end of La Tola's Play, two black women appeared in the park, dressed up with clothes more refined than the usual clothes that blacks wear during the Play—including hats, an expensive watch, and handbags. One of them repeated constantly to everyone around that she wanted to marry a white man. This difference between La Tola and Santo Domingo clearly evokes the use of sex and sexuality as strategies for social advancement.

The socioeconomic context of La Tola in the early twenty-first century is marked by a striking decline following the construction of the road Esmeraldas–Borbón–San Lorenzo that further displaced La Tola as a center for the surrounding area in the Eloy Alfaro canton, to the benefit of the growing importance of Borbón. That decline is very much the result of the decrease in transit of passengers and goods that are now passing through Borbón instead. Many small businesses have closed. The cooperative Buena Esperanza no longer exists. The area around the village where there were cultivated gardens and cattle ranches is now covered by many shrimp farms that generally function with a labor force coming from elsewhere in the country. Outmigration from the village has continued exponentially as the lack of jobs has become more pressing. The local high school now has only three teachers and functions only as a middle school. Many Manabitas and white-mestizos have in-migrated to work in the shrimp farms and to open small cabins for European and North American backpack tourists.

Such a context explains why the Play has not been performed recently. The sectors of the population that used to organize it and perform as blacks, whites, and "Indians" have left the village for Esmeraldas and Guayaquil. One can wonder if the development of the tourism industry in the area could lead one day to the reemergence of a folklorized Festival.

In Santo Domingo, where people seem to have endured an economic downturn, the intensity of the Play has somewhat diminished in the last few years. This is also the result of the growing importance of Protestant churches, which are opposed to the use of images representing God and any scene of Jesus' life. Their leaders claim to interpret the content of the Bible as it should be interpreted, suggesting that any other way—and particularly the traditional Catholic interpretations and imagery—are nothing but an expression of ignorance. This has led those in the village who identify as Catholics to react by claiming that they do indeed know the content of the Bible, which they can also interpret as well as the Protestants. Doña Ermelina, who could be seen as one of the leading Catholics in the village, who wanted to give a more Orthodox content to the Play, insisted on representing the three kings during the first day of the Festival in January 2004. This made the Santo Domingeño Play resemble the Festival as it has been performed in La Tola for many years, where it has always opened with an offering of the three Magi kings to the baby Jesus. The irony in all this is that the Bible doesn't actually talk about kings of different races, but only about Magi, which would all come from the area around Palestine. This makes it difficult to see the inclusion of the three kings in the Santo Domingeño Play as a proof of good interpretation of the Bible's content. In any case, if things continue evolving in that way, and Catholics in Santo Domingo remain attached to the Festival, the representations of the three kings might grow in importance and end up occupying a more central place in the festivities.

I think that one of the most important lessons that the work presented in this book might teach is that scholars who study festivities and celebrations by usually focusing on one single occurrence as performed in one single location should not take for granted that festivities are indeed multilocal. The expression "multilocal" was coined by David Guss (2000) to indicate that what happens in one festival always involves the reality of more than one geographic location—in other words, more than the location where the performance actually takes place. Here, the expression "multilocal" indicates that the reading of the content of a festivity must also be based on the researcher's knowledge of what has been happening in the country, and sometimes even outside of its borders. This is the case, for example, in the act of the arrival of the president in Santo Domingo de Ónzole, when, following an improvisation, Eduardo Baca becomes president of Peru, a country with which Ecuador was at the time still involved in a border conflict.

In the spirit of this book, I would like to use the notion of "multilocality" to additionally mean something slightly different, in order to underscore the undeniable fact that one single festival, ritual, or play always repeats, with a critical distance, the stuff of everyday life of the people involved. In a given cultural area—in this case the northern sector of the province of Esmeraldas—one single festivity is always performed differently in different places. It is therefore absolutely necessary to pay careful attention to the always original local context that surrounds and supports a particular festivity, ritual, or play, or any other cultural practice.

Glossary of Esmeraldian Spanish Terms

alabado(s): Name given to the funerals for adults and to the songs that are sung on these occasions.

arrullo(s): Name given to the ritual performed on saint days to celebrate a particular saint or virgin. The name also refers to the songs that are sung on these occasions and during the chigualos.

batea: A large wooden bowl used for preparing meals and for alluvial gravel panning for gold.

blanqueamiento. Literally, "whitening." It is a concept often linked to the expression *mejorar la raza* ("to improve the race"). Blanqueamiento also refers to the process by which darker skinned people try to marry lighter-skinned individuals to secure upward social mobility.

bombo: "Bass drum" with cloth beater for drum head and palm stick for drum side.

camaronera: Shrimp farm.

catanga: Cylindrical trap made out of tree bamboo used to catch fish and river shrimp.

cepo: Punitive stocks. Cepos are a clear legacy of slavery.

chigualos: Name given to the funerals for children and to the games that are sometimes played on these occasions.

colorados: Light-skinned persons with light and fair brown, red, or even blond nappy hair. The term is associated with the meaning of the Afro-Esmeraldian expression *gente de color*. *Colorado* is sometimes also used as a synonym for *mulatto*.

comadre: Fictive female kin.

compadrazgo: A fictive kinship system relating godparents of a child to the child's parents.

compadre: Fictive male kin.

concha: Edible mussel.

conchera: Woman who gathers conchas.

cuadrillas: Slave gangs used for mining activity during the colonial period.

cucuruchas or cucuruchos: Afro-Esmeraldian women who prepare and participate in the Afro-Esmeraldian Festival of the Kings.

cununo: Percussion instrument played with the hands: a "conga drum."

damajagua: Bark cloth.

damas: Literally, "ladies." Expression used to refer to men cross-dressed as women in the context of the Afro-Esmeraldian Festival of the Kings.

duende: A male forest spirit whom various elders say they have met. The duende is usually described as a small white-mestizo man whose head is always covered with a big hat. He is said to have a big head and, as many Santo Domingeños indicated, has two faces—one in the front and one in the back. He is a good musician and an excellent guitar player. He can fight like no other man can, despite his small size.

entundado: A person who has been victimized by the Tunda.

ferrocarril: A bus mounted on railroad wheels.

fiesteras: Afro-Esmeraldian women who prepare and participate in the Afro-Esmeraldian Festival of the Kings.

fogón: Brazing fire.

gente de color: White people. Afro-Esmeraldian northerners invert the usual terminology found in the urban areas of the country and in most "western" countries in general, where the expression "people of color" or "colored people" refer to black and brown individuals. This could be seen as a way to invert the direction of the racial hierarchy.

guanta: A paca or *Cuniculus paca virgatus*. It looks like a large guinea pig and has a delicious white meat.

guayacán: Tropical wood that is very dense and water resistant.

Guayaquileño(a): A person or a thing from Guayaquil.

hojarasquín: A skirt-like ensemble of palm-tree and coconut-tree leaves attached with a cord.

Manaba or Manabita: A person or a thing from the province of Manabí, located on the coast, south of the province of Esmeraldas. The people from Manabí are usually white or white-mestizos with light-colored hair and sometimes light-colored eyes.

marimba: A locally made xylophone.

marimberos: Musicians who play the marimba.

mestizo(s) or mestiza(s): Mixed race individual who has both white or European (usually Spanish) and indigenous ancestries.

morados: Dark-skinned individuals with "fair" (non-kinky) black hair.

negros azules: The expression in use in Esmeraldas literally means "blue blacks" and refers to unmixed or dark-skinned black persons. It is used to talk about people from the northern sector of the province of Esmeraldas.

Niño Dios: Jesus Christ as an infant.

Oriente: The Amazonian region of the country; Upper Amazon.

Quiteño(a): A person or a thing from Quito.

reyeras: Afro-Esmeraldian women who prepare and participate in the Afro-Esmeraldian Festival of the Kings.

saíno: White-lipped peccary or *Tayassu pecari spiradens.*

Sierra: The central region of the country; the Andes.

Santo Domingeños: A person or a thing from the Esmeraldian village of Santo Domingo.

tagua: A palm nut very popular at the end of the nineteenth century and beginning of the twentieth century, sometimes called "vegetal ivory" on the world markets; tagua was used to produce buttons and other objects before the mass production of plastic.

tambuco: small canon used exclusively to produce a loud noise.

tatabro: Collared peccary or *Peccari tajacu bangsii.* It has a brown meat.

Toleños: A person or a thing from the Esmeraldian village of La Tola.

trigueños: Lighter-skinned persons than the mulattos, with soft, dark hair.

tunda: A female forest spirit who, according to oral tradition, likes to kidnap young boys. She appears generally in the form of the mother or of a female relative of the young boy whom she wants to take away. She cannot hide the fact that one of her legs is deformed; the other leg is normal. Her behind is more voluminous than that of human beings.

unión libre: Consensual union.

zambos: Persons of mixed ancestry with indigenous and black parents. In the province of Esmeraldas, the term is sometimes used to refer to someone who might not have indigenous ancestry but who is light skinned and has light and fair brown, red, or even blond nappy hair. In that way, it is synonymous with *colorado.*

Notes

Introduction

1. Fairly recent serious ethnographies on Ecuadorian peoples include those by Butler (2006); Colloredo-Mansfeld (1999); Corr (2010); Lyons (2006); Weismantel (1998); and Wibbelsman (2009) for the Sierra; Striffler (2002) for the Coast; and Descola (1994); Rival (2002); Uzendoski (2004); and Whitten and Whitten (2008) for the Amazonian region. For overviews of Ecuadorian ethnography and ethnohistory, see de la Torre & Striffler (2008); Whitten, ed. (2003); Whitten and Whitten (2011).

2. In addition to my own work (see the list of cited references) a number of references should be added to these citations if we are to take into consideration the work done in the Pacific lowlands of Colombia; see, among others, Escobar 1997, 2008; Oslender 2002, 2004, 2007a, 2007b, 2008a, 2008b; Restrepo 1996, 2004.

3. Similar to what happens in the Pacific lowlands of Colombia, Afro-Esmeraldian women in various organizations are engaged in sometimes contradictory struggles for both gender and "ethnic" justice (see Asher 1997, 2004, 2009).

4. These categories are mostly mine, or etic, although they are very much informed by local usages.

5. The educated reader will recognize that for the choice of these categories I was inspired by Norman Whitten's work (1974).

Chapter 1. Setting Up the Stage

1. A legend places the relics of the three Kings (Gaspar, Melchior, and Balthazar) in Köln, Germany (see Vacandard 1912, 50; Trexler 1997, 23–33).

2. "Grouped by African ethnic identity (*nación*), Africans and their descendants gathered in the mutual-aid/religious societies called *cabildos* beginning as early as the

sixteenth century in Cuba. Argeliers León writes that the 'blacks called them *cabildos*, choosing this word that had great significance in the colonial Spanish government. The Term *cabildo de negros* came to mean [also] an assembly of blacks.' Strictly speaking, the term *cabildo* did not necessarily refer to a religious organization but could refer to something like a club or mutual aid society, where the term *cofradía* more specifically pointed to a religious brotherhood associated with particular churches. However, in Cuba the term *cabildo* seems to have been more commonly used an could encompass both senses" (Brown 1993, 61).

3. Isidoro Moreno, in accordance with most European scholars, has a greater difficulty than U.S.-based scholars in using the concept of "race." Scholars based in Europe and the United States share the same understanding of "race" as a social and cultural construct. The difference lies in the use, or not, of the term. European-based scholars prefer to use the expression "ethnic groups," which refers for them to both "cultural background and physical appearance." Some even contend that we should not use "race" because "races" do not exist.

4. About the importance of the legend of the three Magi for European "exploration trips" and imperialism, see the chapter four, "*El Dorado*," of Trexler (1997).

5. I have used the English translation published in Bettelheim (1993).

6. "Aguinaldo is the gift of money ritually demanded and received by pre-Lenten (including Christmas) festival maskers from onlookers on the street/road and up in urban balconies. While aguinaldo was probably collected throughout the city, . . . apparently the climax of this practice took place in the *solar* of the palace of the Captain General of the Island (located in Old Havana), a spacious interior courtyard filled with trees, with balconies looming over head on all sides" (Brown 1993, 54).

7. "According to Judith Bettelheim, '[a] *comparsa* is a larger group of *conga* drummers accompanied by paired male and female dancers as well as by smaller groups of line dancers performing a specific choreographed routine' (*conga* being a 'small group of musicians who all play the same rhythm and are followed by neighborhood residents, who dance through the streets with identifying flags or banners'). 'A *comparsa* often includes elements of the *cabildo* . . . such as a King and Queen and decorated banners and *faroles* with specific, identifiable iconography'" (Brown 1993, 65–66).

8. I call the black communities of the province of Esmeraldas and of the Chota-Mira Valley "traditional communities" because they were constituted during the colonial period, unlike the communities found today in Quito, Guayaquil, and the eastern region (*El Oriente*) of the country, which are the result of relatively recent processes of migration. In that sense, there are as well traditional communities—although smaller in size—in Ibarra, the capital city of the province of Imbabura, and in the southern Andean Province of Loja.

9. A *zambo(a)* is a mixed person from black and indigenous parents.

10. This journey of the Arobe in Quito was immortalized in a painting of 1599 by Andrés Sánchez Guallque at the request of Juan de Sepúlveda (*Museo de las Américas*

in Madrid, Spain). The painting presents the Arobe as very dark people standing in elegant Spanish clothing, with gold jewelry as earrings, nose-, and lip rings; each holds a spear in the right hand.

11. At the end of the eighteenth century the annual gold production of New Grenada was 4,140 kilos; of the Vice Kingdom of New Spain, 1,610 kilos; of the Vice Kingdom of Peru, 782 kilos (see more comparisons in West 1952, 5).

12. This is the nut of a palm tree, which has a pulp that when left to dry becomes very hard and white. It was used to make buttons, combs, and other objects before the advent of plastic. Its scientific name is *Phytelephas aequadorialiis*.

Chapter 2. The Village of Santo Domingo de Ónzole and the Period of Preparation of the Festival of the Kings

1. Official representative of the national government in the parish of which he (usually a man) is in charge. The *teniente político* is usually appointed by the provincial Governor, who is himself designated by the president of the republic (Ecuadorian provincial governors are not elected). The teniente is also a judge of the first level.

2. *Cepos*, or stocks, are a clear legacy of slavery, appearing in the earliest and latest documents as typical means of punishing enslaved mineworkers. They were of course used all over Ecuador and Colombia well into modern times as humiliating punishment for petty crimes.

Chapter 3. The Festival of the Kings in Santo Domingo de Ónzole

1. In the past, the expression *baile de cuerda*, which means "dance with cord," referred to dance parties with guitar music. The expression remained as synonymous with any dancing party that is not animated by marimba music.

Chapter 5. Race, Sexuality, and Gender as They Relate to the Festival of the Kings

1. See Whitten 1974, 114–19; for the expression of these gender relations in the Pacific lowlands of Colombia in Marimba songs, see recording 14, "Adiós Berejú," by Norman Whitten in the "Raíces Latinas" CD in the Smithsonian Folkways Latino Roots Collection at http://www.amazon.com/gp/product/B000S9DI8O/ref=dm _sp_alb (accessed July 16, 2012).

2. See the novel *Juyungo*, by Esmeraldian writer Adalberto Ortiz (1983 [1957]).

References

Altschuler, Milton. 1965. "Notes on Cayapa Kinship." *Ethnology* 4:440–47.

Andrade, Xavier. 2001. "Machismo and Politics in Ecuador: The Case of Pancho Jaime." *Men and Masculinities* 3 (3): 299–315.

Antón Sánchez, Jhon. 2007a. *El estado de los derechos colectivos del pueblo Afroecuatoriano: Una mirada desde las organizaciones sobre el derecho al territorio ancestral.* Quito: Ministerio de Coordinación de Desarrollo Social.

———. 2007b. "Afrodescendientes: Sociedad civil y movilización social en el Ecuador." *Journal of Latin American and Caribbean Anthropology* 12 (1): 235n245.

———. 2009. "El Proceso Organizativo Afroecuatoriano: 1979–2009." Unpublished PhD diss., FLACSO-Ecuador.

———. 2010. "Los indicadores sociales afroecuatorianos en la era del Presidente Rafael Correa." *Boletín Informativo-CODAE* 1 (1): 3–7.

Asher, Kira. 1997. "'Working From the Head Out': Revalidating Ourselves as Women, Rescuing our Black Identity; Ethnicity and Gender in the Pacific Lowlands." *Current World Leaders* 40 (6): 106–27.

———. 2004. "'Texts in Context': Afro-Colombian Women's Activism in the Pacific Lowlands of Colombia." *Feminist Review* 78: 1–18.

———. 2009. *Black and Green: Afro-Colombians, Development, and Nature in the Pacific Lowlands.* Durham, N.C.: Duke University Press.

Atencio Babilonia, Jaime, and Isabel Castellanos Córdoba. 1982. *Fiestas de negros en el norte del Cauca: Las adoraciones del Niño Dios.* Cali, Colombia: Universidad del valle.

Bakhtin, Mikhail. 1994 [1965]. "Folk Humor and Carnival Laughter." In *The Bakhtin Reader: Selected Writings of Bakhtin, Medvedev, Voloshinov,* edited by Pam Morris, 194–206. London: E. Arnold.

Barrero, Jacinto. 1979a. "Costumbres, ritualismos y creencias en torno a los muertos en el campo de San Lorenzo." *Apertura* 2:25–49.

———. 1979b. "Creencias y costumbres." *Apertura* 3:26–41.

Barrett, Samuel A. 1925. *The Cayapa Indians of Ecuador*. 2 vols. New York: Heye Foundation.

Bastide, Roger. 1972. *African Civilisations in the New World*. New York: Harper Torchbooks.

Berry, Jason. 2004. *Mardi Gras in New Orleans, USA: Annals of a Queen*. In ¡Carnaval!, edited by Barbara Mauldin, 299–325. Seattle: University of Washington Press.

Bettelheim, Judith, ed. 1993. *Cuban Festivals: An Illustrated Anthology*. New York: Garland.

Botte, Bernard. 1932. *Les origines de la Noël et de l'Épiphanie: Étude historique*. Louvain, Belgium: Abbaye du Mont César.

Bowser, Frederik P. 1974. *The African Slave in Colonial Peru, 1524–1650*. Stanford, Calif.: Stanford University Press.

Brown, David H. 1993. "The Afro-Cuban Festival 'Day of the Kings': An Annotated Glossary." In *Cuban Festivals: An Illustrated Anthology*, edited by Judith Bettelheim, 41–93. New York: Garland.

Browning, Barbara. 1998. *Infectious Rhythm: Metaphors of Contagion and the Spread of African Culture*. New York: Routledge.

Butler, Barbara Y. 2006. *Holy Intoxication to Drunken Dissipation: Alcohol among Quichua Speakers in Otavalo, Ecuador*. Albuquerque: University of New Mexico Press.

Cabello Balboa, Miguel. 1965 [1577]. *Obras (De la entrada que hicieron los negros en la provincia deEsmeraldas)*. Quito: Editora Ecuatoriana.

Carrasco, Eulalia. 1983. *El Pueblo Chachi*. Quito: Abya-Yala.

Carrillo N., Ricardo, and Samyr Salgado A. 2002. *Racismo y vida cotidiana: Estudio de caso de una ciudad de la sierra ecuatoriana*. Quito, Ecuador: Instituto de Antropología UPS.

CESA. 1977. *La Agricultura en las comunidades del Valle del Chota*. Quito, Ecuador: CESA.

———. 1982. *CESA en los grupos campesinos del Valle del Chota: Informe preliminar*. Quito, Ecuador: CESA.

Chávez Gonzalez, Rodrigo. 1971. *El coronel Enrique Valdez Concha y su proyección en el panorama nacional*. Guayaquil, Ecuador: Taller Gráfico de Impresores Asociados.

Ching, Barbara, and Gerald W. Creed, eds. 1997. *Knowing Your Place: Rural Identity and Cultural Hierarchy*. New York: Routledge.

Clark, Kim, and Marc Becker, eds. 2007. *Highland Indians and the State in Modern Ecuador*. Pittsburgh, Pa.: University of Pittsburgh Press.

Colloredo-Mansfeld, Rudi. 1999. *The Native Leisure Class: Consumption and Cultural Creativity in the Andes*. Chicago: University of Chicago Press.

Colmenares, Germán. 1969. *Haciendas de los jesuitas en el Nuevo Reino de Granada, siglo XVIII*. Bogotá: Universidad Nacional de Colombia, Dirección de Divulgación Cultural.

CONADE. 1980. *El estrato popular urbano en Esmeraldas*. Informe de Investigación. Quito: CONADE.

Coronel, Rosario. 1987a. *El valle sangriento 1580–1700, de los señoríos de la coca y del algodón a la aacienda cañera jesuita*. Quito: Facultad Latino-Americana de Ciencias Sociales (FLACSO).

———. 1987b. "Riego colonial: De la coca a la caña en el valle del Chota." *Ecuador Debate* Noviembre (14): 47–68.

———. 1988. "Indios y esclavos negros en el valle del Chota colonial." In *El negro en la historia del Ecuador y del sur de Colombia*, edited by Rafael Savoia, 171–88. Quito: Abya-Yala.

Corr, Rachel. 2010. *Ritual and Remembrance in the Ecuadorian Andes*. Tucson: University of Arizona Press.

Cosentino, Donald. 2004. "'My Heart Don't Stop': Haiti, the Carnival State." In *¡Carnaval!*, edited by Barbara Mauldin, 269–98. Seattle: University of Washington Press.

Costales, Piedad Peñaherrera de, and Alfredo Costales Samaniego. 1959. *Coangue: Historia cultural y social de los negros del Chota y Salinas; Investigación y elaboración*. Quito: Instituto Ecuatoriano de Antropología y Geografía.

———. 1964. *Historia social del Ecuador*. Quito: Editorial Casa de la Cultura Ecuatoriana.

Cresswell, Tim. 2004. *Place: A Short Introduction*. Malden, Mass.: Blackwell.

Cuaderno Afro-Ecuatoriano n 7: Documentos de la esclavitud.

Curtin, Philip. 1969. *The Atlantic Slave Trade: A Census*. Madison: University of Wisconsin Press.

Davis, Natalie. 1975. *Society and Culture in Early Modern France*. Stanford, Calif.: Stanford University Press.

de la Torre, Carlos. 1992. "The Ambiguous Meanings of Latin American Populisms." *Social Research* 59 (2): 385–414.

———. 1996. *El racismo en Ecuador: Experiencias de los indios de la clase media*. Quito: Centro Andino de Acción Popular.

———. 2002a. *Afroquiteños, ciudadanía y racismo*. Quito: Centro Andino de Acción Popular.

———. 2002b. *El racismo en el Ecuador: Experiencias de los indios de clase media*. Quito, Ecuador: Abya-Yala.

de la Torre, Carlos, and Steve Striffler. 2008. *The Ecuador Reader: History, Culture, Politics*. Durham, N.C.: Duke University Press.

Descola, Phillipe. 1994. *In the Society of Nature: A Native Ecology in Amazonia*. New York: Cambridge University Press.

Devisse, Jean, and Michel Mollat. 1979. *The Image of the Black in Western Art*. Volume II. Cambridge: Harvard University Press.

Donoso Pareja, Miguel. 2000. *Ecuador: Identidad o esquizofrenia*. Quito: Eskeletra Editorial.

Drewal, Margaret Thompson. 1992. *Yoruba Ritual: Performers, Play, Agency*. Bloomington: Indiana University Press.

Escobar, Arturo. 1997. "Cultural Politics and Biological Diversity: State, Capital, and Social Movements in the Pacific Coast of Colombia." In *Between Resistance and Revolution: Cultural Politics and Social Protest*, edited by Richard Fox and Orin Starn, 40–64. New Brunswick: Rutgers University Press.

———. 2008. *Territories of Difference: Place, Movements, Life, Redes*. Durham, N.C.: Duke University Press.

Espinosa Apolo, Manuel. 2003. *Mestizaje, cholificación y blanqueamiento en Quito: Primera mitad del siglo XX*. Quito: Universidad Andina Simón Bolivar, Ediciones Abya-Yala.

Estupiñán Bass, Nelson. 1966. *El último río*. Quito: Editorial Casa de la Cultura Ecuatoriana.

Estupiñan Tello, Julio. 1977. *Historia de Esmeraldas*. Portoviejo: Gregorio de Portoviejo.

Fernández, Maria Augusta. 1994. "Latin American Urbanization—Ecuador." In *Latin American Urbanization. Historical Profiles of Major Cities*, edited by Gerard M. Greenfield, 215–51. Westport, Conn.: Greenwood.

Fortes, Meyer. 1958. Introduction to *The Developmental Cycle in Domestic Groups*, edited by Jack Goody, 1–14. Cambridge: Cambridge University Papers.

Freilich, Morris. 1961. "Serial Polygyny, Negro Peasants and Model Analysis." *American Anthropologist* 63 (5): 955–75.

Friedemann, Nina S. de, and Mónica Espinosa Arango. 1995. "Las mujeres negras en la historia de Colombia." In *Las mujeres en la historia de Colombia*, tomo II, Mujeres y Sociedad, edited by Magdala Velasquez Toro, 32–76. Santa Fé de Bogotá, Colombia: Consejería Presidencial para la Política Social, Presidencia de la República de Colombia, Grupo Editorial Norma.

García Salazar, Juan. 1979. *Décimas. Una manifestación de la poesía oral en los grupos negros del Ecuador*. Quito: Centro de Investigación y Cultura del Banco Central del Ecuador, Poligrafiados.

———. 1984. "Poesía negra en la costa de Ecuador: Desarrollo de Base." *Revista de la Fundación Interamericana* 8 (1): 30–37.

———. 1988. *Cuentos y décimas afro-esmeraldeñas*. Quito: Abya-Yala.

Gilroy, Paul. 1993. *The Black Atlantic: Modernity and Double Consciousness*. Cambridge, Mass.: Harvard University Press.

Glissant, Édouard. 1990. *Poétiques de la relation*. Paris: Gallimard.

Gonzalez, Nancie L. 1965. "The Consanguineal Household and Matrifocality." *American Anthropologist* 67 (6): 1541–49.

———. 1970. "Toward a Definition of Matrifocality." In *Afro-American Anthropology*, edited by Norman E. Whitten and John F. Szwed, 231–44. New York: Free Press.

Guerrero, Andrés. 2003. "The Administration of Dominated Populations under a Regime of Customary Citizenship: The Case of Postcolonial Ecuador." In *After Spanish Rule: Postcolonial Predicaments of the Americas*, edited by Mark Thurner and Andrés Guerrero, 272–309. Durham, N.C.: Duke University Press.

Guss, David. 2000. *The Festive State: Race, Ethnicity, and Nationalism as Cultural Performance*. Berkeley: University of California Press.

Hale, Charles R. 1996. "Introduction." *Journal of Latin American Anthropology* 2 (1): 2–3.

———. 1999. "Travel Warning: Elite Appropriations of Hybridity, Mestizaje, Antiracism, Equality, and Other Progressive-Sounding Discourses in Highland Guatemala." *Journal of American Folklore* 112 (445 [Summer 1999]): 297–315.

———. 2002. "Does Multiculturalism Menace? Governance, Cultural Rights and the Politics of Identity in Guatemala." *Journal of Latin American Studies* 34:485–524.

———. 2004. "Rethinking Indigenous Politics in the Era of the 'Indio Permitido.'" *NACLA Report on the Americas* 38 (2): 16–20.

———. 2005. "Neoliberal Multiculturalism: The Remaking of Cultural Rights and Racial Dominance in Central America." *PoLAR: Political and Legal Anthropology Review* 28 (1): 10–28.

———. 2006. *Más Que un Indio: Racial Ambivalence and Neoliberal Multiculturalism in Guatemala*. Santa Fe, N.M.: School of American Research.

Handelman, Don. 1990. *Models and Mirrors: Towards an Anthropology of Public Events*. Cambridge and New York: Cambridge University Press.

Harris, Max. 2003. *Carnival and Other Christian Festivals: Folk Theology and Folk Performance*. Austin: University of Texas Press.

Harvey, David. 1996. *Justice, Nature and the Geography of Difference*. Malden, Mass.: Blackwell.

Herlihy, Laura Hobson. 2007. "Matrifocality and Women's Power on the Miskito Coast." *Ethnology: An International Journal of Cultural and Social Anthropology* 46 (2): 133–49.

Herskovits, Melville J. 1938. "Les noirs du Nouveau-Monde: Sujet de recherches africanistes." *Journal de la Société des Africanistes* 8: 65–82.

Hidalgo Alzamora, Laura. 1982. *Décimas Esmeraldeñas*. Quito: Banco Central del Ecuador.

Hooker, Juliet. 2005. "Indigenous Inclusion/Black Exclusion: Race, Ethnicity and Multicultural Citizenship in Latin America." *Journal of Latin American Studies* 37:285–310.

Huizinga, Johan. 1976. "Nature and Significance of Play as a Cultural Phenomenon." In *Ritual, Play, and Performance*, edited by Richard Schechner and Mady Schuman 46–66. New York: Seabury.

Hutcheon, Linda. 1985. *A Theory of Parody: The Teaching of Twentieth Century Art Form*. New York: Methuen.

Jácome B., Nicanor. 1978. *Un modelo diferente de vinculación al mercado mundial: El caso de Esmeraldas, segundo encuentro de historia y realidad económica y social del Ecuador*. Tomo III. Cuenca: Universidad de Cuenca y Banco Central del Ecuador.

Jácome B., Nicanor, and Vicente Martínez Fissau. 1979. "La formación del estrato popular de Esmeraldas en el contexto del desarrollo provincial." *Revista de Ciencias Sociales* (Quito) III (10–11): 89–144.

Kimerling, Judith. 1991. *Amazon Crude*. New York: Natural Resources Defense Council.

Klumpp, Kathleen. 1970. "Black Traders of North Highland Ecuador." In *Afro-American Anthropology: Contemporary Perspectives*, edited by Norman E. Whitten Jr. and John F. Szwed, 245–62. New York: Free Press.

Landau, Brent. 2010. *Revelation of the Magi: The Lost Tale of the Wise Men's Journey to Bethlehem*. New York: Harper One.

Lane, Kris. 2002. *Quito 1599: City and Colony in Transition*. Albuquerque: University of New Mexico Press.

———. 2003. "Haunting the Present: Five Colonial Legacies for the New Millenium." In *Millenial Ecuador: Critical Essays on Cultural Transformations and Social Dynamics*, edited by Norman E. Whitten Jr., 75–101. Iowa City: University of Iowa Press.

LeCount, Samaké Cynthia. 2004. "Dancing for the Virgin and the Devil: Carnaval in Oruro, Bolivia." In *¡Carnaval!*, edited by Barbara Mauldin, 173–202. Seattle: University of Washington Press.

Lyons, Barry. 2006. *Remembering the Hacienda: Religion, Authority and Social Change in Highland Ecuador*. Austin: University of Texas Press, 2006.

Massey, Doreen. 1997. "A Global Sense of Place." In *Reading Human Geography*, edited by Trevor Barnes and Derek Gregory, 315–23. London: Arnold.

Mauldin, Barbara, ed. 2004. *¡Carnaval!*. Seattle: University of Washington Press.

McDonnel, Kilian. 1996. *The Baptism of Jesus in the Jordan: The Trinitarian and Cosmic Order of Salvation*. Collegeville, Minn.: Liturgical.

Miller, Marilyn Grace. 2004. *Rise and Fall of the Cosmic Race: The Cult of Mestizaje in Latin America*. Austin: University of Texas Press.

Mintz, Sidney Wilfred, and Richard Price. 1992. *The Birth of African-American Culture: An Anthropological Perspective*. Boston: Beacon.

Montaño, T. Valther Ernesto. 1982. *Economia y producción en la provincia de Esmeraldas*. Esmeraldas, Ecuador: Banco Central del Ecuador.

Moreno, Isidoro. 1981. "Control político, integración ideológica e identidad étnica: El sistema de cargos en las comunidades indígenas americanas como adaptación de las cofradías étnicas andaluzas." *Primeras Jornadas de Andalucía y América* 1:249–65.

———. 1985. *Cofradías y hermandades andaluzas, estructura, simbolismo e identidad.* Sevilla: Andaluzas Unidas.

———. 1997. *La antigua hermandad de los negros de Sevilla: Etnicidad, poder y sociedad en 600 años de historia.* Sevilla: Universidad de Sevilla and Consejería de Cultura de la Junta de Andalucía.

———. 1999. "Festive Rituals, Religious Associations, and Ethnic Reaffirmation of Black Andalusians: Antecedents of the Black Confraternities and Cabildos in the Americas." In *Representations of Blackness and the Performance of Identities*, edited by Jean M. Rahier, 3–17. Westport, Conn: Bergin & Garvey.

Morris, Pam, ed. 1994. *The Bakhtin Reader: Selected Writings of Bakhtin, Medvedev, Voloshinov.* London: E. Arnold.

Nájera-Ramirez, Olga. 1997. *La Fiesta de los Tastoanes: Critical Encounters in Mexican Festival Performance.* Albuquerque: University of New Mexico Press.

Nunley, John. 2004. "Playing Mas: Carnival in Port of Spain, Trinidad and Tobago." In *¡Carnaval!*, edited by Barbara Mauldin, 239–65. Seattle: University of Washington Press.

Ortiz, Adalberto. (1957) 1983. *Juyungo.* Quito: Seix Barral.

Ortiz, Fernando. 1920. "La fiesta afrocubana del 'Día de Reyes.'" *Revista Bimestre Cubana* XV (January–June): 5–26.

Oslender, Ulrich. 2002. "The Logic of the River: A Spatial Approach to Ethnic-Territorial Mobilization in the Colombian Pacific Region." *Journal of Latin American Anthropology* 7 (2): 86–117.

———. 2004. "Fleshing Out the Geographies of Social Movements: Black Communities on the Colombian Pacific Coast and the Aquatic Space." *Political Geography* 23 (8): 957–85.

———. 2007a. "Spaces of Terror and Fear on Colombia's Pacific Coast: The Armed Conflict and Forced Displacement among Black Communities." In *Violent Geographies: Fear, Terror, and Political Violence*, edited by Derek Gregory and Allan Pred, 111–32. New York: Routledge.

———. 2007b. "Violence in Development: The Logic of Forced Displacement on Colombia's Pacific Coast." *Development in Practice* 17 (6): 752–64.

———. 2008a. *Comunidades negras y espacio en el Pacífico colombiano: Hacia un giro geográfico en el estudio de los movimientos sociales.* Bogotá: Instituto Colombiano de Antropología e Historia.

———. 2008b. "Another History of Violence: The Production of 'Geographies of Terror' in Colombia's Pacific Coast Region." *Latin American Perspectives* 35 (5): 77–102.

Palacios Preciado, Jorge. 1978. *La esclavitud y la sociedad esclavista: Manual de historia de Colombia.* Instituto Colombiano de Cultura. Bogotá: Procultura.

Pavy, Paul David III. 1967. "The Provenience of Colombian Negroes." *Journal of Negro History* 52:36–58.

———. 1968. "The Negro in Western Colombia." PhD diss., Department of Anthropology, Tulane University.

Pereira de Magalhães Gomes, Núbia, and Edimilson de Almeida Pereira. 2000. *Negras raízes mineiras: Os arturos*. Belo Horizonte, M.G.: Mazza Edições.

Phelan, John Leddy. 1967. *The Kingdom of Quito in the 17th Century: Bureaucratic Politics in the Spanish Empire*. Madison: University of Wisconsin Press.

Polo, Rafael. 2002. *Los intelectuales y la narrativa mestiza en el Ecuador*. Quito: Universidad Andina Simón Bolívar, Sede Ecuador.

Pradier-Fodéré, Camille. 1897. *Lima et ses environs*. Paris: A. Pedone.

Price, Richard, and Sally Price. 2003. *The Root of Roots; or, How Afro-American Anthropology Got Its Start*. Chicago: Prickly Paradigm.

Prior, Marsha. 1997. "Matrifocality, Power, and Gender Relations in Jamaica." In *Gender in Cross-Cultural Perspective*, edited by Caroline B. Brettell and Carolyn F. Sargent, 331–50. Upper Saddle River, N.J.: Prentice Hall.

Quiroga, Diego. 1994. "Saints, Virgins, and the Devil: Witchcraft, Magic, and Healing in the Northern Coast of Ecuador." PhD diss., Department of Anthropology, University of Illinois at Urbana-Champaign.

Rabelais, Francois, and Donald Murdoch Frame. 1991. *The Complete Works of François Rabelais*. Berkeley: University of California Press.

Rahier, Jean Muteba. 1987. *La Décima: Poesía oral negra del Ecuador*. Quito: Abya-Yala and Centro Cultural Afro-Ecuatoriano.

———. 1994. "La Fête des Rois Afro-Esméraldienne (en République de l'Equateur)." Thèse de Doctorat, Département de Sociologie, Université de Paris X, Nanterre, France.

———. 1998. "Blackness, the 'Racial'/Spatial Order, Migrations, and Miss Ecuador 1995–1996." *American Anthropologist* 100 (2): 421–30.

———. 1999a. "Blackness as a Process of Creolization: The Afro-Esmeraldian Décimas (Ecuador)." In *The African Diaspora: African Origins and Self-Fashioning*, edited by Isidore Okpewho, Carole Boyce Davies, and Ali Mazrui, 290–314. Bloomington: Indiana University Press.

———. 1999b. "Body Politics in Black and White: Señoras, Mujeres, Blanqueamiento and Miss Esmeraldas 1997–1998, Ecuador." *Women and Performance: A Journal of Feminist Theory* 11 (1, 21): 103–19.

———. 1999c. "Mami, ¿qué será lo que quiere el negro? Representaciones racistas en la revista Vistazo, 1957–1991." In *Ecuador racista: Imágenes e identidades*, edited by Emma Cervonne and Fredy Rivera, 73–110. Quito: FLACSO-Sede Ecuador.

———. 1999d. "Presence of Blackness and Representations of Jewishness in the Afro-Esmeraldian Celebrations of the Semana Santa (Ecuador)." In *Representations of Blackness and the Performance of Identities*, edited by Jean M. Rahier, 19–48. Westport, Conn.: Bergin & Garvey.

———, ed. 1999e. *Representations of Blackness and the Performance of Identities*. Westport, Conn.: Bergin & Garvey.

———. 2003a. "Métis/Mulâtre, Mulato, Mulatto, Negro, Moreno, Mundele Kaki, Black, . . . : The Wanderings and Meanderings of Identities." In *Problematizing*

Blackness: Self-Ethnographies by Black Immigrants to the United States, edited by Percy C. Hintzen and Jean M. Rahier, 85–112. New York: Routledge.

———. 2003b. "Racist Stereotypes and the Embodiment of Blackness: Some Narratives of Female Sexuality in Quito." In *Millennial Ecuador: Critical Essays on Cultural Transformations and Social Dynamics,* edited by Norman E. Whitten, 296–324. Iowa City: University of Iowa Press.

———. 2008. "Fútbol and the (Tri-)Color of the Ecuadorian Nation: Ideological and Visual (Dis-)Continuities of Black Otherness from Monocultural Mestizaje to Multiculturalism." *Visual Anthropology Review* 24 (2 [Fall]): 148–82.

———. 2010. "The Ecuadorian Victories in the 2006 FIFA World Cup and the Ideological Biology of (Non-)Citizenship." In *Global Circuits of Blackness: Interrogating the African Diaspora,* edited by Jean M. Rahier, Percy. C. Hintzen, and Felipe Smith, 29–45. Urbana: University of Illinois Press.

———. 2011. "From *Invisibilidad* to Participation in State Corporatism: Afro-Ecuadorians and the Constitutional Processes of 1998 and 2008." *Identities: Global Studies in Culture and Power* 18 (5): 502–27.

Ramos Tinhorão, José. 2000. *As festas no Brasil colonial.* São Paulo, Brasil: Editora 34.

Real, Katarina. 2004. "Evoé! The Carnaval of Recife and Olinda in Pernambuca, Brazil." In *¡Carnaval!,* edited by Barbara Mauldin, 203–38. Seattle: University of Washington Press.

Restrepo, Eduardo. 1996. "Los tuqueros negros del Pacífico sur colombiano." In *Renacientes del Guandal "Grupos Negros" de los Ríos Satinga y Sanquianga,* edited by Jorge Ignacio del Valle and Eduardo Restrepo, 243–348. Bogotá: Biopacífico-Universidad Nacional de Colombia.

———. 2004. "Ethnicization of Blackness in Colombia." *Cultural Studies* 18 (5): 698–753.

Rival, Laura. 2002. *Trekking through History: The Huaorani of Amazonian Ecuador.* New York: Columbia University Press.

Roach, Joseph. 1996. *Cities of the Dead: Circum-Atlantic Performance.* New York: Columbia University Press.

Rueda Novoa, Rocío. 1990. *Zambaje y autonomía: La historia de Esmeraldas siglos XVI–XIX.* Maestría en Historia Andina, FLACSO-Universidad del Valle.

———. 2001. *Zambaje y autonomía: Historia de la gente negra de la Provincia de Esmeraldas (Siglos XVI–XVIII).* Quito: Taller de Estudios Históricos (TEHIS), Municipalidad de Esmeraldas y Ediciones Abya-Yala.

Safa, Helen. 1995. *The Myth of the Male Breadwinner: Women and Industrialization in the Caribbean.* Boulder, Colo.: Westview.

———. 2009. "Hierarchies and Household Change in Postrevolutionary Cuba." *Latin American Perspectives* 36 (1): 42–52.

Savoia, Rafael. 1988. *El negro en la historia del Ecuador y del sur de Colombia: Actas del Primer Congreso de Historia del Negro en el Ecuador y Sur de Colombia.* Quito: Abya-Yala.

———. 1992. *El negro en la historia: Raíces africanas en la nacionalidad ecuatoriana (500 Años)*. Quito: Afroamerica (Centro Cultural Afroecuatoriano).

Schechner, Richard. 1985. *Between Theater and Anthropology*. Philadelphia: University of Pennsylvania Press.

Schubert, Grace. 1981. "To Be Black Is Offensive: Racist Attitudes in San Lorenzo." In *Cultural Transformations and Ethnicity in Modern Ecuador*, edited by Norman E. Whitten Jr. Urbana: University of Illinois Press.

Schultz, Emily and Robert Lavenda. 2001. *Cultural Anthropology: A Perspective on the Human Condition*. Mountain View, Calif.: Mayfield.

Sharp, William Frederick. 1976. *Slavery on the Spanish Frontier: The Colombian Chocó, 1680–1810*. Norman: University of Oklahoma Press.

Silva, Erika. 1995. *Los mitos de la ecuatorianidad. Ensayo sobre la identidad nacional*. Quito: Abya-Yala.

Smith, Michael G. 1962. *West Indian Family Structure*. Seattle: University of Washington Press.

Smith, Raymond T. 1956. *The Negro Family in British Guiana*. London: Routledge & Kegan.

———. 1969. *Migration and Modernization: Adaptive Reorganization in the Black Carib Household*. Seattle: University of Washington Press.

Striffler, Steve. 2002. *In the Shadow of State and Capital: The United Fruit Company, Popular Struggle, and Agrarian Restructuring in Ecuador*. Durham, N.C.: Duke University Press.

Stubbs, Jean. 1993. "The Afro-Cuban Festival 'Day of the Kings': Fernando Ortiz." In *Cuban Festivals: An Illustrated Anthology*, edited by Judith Bettelheim, 3–7. New York: Garland.

Stutzman, Ronald Lee. 1974. "Black Highlanders: Racism and Ethnic Stratification in the Ecuadorian Sierra." PhD diss., Department of Anthropology, Washington University, St. Louis.

———. 1981. "El Mestizaje: An All-Inclusive Ideology of Exclusion." In *Cultural Transformations and Ethnicity in Modern Ecuador*, edited by Norman E. Whitten, 45–94. Urbana: University of Illinois Press.

Taussig, Michael. 2004. *My Cocaine Museum*. Chicago: The University of Chicago Press.

Terán, Emilio Maria. 1896. *Informe al jefe supremo general Eloy Alfaro, sobre la deuda Anglo-Ecuatoriana*. Quito: Imprenta Nacional.

Trexler, Richard. 1997. *The Journey of the Magi: Meanings in History of a Christian Story*. Princeton, N.J.: Princeton University Press.

Tuan, Yi-fu. 1977. *Space and Place: The Perspective of Experience*. Minneapolis: University of Minnesota Press.

Turner, Victor. 1977. "Frame, Flow and Reflection: Ritual and Drama as Public Liminality." In *Performance in Postmodern Culture*, edited by Michel Benamou and

Charles Caramello, 33–55. Madison, Wisconsin. Center for Twentieth Century Studies, University of Wisconsin.

Uzendoski, Michael. 2004. *The Napo Runa of Amazonian Ecuador*. Urbana: University of Illinois Press.

Vacandard, Elphège. 1912. *Études de critique et d'histoire religieuse. IIIème série: Les fêtes de Noël et de l'Épiphanie*. Paris: J. Gabalda.

Van Assche, Robert. 1974. *Histoire de la fête de l'Épiphanie*. Paris: Cercle Ernest-Renan.

Vickers, William T. 2003. "The Modern Political Transformation of the Secoya." In *Millennial Ecuador: Critical Essays on Cultural Transformations and Social Dynamics*, 46–74. Iowa City: University of Iowa Press.

Wade, Peter. 1993. *Blackness and Race Mixture: The Dynamics of Racial Identity in Colombia*. Baltimore: Johns Hopkins University Press.

Walsh, Catherine. 2010a. "Development as Buen Vivir: Institutional Arrangements and (De)Colonial Entanglements." *Development* 53 (1): 15–21.

———. 2010b. "Re-presentando el estado plurinacional e intercultural: Avances y enredos en el Ecuador." Talk presented at LASA, Toronto, October 8.

Walsh, Catherine, and Juan García Salazar. 2002. "El pensar del emergente movimiento afroecuatoriano: Reflexiones (des)de un proceso." In *Prácticas intelectuales en cultura y poder*, edited by Daniel Mato, 1–14. Buenos Aires: CLACSO.

Weismantel, Mary. 1998. *Food, Gender and Poverty in the Ecuadorian Andes*. Long Grove, Ill.: Waveland.

West, Robert C. 1952. *Colonial Placer Mining in Colombia*. Baton Rouge: Louisiana State University Press.

———. 1957. *The Pacific Lowlands of Colombia: A Negroid Area of the American Tropics*. Baton Rouge: Louisiana State University Press.

Whitten, Norman E. Jr. 1965. *Class, Kinship and Power in an Ecuadorian Town: The Negroes of San Lorenzo*. Stanford: Stanford University Press.

———. 1970. "Strategies of Adaptive Mobility in the Colombian-Ecuadorian Littoral." In *Afro-American Anthropology*, edited by Norman E. Whitten and John F. Szwed, 329–44. New York: Free Press.

———. 1974. *Black Frontiersmen: A South American Case*. Cambridge, Mass.: Schenkman.

———. 1981. Introduction to *Cultural Transformations and Ethnicity in Modern Ecuador*, edited by Norman E. Whitten, 1–41. Urbana: University of Illinois Press.

———. 2003a. Introduction to *Millennial Ecuador: Critical Essays on Cultural Transformations and Social Dynamics*, edited by Norman E. Whitten, 1–45. Iowa City: University of Iowa Press.

———. 2003b. "Symbolic Inversion, the Topology of 'el mestizaje' and the Spaces of 'las razas' in Ecuador." *Journal of Latin American Anthropology* 8 (1): 52–85.

———, ed. 2003. *Millennial Ecuador: Critical Essays on Cultural Transformations and Social Dynamics*. Iowa City: University of Iowa Press.

Whitten, Norman E. Jr., and Dorothea Scott Whitten. 2008. *Puyo Runa: Imagery and Power in Modern Amazonia*. Urbana: University of Illinois Press.

———. 2011. *Histories of the Present: People and Power in Ecuador*. Urbana: University of Illinois Press.

Whitten, Norman, Dorothea Scott Whitten, and Alfonso Chango. 2003. "Return of the Yumbo: The Caminata from Amazonia to Andean Quito." In *Millennial Ecuador: Critical Essays on Cultural Transformations and Social Dynamics*, edited by Norman E. Whitten, 184–216. Iowa City: University of Iowa Press.

Wibbelsman, Michelle. 2009. *Ritual Encounters: Otavalan Modern and Mythic Community*. Urbana: University of Illinois Press.

Wilson, Leon Conrad. 1989. "Family Structure and Dynamics in the Caribbean: An Examination of Residential and Relational Matrifocality in Guyana." PhD diss., Department of Anthropology, University of Michigan. Ann Arbor: University Microfilms.

Wilson, Peter. 1969. "Reputation and Respectability: A Suggestion for Caribbean Ethnology." *Man, New Series* IV (1): 70–84.

———. 1973. *Crab Antics: The Social Anthropology of English Speaking Negro Societies of the Caribbean*. New Haven, Conn.: Yale University Press.

Yuen, Edward. 1996. "Social Movements, Identity Politics and the Genealogy of the Term 'People of Color.'" *New Political Science* (38/39): 97–107.

Index

JEAN MUTEBA RAHIER is an associate professor of anthropology and the director of the African & African Diaspora Studies Program at Florida International University. He is the coeditor of *Global Circuits of Blackness: Interrogating the African Diaspora.*

The University of Illinois Press
is a founding member of the
Association of American University Presses.

————————————————————————

Composed in 10.5/13 Minion Pro
with Clearface Gothic display
by Celia Shapland
at the University of Illinois Press
Manufactured by Thomson-Shore, Inc.

University of Illinois Press
1325 South Oak Street
Champaign, IL 61820-6903
www.press.uillinois.edu